THE BIG BAD BRUINS—

Led by the Greatest Ever!

Never before has there been such a lethal lineup on the ice—and the wonder of it is, this rough, tough, all-stops-out crew led by Bobby Orr is still picking up speed.

That's Bobby Orr,[4] the game's greatest superstar . . . followed by Derek Sanderson,[16] the snarling Dead-End Kid who swings hard on the ice and off . . . Phil Esposito, the big boy with brains to match his brawn . . . Ted Green, the most feared "policeman" in the NHL . . . and all the other bruising Bruins.

Here is the story of the team, the men, and the birth of a legend.

BOBBY ORR AND THE BIG, BAD BRUINS

by Stan Fischler

A DELL BOOK

Published by
DELL PUBLISHING CO., INC.
750 Third Avenue
New York, New York 10017

Dell ® TM 681510, Dell Publishing Co., Inc.

Reprinted by arrangement with
Dodd, Mead & Company
New York, New York
Printed in the U.S.A.
First Dell printing—November 1970

Contents

Introduction

At 5 A.M. on Monday, May 11, 1970, it was reported that the Parry Sound, Ontario, fire brigade had put its men on stand-by alert for fear that the resort hamlet might be burned down early that morning.

Needless to say, nobody would set Parry Sound afire in anger. The fear was rooted in the fact that exuberant citizens might do *anything* to celebrate the latest feat of their conquering hero, Robert Gordon Orr.

By now Bobby's superhuman accomplishments are taken for granted by the Orr-watchers of the world, but on Sunday afternoon, May 10, 1970, Bobby rapped a six-ounce hunk of hard rubber past St. Louis Blues goalie Glenn Hall, and the Boston Bruins had won the Stanley Cup!

Just how monumental that accomplishment was depends on your set of values. There was no denying that it was the first time in 29 years that hockey's world championship had returned to Boston. To many inhabitants of North America this was as exciting an event as the winning of World War II.

Hundreds of thousands of Bostonians poured onto the streets to hail their heroes. The State of Massachusetts proclaimed a "Bruins Week." And in Canada, a Conservative Member of Parliament rose in the House of Commons to praise Orr.

The uproar over the Bruins had been developing throughout the 1969–70 National Hockey League season until it reached its crescendo in May. What made it all the more remarkable was that the furor had been generated by a relatively simple Canadian boy who articulates little in the dressing room but filibusters mightily on the ice.

It is not enough to say that Orr was the first defenseman ever to lead the National Hockey League in scoring; nor that he was the winner of the Norris Trophy, Hart Trophy,

Conn Smythe Trophy and the Art Ross Trophy all in one season; nor that he set records for most points and most goals by a defenseman; nor that he was the first defenseman to score 100 points in a season; nor that he set the record for assists.

To understand the significance of Orr to his profession, one must listen to a professional observer of the sporting scene, yet one who is not obsessed by hockey alone. Larry Merchant, the creative sports columnist of the *New York Post*, is such a man. After watching Bobby single-handedly demolish the New York Rangers in April 1970, Merchant remarked:

"It is clear that Orr is at least hockey's sixth dimension. He is one of those rare athletes who revolutionizes his game, as Babe Ruth did, as Bill Russell did. Bobby Jones once said of Jack Nicklaus, 'He plays a game with which I am not familiar.' Orr plays hockey in a way that makes old-timers feel like dinosaurs too."

The insiders, the "hockey men," look for different things. Mostly, they look for flaws in Orr's armament, and they react with varying forms of astonishment. "Orr is the first one up the ice," says New York Ranger general manager–coach Emile Francis, "and the first one back." Chicago Black Hawks defenseman Doug Jarrett puts it another way: "I saw him at the blue line. Then he was on top of me. He shot the puck and it hit me in the leg pads. When that puck hit it was like a bullet."

In the writing business, temptation always pushes the reporter to exaggeration, and so inevitably the newspapermen have perhaps exaggerated Orr's abilities. The fact remains that he has yet to lead Boston to first place—Chicago edged the Bruins in 1970—and he has proven himself vulnerable as a *defensive* defenseman. Also, there is the indisputable evidence that the diluted, expanded version big-league hockey today sorely lacks the competitive quality of past decades when such lions as Maurice "Rocket" Richard, Howie Morenz and Eddie Shore roamed the rinks. This, of course, is no fault of Bobby Orr. But one thing is certain: none of hockey's immortals ever attracted as much attention in so short a time as Orr.

Likewise, few teams have risen from the ashes as dramatically as the Bruins. They are, in fact, a collection of virtuosos, some very talented, some very funny, and some very underrated. Under coach Harry Sinden's guidance in 1969–70 they reached the summit; and they did so despite the injury that nearly cost Ted Green his life and side-lined him for the entire season.

Sinden's abrupt departure after the Stanley Cup triumph left a sour taste in Boston and put the onus on Tom Johnson, the rookie coach of the Bruins. Duplicating the feats of 1970 will be more than a simple task; but with Bobby Orr to skate for him, Johnson has a large head start.

Some readers may regard portions of the book as being harsh to the Boston team, but this is the inevitable consequence of a candid history of this forty-five-year-old organization. It is an asset of the book, I think, that it lacks partiality in favor of the team. In that regard the philosophy of political columnist Walter Lippmann provided the guideline:

"Cronyism is the curse of journalism. After many years, I have reached the firm conclusion that it is impossible for an objective newspaperman to be a friend of a President [or coach]. Cronyism is a sure sign that something is wrong and that the public is not getting the whole journalistic truth."

Many years ago Conn Smythe, then managing director of the Toronto Maple Leafs, invented what developed into a new hockey cliché. "If you can't beat 'em in the alley," said Smythe, "you can't beat 'em on the ice."

The Boston Bruins have proven that they can do it both ways, which explains, more than anything else, why this book was written.

Stan Fischler
New York City, June 1970

PART I

Bobby Orr

1. The Wunderkind

"Ah, but a man's reach should exceed his grasp,
Or what's a heaven for?"
—Robert Browning, "Andrea del Sarto"

It was 8 P.M. on December 16, 1968, a miserable, rainy night. A gleaming silver Buddliner had just applied its brakes, screeching to a halt on the wet tracks outside Boston's grubby North Station, and snorting as the engineer stopped the diesel engine. A handful of commuters walked through the high-ceilinged waiting room. Although it was early in the evening a funereal air had enveloped the railroad station, but the three men running up the cement ramp were oblivious to the rain and the quiet.

They were late for the Bruins-Black Hawks hockey game being played next door in Boston Garden, a high-domed arena linked to North Station like a Siamese twin. They were late, but not too late. As their tickets were halved by the gateman, the clock showed that only two minutes had elapsed in the first period. Suddenly, the men were in a new continent. The silence of the railroad station was replaced by noises suggesting a pride of lions at dinnertime. There were 14,653 of them in the cage known as a hockey rink that night. Over and over they bellowed with a sound that was to multiply in decibels as the evening progressed, because something very special was about to happen. Within the hour, Robert Gordon "Bobby" Orr, the Boston Bruins defenseman, would ascend to the plateau of superstardom in Boston hockey. He would reach an inner circle occupied by only one other player, Eddie Shore, the Bruins Lochinvar of the late twenties and thirties.

It was a night Boston fans had been anticipating; it was just that they weren't quite sure when it would happen. For two years Orr had been orchestrating the Bruin symphony in a relentless crescendo, always challenging the Shore legend. When Bobby was signed by the Bruins as an eighteen-year-old, with the biggest build-up in the history of the National Hockey League, the Bruins were groping aimlessly in the NHL cellar. In the six seasons prior to Orr's rookie year Boston had finished last five times and next to last once.

Within two years Orr had won the Calder Trophy as rookie of the year, the Norris Trophy as the league's best defenseman, and was named to the First All-Star Team. It was no coincidence that the Bruins climbed to third place in 1967–68, and in 1968–69 they were a very solid bet to challenge for first place and the Stanley Cup, all because of Orr.

But comparing him to Hall-of-Famer Shore is like comparing the young Mickey Mantle to Babe Ruth. In three years Orr had accomplished more than Shore did in a similar space of time, but Bobby knew he must continue extending himself: the conquests must go on until every one of Shore's numerous feats were duplicated or bettered. Prior to December 16, 1968, he had failed to match one very special achievement of Shore's. On February 24, 1931, the man they had lionized in Boston had scored the second, fourth, and fifth goals in a 5—1 win over the Philadelphia Quakers at the Arena in Philadelphia.

It was the first three-goal "hat trick" ever scored by a Bruins defenseman and the only one ever carved by Shore in his long Bruins career. Monumental as it was, Shore's performance was sullied by the fact that he scored his goals against the Quakers, one of the worst teams ever to skate in the NHL, a team that departed that same year after winning only four games.

Orr, on the other hand, was skating against the awesome Chicago Black Hawks with Stan Mikita and Bobby Hull, a club that was contending for first place along with the Bruins. The Black Hawks already had gone ahead, 1—0, on a goal by Eric Nesterenko at 1:23 of the first period. But Pat Stapleton of Chicago was penalized at 3:14, and Orr was dispatched to the ice by coach Harry Sinden to guide the Bruins power play.

Bobby gracefully lifted his 5-foot-11 185-pound frame over the wooden boards with one hand and glided to his position at the face-off circle. "Go with it, Bobby!" a middle-aged man in the expensive red seats screamed. It was as if there were a spotlight on his big number four, even though the kliegs were beaming on everybody. He has the knack of arresting one's attention; the combination of blue eyes, blond hair dipping down over his forehead, and the overstuffed knee and leg pads stamped him as unique on looks alone.

Boston captured the puck from the face-off. It moved out of the Bruins zone, from Derek Sanderson to Ed Westfall. Moving up behind them was Orr. As Bobby crossed the blue line Westfall dropped the puck to him. The first and then the second Black Hawk penalty killer charged Orr, but he brushed them aside as if they were annoying mosquitoes and moved into shooting range. His shot was stunning, so quick that goalie Dave Dryden's right hand never moved as the rubber hit the webbing in the upper right corner at 3:42.

Three Bruins penalties within the next five minutes stalled the Boston offensive. But when Ted Green emerged from the penalty box at 8:25, the Bruins returned to their full complement of five skaters. Within seconds Orr had switched on the attack by snaring the puck in front of his own net. This time Bobby had nearly three quarters of the rink to go, and there was some doubt that he'd make it. But he flashed past the Black Hawks one by one, like a locomotive passing telegraph poles. Goalie Dryden braced himself in the goal crease as Orr circled the Chicago defense. Orr flipped his wrist. It was a casual, almost invisible flip, the way he might crack his knuckles while carrying on a conversation, but the puck blurred past Dryden's bulky leather pads and into the net. While the Garden seemed to tremble under the ovation, Milt Schmidt, the Bruins' general manager, sat beaming quietly in the stands. As a Bruins center in the thirties and forties he had known such cheers, but never in his life had he seen so much talent crammed into one player.

"You watch him every game," said Schmidt, rubbing his craggy nose, "and you say, 'there's the best play he's ever made.' Then you look again and he's doing something even better."

The Bruins surged ahead, 4—1, but the Black Hawks were tenacious that night. By the seven-minute mark of the second period the score was only 5—4 in Boston's favor, and when Don Awrey was penalized at 8:00 it appeared the lead would collapse. This time Orr was sent out on a defensive mission. He had to defuse Chicago's heavy artillery, which he did by hurling his body in front of the shots, deflecting them harmlessly to the corner.

"He oughta get his name on the Vezina Trophy," snapped Phil Esposito, turning to Johnny McKenzie on the Bruin bench. "He blocks more shots than the goalies."

Chicago's attack was neutralized, and at ten minutes of the period Awrey stepped out of the penalty box. Precisely at that moment Orr had the puck and moved on a direct line to the Chicago net. At first it seemed as if he'd try to bisect the Black Hawk defense and work his way right up to the net, but as he crossed the blue line his stick went up, then down, and the puck was invisible until, after a forty-five-foot flight, it landed in the back of the net. The goal, Boston's sixth, proved to be the winner, and the crowd reacted as if it were recreating the ovation in Scollay Square the day World War II ended. It was, in fact, a demonstration that in forty-five years had never before been seen in Boston Garden.

One by one, hats began floating into the air and onto the ice. Soon, the shower of fedoras, fishing caps, and rainhats became a torrent until more than fifty headpieces had landed on the ice. The once milky surface looked as if it had a giant case of freckles. For more than ten minutes the capacity crowd toasted Orr with a standing ovation.

Orr responded by invading Chicago territory a dozen more times during the game; he barely missed scoring another goal by the margin of a goal post or because of a devilishly brilliant save by Dryden. After the game had ended and the Bruins had won, it was established that Bobby's third goal was the winner; the question was raised that has been raised since Orr was fourteen years old—what more can the boy do?

"The way it is now," said veteran Boston hockey writer Tom Fitzgerald, "the fans want to take him to the Charles River and see him walk on the water."

Bruins players would put their money on Orr gliding across the waves. They have seen so much of Bobby in just a few years that they don't doubt he can do *anything*. One night Orr took a pass from goalie Cheevers and detonated a ninety-foot shot that was so fast—despite its distance— that Detroit goalie Roger Crozier stood dumbfounded as it went by. Cheevers, who had never received a point in his career, was awarded an assist on the play. "It's easy," the goalie explained, "to get an assist with Orr."

This means that at his present rate of hockey growth,

Bobby Orr will be the greatest all-around player the game has ever known. He is already regarded by some as a better defenseman than Doug Harvey was in his All-Star prime at Montreal, and Harvey, until recently, was considered the best of the moderns. Offensively, Orr is so good that he was the second-leading scorer on the Bruins at midseason 1968–69, before being sidelined with an injury. His shot is one of the hardest and most accurate in the league. He is one of the fastest and strongest skaters and a deft body-checker, who can play tough with the most sinister of them. His passes are perfectly synchronized and his grasp of the game is encyclopedic. He logs more ice time than any other Bruin, not only taking a regular turn but also killing penalties and working the power play, and he could play goal if he wanted to.

"One night," said Wren Blair, general manager of the Minnesota North Stars, "I saw what Bobby could do if he wanted to be a goalie. I was coaching Oshawa, and we were down a goal to the Toronto Marlboros. We pulled our goalie in the last minute of play but Jim McKenny of the Marlboros broke free for a shot at the empty net. Instinctively, Bobby raced back into the net. McKenny came in alone and tried to fake him, then shot. Like an experienced goalie Bobby stood his ground and blocked the shot with his chest."

Once a naive kid, Bobby Orr has developed into a sophisticated young businessman who may be a millionaire before he's thirty. Armed with a $400,000 contract, the blue-eyed blond defenseman is the highest-paid player hockey has known. He came to Boston in 1966 as the most widely advertised skater ever to reach the NHL and was immediately confronted with inhumanly demanding challenges. He was taken on by stick-swinging opponents, frustrated and demanding fans, and an impatient and frugal management. He met them all head on—and topped everybody.

Tormented by a series of punishing injuries that leave his career in doubt every time he steps on the ice, he has nevertheless emerged as one of the best total hockey players in the world—if not *the* best. He is the balance wheel of the Bruins and the man who backed the NHL establishment against the wall and made it cry uncle.

His feats have compelled writers to search for new adjectives. "Imagining a better hockey player," says Hall-of-Famer Bill Chadwick, "is beyond my comprehension."

The Bruins' manager, Milt Schmidt, is more conservative. "He's almost unbelievable," says Schmidt. "He can do everything. The fact is, we have yet to find out what he can't do."

Bobby Orr's weakness is that he's incapable of doing anything *ordinary* on the ice. His slap shot flies at upward of 110 miles an hour, among the speediest in the league; his skating style is amazingly strong and flexible; and his strength is such that one night he actually lifted Gordie Howe, supposedly the strongest man in hockey, out of the goal crease and hurled him to the ice. If it's possible, he's better offensively than he is on defense. He not only commands the Bruin attack but he also scores goals, from everywhere and in every way. Consider two he once made against the Chicago Black Hawks.

The score was tied 3—3 with two minutes left in the game. Orr snared the puck behind his net, took a deep breath, and plunged forward, outskating Chicago's three forwards. As he bulled his way past the defense he was tripped, but he slid forward into the Black Hawk net with the puck rolling ahead of him.

In the second instance he also moved the puck from behind the net but then seemed to stop nonchalantly as if he was looking for someone to whom to feed a pass. Suddenly he was thirty feet away from his original location. "All he needs," says Schmidt, "is one stride and he's away." As he crossed the Chicago blue line a defenseman came at him. Orr's body tilted precariously as if it had for the moment been broken at the hip. He was around the defense but far to the right, too far to find an opening. Yet he shot the puck off his backhand, the most difficult side, and the puck drove so hard it struck goalie Dave Dryden's stick, climbed six inches over the black-taped blade, and rolled into the net.

This may help explain why Orr at nineteen and in his first year won the Calder Trophy as the best rookie and was a Second All-Star defenseman—the youngest ever in both cases. In the 1967–68 season he was the outstanding player in the All-Star game, was named to the First All-Star team and won the Norris Trophy as the best defenseman, a feat he again accomplished in 1968–69. It's worth remembering that neither Gordie Howe nor Bobby Hull won the rookie award, and that when the superb Jean Beliveau was twenty he was still playing amateur hockey.

By midseason 1968–69 Orr was a unanimous choice for the Norris Trophy and First All-Stars, at defense, and he won these awards with ease at the end of the season. He also broke (by one goal) the goal-scoring record (20) for a defenseman made by Flash Hollett twenty-four years ago.

But that's only for starters. In Boston, Bobby ranks first or second in civic popularity, along with Cardinal Cushing. Perhaps most significant is that Orr, whom they revere in Massachusetts as "Super Boy," personally rescued the defeat-riddled Bruin franchise, and now that he's completed the reclamation he is being asked to win Boston its first Stanley Cup since 1941—which was seven years before Bobby was born.

To some observers this may be regarded as an excessive demand but, as Schmidt says, "Don't ask what Orr can do, ask what he can't do." When Bobby was fourteen—too young to own a driver's license—he was virtually commanded to revive the Bruins even though he was four years away from playing for them. The desperate Bruins management banked everything on the towheaded prodigy from Parry Sound, Ontario. "Patience, patience," urged Bruins president Weston Adams as the Boston club plumbed new depths of incompetence. Adams, himself, had worked long and hard to revive his team and he above all hopefully watched Orr develop.

Rejuvenating the Bruins was only one of Orr's assignments. He was also asked to outdo the greatest Bruin of them all, Eddie Shore. Back in 1966 the then Bruins manager Hap Emms laid it on the line. "Orr could be another Shore." Others said he should be, and that really put undue pressure on the lad. "All that did," Bobby said, "is put me on the spot. I had the feeling that some people would expect too much." To suggest that Orr could even approach Shore's achievements was a bit much, but the idea quickly caught fire; Bobby was left with the choice: either produce or produce.

Both defensively and offensively he did everything asked of him and fortunately, nobody so far has asked him to play goal. But he works in his own way. Late in December, 1968, during a game against Montreal his head blocked a shot by

Jacques Lemaire, and since Orr isn't quite Superman, he was sliced for five stitches over the right eye. By the time the game had ended the swelling had inflated to such an extent that his visibility was zero on that side.

This created a grave situation for the Bruins. They had played Montreal to a 0—0 tie that night at the Forum and were to meet them again the following night in Boston. The Bruins were only one point behind Montreal in first place in the Eastern Division, but without Orr their chances for annexing the top would be small.

At 10 A.M. on Sunday morning Bobby eased his car into an empty stall at the North Station parking lot. In his raincoat he resembled a Harvard senior as he walked under the "el" tracks on Causeway Street. As an MTA trolley car lumbered overhead he turned left and walked through the empty waiting room. Bobby waved to the old lady behind the newsstand counter and walked up the ramp linking the station to Boston Garden, then through the players' gate and into the gleaming, renovated dressing room. This was Bobby Orr's world, and his nostrils twitched as he inhaled the liniment fumes.

"Hey, Dan," he greeted trainer Dan Canney, "what can ya do for me?"

Canney sat him down and studied the ugly apple hanging over his eye. "Tsk, tsk . . . we'll give you some heat."

While Canney applied hot packs to his forehead, a friend sat down next to Orr and suggested he'd be better off staying home in bed. "I feel lousy," Orr said. "I wish there was no game. But, it's a funny thing; sometimes you play your best on days like this."

He wore a white turtleneck sweater that intrigued a visitor. It seemed as if Orr had forgotten to remove a wooden hanger from inside the sweater, until he realized that Orr's shoulders are almost perfectly squared. His hands are big and, as Canney worked on him, he'd bite the nail of his right index finger and fidget, crossing one leg over another and then reversing them.

Finally the hot packs eased the swelling. "Go home," said Canney. "Rest, and we'll see how it is tonight."

Orr walked back to the car. Why didn't he beg off tonight? The eye was as good as closed, and you don't play big-league hockey with one eye. But he wouldn't think of it; there was an obligation for one thing. There was also a $400,000 contract, and an irresistible wanting to be *in* the game as much as possible, whether he could see out of the bum eye or not.

He steered the car through Callahan Tunnel and out toward his house in Nahant. "You get the hell knocked out of you," he said, "but believe it or not, you enjoy it. If I didn't enjoy it, I wouldn't be able to put out 100 per cent."

He gunned the car past a row of oil storage tanks, around a traffic circle, and finally across a causeway leading to the house he shared with players Gary Doak and Ed Johnston and assistant trainer John Forrestall. His congenital calm bothered the listener. Doesn't he worry? The demands, game after game, the threat of injury to his oft-repaired legs?

He moved the car up the steep hill overlooking Nahant Bay. "Maybe I don't show it," he said, "but I worry. About my health; the legs. I was worried at the start of this year that I might not be able to play. I mean you get a little doubt and you worry. Lately I've been throwing up. The doctor says it's just nerves—I've been getting worked up too much."

"You mean they're all expecting too much from you?"

"There are people who say I'm not worth that much money. You get it a lot of ways. I used to have a brush cut but I let my hair grow. Now some people bug me about getting a haircut. At the games you get a few wolves here and there. But you've got to take the good with the bad. But just about everybody has been super—SU-PER! I mean, there's just no easier way of making a living."

He spent the afternoon relaxing with his teammates. Although the game wouldn't begin until 7:30 P.M. Orr made certain he was at the rink by 6 for more hot packs. When teammate Derek Sanderson arrived he walked straight to the toilet and vomited. Soon he recovered and returned to the bench near Orr.

"Whatsa matter, Turk?" snapped Orr.

"Bad tuna-fish sandwich. I threw up eleven times already."

"Turk," Bobby replied, "five bucks says you'll score tonight."

An hour later the two were at center ice. NHL President Clarence Campbell was there to present Orr and Sanderson the Norris and Calder Trophies, respectively. When Orr's name was mentioned the applause was prolonged, a much lengthier ovation than Sanderson received. Bobby bowed his head, obviously uncomfortable.

"I wanted to hide," he said later, "but there was no place to go."

Teammate Phil Esposito yelled at him, "Willya tell them to stop, we gotta get home tonight."

The crowd couldn't tell that Bobby was able to see out of only one eye. The presentation and the ovation made it clear that on this night of all nights they expected something special, even from a man with 50 per cent vision. Orr's performance that night provided an excellent study of his style under the most trying conditions.

Montreal was first to attack. Smallish Henri Richard one-stepped his way into Bruins territory along the left boards, passing the puck as he crossed the blue line. Although Richard no longer had possession of the puck he *was* skating on Orr's turf, and Bobby let him know it. As the Montreal center skated by, Orr quickly but menacingly waved his stick in front of Richard's face. No harm was meant, just a dose of intimidation—the kind that made Shore so feared when he patrolled the same ice.

Minutes later Orr collided with Ted Harris, the tall Montreal defenseman, but the war ended as quickly as it started and no penalties were called by referee John Ashley. Now Jacques Lemaire of the Canadiens swooped over the blue line. A night earlier Lemaire's shot had nearly blinded Orr. The Canadiens center wound up and slapped the puck, but it never reached the net. Orr had hurled his body feet first, like Lou Brock stealing second, and deflected the rubber to the sideboards.

Still, the Bruins were not "jumping," as they say in hockey rooms, and by the time the game was fifteen minutes old the Canadiens were ahead, 3—0. Phil Esposito scored for Boston at 18:00 of the first period, but the Canadiens got another goal early in the second period. The score, 4—1 for Montreal. If the Bruins were going to go anywhere this night the Canadiens' attack had to be stopped. Orr knew that the one way to stop it was to stop Jean Beliveau.

Out of the corner of his good eye Orr detected Beliveau accelerating along the right wing. Bobby skated backward, swishing his hips back and forth as if he were doing a grotesque Frug. Beliveau tried to run the blockade by sprinting past Orr in front of the Montreal bench. It was the battle-ship Beliveau (6-3, 205 pounds) against the pocket battle-ship Orr (5-11, 185). Big Beliveau didn't have the speed to make it, and Bobby rammed him amidships with his hip and shoulder.

The initial jolt abruptly snapped Beliveau's head back. The impact of Orr's follow-through crunched Beliveau against the boards so that he was draped over the bench, his eyes staring wildly and embarrassingly eye-to-eye with his teammates. By now Beliveau had lost the puck, but Bobby wasn't finished with the demolition. He contemptuously shoved his elbow into Beliveau's face and then skated tri-umphantly back to the action. "The kid's tough," says ex-referee Chadwick, "and that's one of the signs of a great one, like Howe or Richard."

From that moment on the Canadiens were a dead hockey team. All that remained was to penetrate Montreal's goalie Tony Esposito. At 6:56 of the second period Wayne Cash-man scored for the Bruins, and at 8:43 Phil Esposito beat his brother to trim the lead to 4—3. The intermission buzzer interrupted the assault, but the Bruins were now alive.

Before the third period was one minute old Sanderson had scored, making it 4—4. The crumbling Canadiens would settle for a tie. They regrouped their defense and battled the Bruins on even terms until the seventh minute of the period. Boston's momentum was halted and now the Canadiens were back on the offensive.

"You wonder what you can do to swing the pendulum," says coach Sinden. "You look along the bench and there he is and you say, 'Bob, get out there!' And suddenly you've changed the whole flow."

The numbers on the bulky clock overhanging center ice flashed 7:00 when Orr took the ice. John McKenzie set him in motion with a short pass in his own zone. Both Henri Richard and Bobby Rousseau, two of the fastest skaters in the NHL, veered sharply to their left to intercept the Bruin, but as they approached, Orr left them in the dust.

"He's going into his passing gear," said Boston's assis-tant general manager Tom Johnson, "that's what gives him the agility nobody else in the league has."

Defenseman Ted Harris had Orr lined up at center ice in almost the identical spot and in the same way that Bobby stopped Beliveau a period earlier. Harris rumbled in and got a piece of Orr but Bobby was moving too fast. "I almost fell a couple of times," he admitted later. By now the momentum had carried him too far and too deep into the Montreal zone for a shot on goal. His injured eye limited his passing vision, so, he later explained, "there was only one thing to do."

He nursed the puck on the backhand side of his stick blade behind the net from the right side. Without warning he swerved to the left as he reached the left side of the net. Goalie Esposito fixed his eye on the puck, expecting a centering pass. But as Orr moved out, his good left eye picked up an opening in Esposito's armor. True, it wasn't much, just about five inches between his fiber-encrusted goalie skate and the red iron goalpost.

"I noticed he wasn't against the post," said Orr, "and I remembered what our forward Tommy Williams always did in practice."

Bobby swung counterclockwise and shoveled the puck into the gap. As he watched the black disk slide over the line he threw an emphatic punch at the air with his right hand, a symbolic sock-it-to-'em. The red light was on, and the Bruins pounded the wooden boards with their thick, leather gauntlets.

"That kid," said Turk Sanderson to Dallas Smith, "ain't human."

Orr returned to the bench, grabbed the white plastic water container, and squeezed five spurts of water into his throat. Returning to the blue line, he finished the game without appearing to need a second wind. Boston won the game, 7—5, and as Orr clomped over the rubber mat to the dressing room the fans were chanting the new Boston war cry, "We're Number One!"

A half hour later he sat on the dressing room bench surrounded by reporters. A listener cut in, "Have you ever scored a prettier goal?"

He waited several seconds before answering. Whenever possible he tries to deflect the spotlight away from himself, and that's when the sugar-coated monologue flows. "No," he said, removing a towel from his neck, "it's not what I did. It's what the team did out there. We're a team. We stick together. Everybody does his job. That's why we're winning."

His injured eye appeared sewn up tight for the evening. The throbbing was intense so he distracted himself. "Hey, Turk," he yelled across the room, "I told you you weren't sick . . . but if you were, maybe you should get sick more often."

Sanderson laughed. He had scored two goals that night, but he wasn't talking about the goals, he was talking about Orr. "I sit on the bench," he said, "and watch him all the time. I hope he can play till he's fifty-six."

A newcomer to the scene wondered whether the Bruins were just staging a put-on for his benefit. Nobody could be *that* nice a guy. But wherever you go they tell you he is. Charles Mulcahy, the Bruins vice president and general counsel, told how Orr got two thirds of a fee for doing a hockey movie and insisted his cut be trimmed to one third, with the other third to go to his teammates. Herb Ralby, the Bruins publicist, told about the time a kid came to Boston from Parry Sound, and Bobby personally provided room and board and other guidance.

If one Bruin had cause to think twice about Orr, it was defenseman Ted Green. For years Green had had a monopoly on hockey ink in Boston. Bobby's arrival pushed Green into relative obscurity. What did "Terrible" Ted have to say?

"The kid is super. He's got moves that take the rest of us five years to pick up. I enjoy watching the kid as much as anybody."

Maybe a writer would put the rap on him. Trent Fayne, a hard-nosed Toronto reporter, put it simply: "Sometimes Orr seems more like an invention than a real, live boy. He is polite, good-natured, relaxed, modest, generous, thoughtful, and adjusted."

But there are people who resent and are jealous of Orr. These are his opponents, the people from whom he takes money when he beats them. He was warned before he stepped on an NHL rink that they'd be running at him, that they'd resent his fat salary, and that they'd test his guts. Right from the start they came, with sinister spears in the stomach, subtle butt-ends that crush the ribs, elbows to the jaw, and crosschecks. Pretty-boy Bobby would be the woodchopper's mark.

"I hate when they use the stick on you," he said. "If a guy wants to beat hell outa me with his fists that's okay, but not with the stick. They got me right away, in my second exhibition game of my rookie year—three times in the stomach and once behind the leg. I don't like that."

What does an eighteen-year-old rookie do when a veteran twice his age shoves a stick into his ribs? The kid watched Ted Green and he learned fast. "You've got to protect yourself," Bobby explained. "If they see you backing up, you're finished."

In time he adopted the philosophy that has guided Gordie Howe. By crunching any opponents who mistreated him Howe made it quite clear that it was perilous to quibble with him. Orr has done likewise and consequently he sullied his lily-white image. Anyone who thought he was pure Boy Scout revised his thinking after November, 1967, when Orr belabored Brian Conacher, then a Toronto Maple Leaf forward.

It started when Conacher came at Orr with his stick upraised and crashed it against Bobby's head. The Bruin defenseman fell to his knees, dazed by the blow. "I felt," he recalled, "that he was too far away for it to have been an accident."

John McKenzie of the Bruins pursued Conacher and brought him down, but Orr wasn't satisfied. He got to his feet and skated over to Conacher, who had been wrestled to the ice by McKenzie. "That," said Bobby, "is when I got into a lot of trouble."

A Toronto player hauled McKenzie away from Conacher, but Orr jumped in and pummelled him beyond the call of duty, at least as far as some viewers were concerned. Some critics spanked Bobby for his explosion and suggested he concentrate on hockey rather than boxing. It wasn't exactly a new theme. Schmidt had been hounding him to stay out of fights if he could help it, and Sinden warned opponents they'd be damaged if they pestered Orr. "People are crazy if they want to fight with him," said Sinden. "He's got about the quickest hands I've ever seen in hockey."

Until Orr came along, Ted Harris of the Canadiens had been rated among the top three fighters in the NHL. He clashed with Bobby in Orr's rookie year, and twice Harris was dispatched to the ice like a bag of mail. Within a year Orr decisioned Vic Hadfield, Reg Fleming, and assorted other ruffians. The mention of these triumphs by a friend only embarrassed him.

"You do funny things when you're scared," he joked. "Okay, seriously, I'd rather play hockey, but I'll never back away."

Some opposing coaches decided to exploit Orr's refusal to turn the other cheek. One of the most successful was Keith Allen of the Philadelphia Flyers. Early in the 1968–69 season Allen watched gleefully as his forward Gary Dornhoefer twice provoked Orr and lured him into a couple of fights. Orr received two major penalties and an automatic game misconduct that removed him for the night. It was enough to give the Flyers a 4—2 win over Boston, but Bobby insisted he *had* to punch Dornhoefer.

"He damned well deserved it," said Orr, who suffered a badly bruised hand after the bout. "He was spearing me all night and I wasn't going to stand for it."

Some critics contend that Orr's iron fist is necessary in the NHL jungle where one's health is often measured by the ferocity of a bodycheck, a roundhouse right, or, if necessary, a spear in the stomach. For Bobby, they say, it is especially necessary, because he is protecting a body that within three NHL years had been riddled with a succession of freak injuries. He knows that the next one—which might well be the result of a sneaky trip or an elbow after the whistle—could mean the end of his career.

"The strange thing," he said, "is that I never got hurt in junior hockey, hardly a cut or anything much, and I kept all my teeth."

He began beating a steady path to the hospital in August, 1967, when he suffered torn ligaments in his right knee during a benefit exhibition game at Winnipeg. The Bruins management, which rushes for the penicillin whenever Bobby coughs, was furious because they hadn't known about the game and wouldn't have given Orr permission to play in it. In retrospect Bobby agreed that he had erred, but, "after all," he pointed out, "it was a benefit game for oldtime hockey players."

Orr recovered in time to start the season with Boston, but the big blow was yet to come. During a game against the Maple Leafs in December, 1967, Orr was dropped to the ice by a violent but legitimate bodycheck delivered by Frank Mahovlich. At first the Bruin management announced that their *wunderkind* had suffered a fractured collarbone, but they were telling only a fraction of the story. Later in the month it was learned that he had also suffered a shoulder separation that was much more serious than the broken collarbone, and that was followed by a knee injury that sidelined him.

By now the well-cultivated hockey grapevine was sprouting a rumor that Orr was injury prone. Bruins Coach Harry Sinden viewed the problem from another perspective.

"I've never seen him when he isn't trying to live up to his reputation," said the coach. "What this means is that he won't tell anyone when he's injured. Unless you catch him off guard or some bones are broken, you never know if he's hurt. All he ever says is 'I'm all right, I'm all right.' "

But the Bruins were in a neck-and-neck race for second place with the Rangers, and Orr was desperately needed. On March 24, a week before the season was to end, Bobby was rushed into action against the Red Wings at Olympia Stadium.

The pressure on him was tremendous and, curiously, his safety valve turned out to be a referee, Bill Friday. In the second period Orr quarreled with Friday, seemed to deliver a "choke-up" sign to his throat, and was promptly tagged with a ten-minute misconduct penalty. As Friday delivered the sentence, Orr stormed into the penalty box and slammed the door so hard it thrust the protective glass against Friday's nose.

"That's another ten minutes for you, Orr," snapped Friday. "You're out of the game."

Bobby had blown his fuse; nothing worse could happen now so he broke into a grin. "Bill, I didn't know you were there," he told Friday, "and if I had, I'd have hit you *harder* than that."

Without Orr the Bruins lost the game to Detroit, 5—3, and then returned to Boston, where they were defeated by the Rangers, 5—4. Judging by his mediocre play, Bobby had been returned to the lineup prematurely, and nothing he did in the playoff series against Montreal suggested otherwise. The Bruins were eliminated in four straight games. But that was only the beginning of evidence that he shouldn't have played.

Soon after that season ended he began feeling strange sensations in the knee. He refused to admit he was in trouble again but all signs told him the optimism of February was turning to pessimism in June. The fears were confirmed when Dr. John Palmer of Toronto ordered a second operation on the left knee, this time to remove a cartilage chip.

For a time, late in the summer of 1968, it appeared that Bobby's recovery would not be complete, but he returned to the Bruins' lineup before training camp had ended. He was to be the catalyst for one of the most exciting and successful seasons in Boston hockey history. It was to be a season of many landmarks and many records for Bobby and the Bruins, but nothing symbolized the pulsating campaign as much as Orr's performance on Thursday night, March 20, 1969 at Boston Garden.

That night the Bruins were trailing Chicago, 5—4, in the final minute of play. A loss to the Black Hawks would mean that Boston would be eliminated from the battle for first place. As the timeclock relentlessly ticked off the final seconds of play, the Bruins hurried into the Chicago zone. With four seconds remaining the puck went to Fred Stanfield, who was standing just inside the blue line near the left boards. He clouted the puck and it flew toward the goal mouth, but Black Hawk defenseman Pat Stapleton hurled his leg in front of the black blur.

As the puck fell in front of the net, Orr swooped down and pushed the disk over the goal line. The red light announced the tying goal, just one second before the end of the game! On his twenty-first birthday Bobby Orr had scored his twenty-first goal, breaking the NHL record and saving the Bruins from almost certain elimination from their first-place challenge.

When the final buzzer sounded, Chicago's Bobby Hull, who had scored a record-breaking fifty-fourth and fifty-fifth goal in the same game, only to be overshadowed by Orr, skated over to his young foe and pumped his hand.

"He scored in the clutch," Hull said, moments later. "The kid proved he is a great one."

2. How It All Started

It would hardly be stretching a point to say that Orr began achieving the near-impossible from the day he was born. Last-second histrionics, such as the goal at 19:59 of the final period against Chicago, seem to be second nature to Bobby. Certainly, the physicians and nurses at St. Joseph's General Hospital on the perimeter of Parry Sound were not overly optimistic on the night of March 20, 1948, when Arva Orr gave birth to her third of five children.

"The infant may not live," was the ominous comment of a nurse as she left Arva in the delivery room, "but the mother appears to be all right."

Such pessimism was to surround Bobby in succeeding years as he began challenging the hitherto unassailable. Almost always, and often in seemingly cliché-like fashion that inspired comparisons with Frank Merriwell, he came through. While the complicated birth did inspire temporary anguish in Parry Sound, it was only a matter of hours before Robert Orr took a turn for the better.

Those familiar with the leathery Orr stock were not surprised at the baby's recovery and healthy development. The strength and durability are traceable to Robert Orr, Bobby's grandfather on his father's side, for whom Bobby was named. Before emigrating from his native Ireland to Parry Sound, Robert Orr played a strong brand of professional soccer in Ballymena, Ireland, and was quick to pursue an interest in hockey during his later years, especially when Bobby started playing.

"He used to watch any game they put on television," said Bobby. "When the hockey season ended in 1965–66, you could see the change right away. You could see the life just go out of him, and he died a few weeks later."

With the encouragement of a venerable athlete like Robert Orr and an equally superb hockey player like

Bobby's father, Doug, it was inevitable that young Bobby would take to the ice. It was only a question of when and how well he'd perform. To some friends of the family, those who remember his father Doug as a skater, it would only be just for Bobby to reach the NHL. To this day they insist that Doug could have gone all the way, if circumstances were different. But World War II was thundering across the Atlantic in 1942 when Doug was coming to full flower as a stick-handler, and he had the kind of ideas you'd expect from a seventeen-year-old.

"I was young and I wanted to travel," Doug explained, "so I joined the Navy."

Ironically, he probably could have become a member of the Boston Bruins if he had not entered the armed forces. Doug had played junior hockey with Pete Horeck, a small but fleet forward from Capreol, Ontario, a railroad town some 150 miles north of Parry Sound. Horeck played right wing on a line with Doug on the left. One evening Harold "Baldy" Cotton, the chief scout of the Boston Bruins and a former NHL star in his own right, watched Orr's team in action. He was impressed with both Horeck and Orr and suggested they audition in the Bruin farm system. It was a tempting offer and Horeck agreed, but Doug Orr declined.

"Even after Cotton talked to us," Doug told George Sullivan of the Boston *Herald-Traveler,* "I had a chance. When Pete reported to the Atlantic City Seagulls [of the Eastern Hockey League] and I hadn't left for the Navy yet, he wrote that everything was all set for me there if I wanted to report. But I was young and set on going to sea. I spent three years on a corvette running between Newfoundland and Ireland.

"Could I have made the NHL? I don't know. Maybe. A lot of hockey people told me I could have. It was a lot easier to make the league in those days. Anyway, I didn't. But every time I look back and see the if's—well, I've just tried to make sure Bob didn't make the same blunders."

The fact is Doug Orr underestimated his chances for major-league stardom. Many respected observers said he was a better all-round player than Horeck, and he was bigger, an important factor in rating NHL potential.

"I'll tell you," Doug once said, "I *could* skate better than Pete. I'll tell you that if I do say so myself."

Horeck went on to a successful if not stupendous NHL

career. He moved quickly up the ladder from Atlantic City to Cleveland in the American League in 1943–44 and reached the NHL a year later with the Chicago Black Hawks. He later played for Detroit and Boston; although he was never an extraordinary player he managed to hold his own—like a consistent .270 hitter in baseball.

"Pete played a lot of years," said Doug. "He made a pile of money and opened a jewelry shop in Sudbury."

The double irony of the Horeck-Orr story is that Bobby probably wouldn't have reached the NHL if his father had taken up professional hockey. For if Doug had followed Horeck's trail, Bobby would never have had the opportunity to obtain ice time in Cleveland or Chicago or Detroit or Boston on which to hone his skating to the sharpness it later obtained in Parry Sound. So Shakespeare's immortal phrase, "Sweet are the uses of adversity" was applicable in the case of Doug Orr.

Just before joining the Navy, Doug married Arva Steele, a pretty young girl from Callendar, Ontario, a town that once made headlines as the birthplace of the Dionne quintuplets. At the end of the war, Doug and Arva settled in Parry Sound and began raising a family. Their first child was a girl, Pat, followed two years later by a boy, Ron, and then Bobby, Penny, and Doug.

By the time Doug senior had stowed away his Navy-blue uniform he considered himself too old to pursue a hockey career. Besides, there were mouths to feed and a mortgage to pay. Lesser types might have been resentful of what-might-have-been, but Doug got a job and went about enjoying life in Parry Sound. If you're Doug Orr that's not very difficult, and being in Parry Sound doesn't hurt either.

There are unquestionably hundreds of more attractive towns in the world than Parry Sound; but not very much more. The Iroquois and Huron Indian tribes were the first to enjoy the fishing from the waters of Georgian Bay and to reap the bounty of a flourishing fur trade in the area 150 miles north of Toronto (then called York). The rival tribes warred over the fur and, in time, the Ojibways established a village on Parry Island in the harbor of what is now the town of Parry Sound.

The town was established in the middle of the nineteenth century as a lumbering camp, abuzz with sawmills, of which only one is left today. The mills had to be serviced and soon the Canadian National and Canadian Pacific Railroads extended their track to Parry Sound. The town's railroading heritage today remains as prominent as anything in the vicinity. Parry Sound's most significant structure is an enormous black steel trestle, erected by the Canadian Pacific, that overlooks the population of 6,075.

The natives would rather talk about the pickerel and trout in Georgian Bay or point out the outline of the fir trees lining the north shore, but nothing else catches the eye as much as the trestle, one of the largest of its kind east of the Rockies. One foundation of the span is anchored in Belvedere Hill and the other is based in Tower Hill. Between flows the Seguin River, which funnels its water into the Sound.

Because Belvedere Hill boasts the best view of Parry Sound it was only natural that the town's wealthiest people built their homes there. The closest Bobby came to living on Belvedere Hill was the summer he worked as a bellhop at the old Belvedere Hotel. He was thirteen at the time and earned a dollar a day, but that summer he earned $500 in tips. A year later the hotel burned down.

The Orr family grew up on the other side of the river— and the tracks—at 24 Great North Road. It is an eight-room stucco house, unobtrusive in almost every way and typically Canadian, or even American, for that matter. There was nothing distinctive about it except its warmth, both physical and spiritual.

Simple people with simple tastes, the Orrs enjoyed their children, their neighbors and, most of all, a good laugh. Bobby's father worked at Canadian Industries Ltd., an explosives firm, loading crates. When Arva wasn't taking care of her children, she worked as a waitress in the Brunswick Motor Hotel coffee shop. Once a child was old enough to walk there were plenty of things to do in Parry Sound, and Bobby did them all. In the summer he fished, swam, and camped in and around the Bay; in the winter there was skiing, hunting, and ice fishing. But most of all there was hockey.

Even by Canadian standards Parry Sound is a cold-weather town, the kind that produces the best hockey players. In midwinter the temperature has been known to tip to forty below zero, and it may hover for days around the zero mark. The icicles on the Orr house hang six feet long from the rooftop, and the Seguin River has been known to freeze solid from as early as mid-December until April. Any hockey scout will tell you that that's where you'll find the best stick-handlers.

There's nothing formal about hockey on the Seguin, or on the Sound, which also freezes solid. They call the sport *shinny* up there, and its trademark is madness. The idea is to get the puck and retain it as long as possible while a tribe of two to two dozen kids tries to get it away from you. If you want to keep the puck you first have to learn how to skate, then you have to learn how to stick-handle, and then, if you really want to be king of the hill, you have to use your brains. For Bobby Orr, learning began at the age of four, first on the Seguin River and then on the Sound.

Nobody would have predicted that the tiny blond four-year-old had big-league potential. If anything, he looked more like a miniature clown right out of the Ice Follies. His first steps were tentative and clumsy as his little blades cut into the three-foot-deep ice. His ankles curved precariously inward, and he appeared to be fighting a losing battle against gravity. But somehow he managed to remain upright.

"At first," said his father, "he was skating on his ankles. But he learned fast and a year later he had improved a great deal. He learned to skate and pretty soon he could stick-handle. It all seemed to be natural to him."

More important than that, he enjoyed it and was willing to put up with the travail that goes with learning hockey outdoors. His skates contained no special insulation to warm his feet. On frigid days the cold would get to his toes, and the moments after opening the laces on his boots caused him the most excruciating pain. But this was balanced by the exquisite joy of gliding swiftly over the ice, the blades crunching audibly as he pursued the puck.

Not a day went by when Bobby wasn't out on the ice. Sometimes he'd play with his immediate neighbors, other times with the Indian boys from Parry Island, who came onto the ice with freshly cut saplings for sticks. Occasionally, Doug would work the night shift at Canadian Industries and have his days free to watch his son dipsy-doodle on the ice. Memories of his five-year-old mastering the game have stayed in Doug's mind.

"By his second year he had the moves of a natural," said Doug. "He was a strong skater, although not that fast. But his stick-handling already was developing nicely. He had the puck a lot of the times, but he was a little fella in those days. We used to think he was the smallest defenseman in Canada."

But Doug Orr was realistic enough to understand that Bobby was like thousands of kids across Canada and the northern United States who are precocious in their early hockey days. "We couldn't have dreamed of the future he'd have," Doug admitted.

For one thing, little guys aren't especially desirable in the NHL anymore, and for too long Bobby was downright small. Fortunately it never deterred him. He soon outgrew the outdoor games and at age five joined the league sponsored by the Parry Sound Minor Hockey Association. There he would play in a regulation-sized rink with real metal and twine nets for goals instead of a pair of rocks on the ice.

The facade of the Parry Sound Memorial Community Center reminds a visitor of an abandoned aircraft hangar. It was built shortly after World War II, but its trappings are more suited to an earlier time. The structure doesn't have a heating system, which means that in midwinter spectators occupying the 1,200 seats must be well clothed and preferably armed with fuel of some sort. For the players, however, the clean cold air is a catalyst to help them skate faster and shoot harder.

Just about anybody willing to lace on a pair of skates can play in the Community Center. Organized hockey starts with the Minor Squirt division for kindergarten youths and progresses to Squirt (six and up), PeeWee, Bantam, Midget, Junior C, and Intermediate, the latter for men over 20 years old. A trend soon became obvious. Doug Orr's smiling, little blond son began dominating nearly every game he played in every division he joined.

Sure, he was Lilliputian compared to some of his peers, but his talents were Gulliverian by comparison. Already he was showing a style, something most young hockey players don't acquire until their early or mid-teens. He would leap forward like an impala with the puck on his stick, and he confounded opponents with a repertoire of head fakes— "dekes," as they're called in Canada—that baffled his coaches and friends. But most of all it was his skating, combining a bullishness with a balletlike turn of foot. To the

good folk of Parry Sound he was a wonder; but Parry
Sound was far from the madding professional hockey
crowd, and some questioned whether the Orr genius would
triumph. The answer was supplied in the spring of 1960.

At twelve, Bobby was 5-2, and weighed 110 pounds.
Technically, he was young enough and small enough to
play PeeWee hockey. But the coaches in Parry Sound were
practical men and they realized the lad was good enough to
play in more advanced company, so he was permitted to
skate with older and bigger players in the Bantam Division.

Parry Sound's Bantam sextet was a good one in 1959–60.
It qualified for the all-Ontario Bantam championship tournament to be held in Gananoque, 18 miles east of Kingston
and 300 miles south of Parry Sound. Normally, such compe-
titions are unlikely to attract professional hockey men because the players are still relatively young and too immature to be judged on their potential capabilities. But 1960
was not a normal year for the Boston Bruins. The club had
finished out of the Stanley Cup playoffs for the first time
in four years and, worse still, there were ominous indications, which were later proven correct, that the NHL team
was in for a long depression out of the playoffs.

It was a time for the Boston organization to find young
players and find them anywhere. In the spring of 1960 a
Bruin Expeditionary Force went searching for talent. The
group consisted of Boston hockey officials from president
Weston Adams down the executive line to Lynn Patrick,
Phil Watson, Milt Schmidt, Hap Emms, and Wren Blair.
One of their ports of call was a tiny rink that could have
been mistaken for an overlong Quonset hut, in Gananoque,
Ontario.

Word had been spreading along the local hockey grapevine that a couple of Gananoque defensemen named Rick
Eaton and Doug Higgins had extraordinary talent and
couldn't miss with the pros. The reports on Eaton and Higgins were emphatic enough to woo a scout from the Montreal Canadiens' organization, not to mention the B.E.F. As
far as can be determined Eaton and Higgins were never
heard from again, but Bobby Orr was discovered around the
fifteen-minute mark of the first period.

Blair, a young, unknown but insightful hockey executive
who was then general manager and coach of the Kingston
Frontenacs, Boston's farm team in the now-defunct Eastern

Pro League, nudged Patrick as the Parry Sound team organized an attack. "Do you see what I see?" he asked.

"I see what you see," acknowledged Patrick. "Who is he?"

"You got me."

Blair got up and walked around the rink. When he returned his face was noticeably bright. "That number two is a kid named Orr, Bobby Orr."

Patrick was fascinated but concerned. He wondered whether any of his competitors in the NHL held sponsorship rights in the Parry Sound area. If any of them did, that team and not the Bruins would have first claim on any of the players. "Good news," added Blair. "Nobody is sponsoring them."

Parry Sound lost the final game of the tournament to the Scarboro Lions, 1—0, but there was absolutely no question who had been the dominant player.

"Orr skated rings around everybody on the ice," Blair later explained. "He had the puck all the time, and he played the whole game except for a two-minute penalty."

That meant fifty-eight minutes of hockey, the way they used to play in the twenties and early thirties, but which had become obsolete. Obviously, even at twelve Orr was a throwback and a prodigy in hockey. Although his team lost, Bobby was voted the most valuable player in the tournament and the B.E.F. began taking serious steps to acquire him. Perhaps it was absurd to expect that a twelve-year-old had the earmarks of a great one, but the Bruins weren't going to take any chances. After all, there always was a possibility that he *might* be as good as they hoped.

Tow-headed Bobby, of course, was oblivious to the behind-the-scenes machinations being conducted by the Bruins. The NHL? Oh, he followed the broadcasts of Foster Hewitt on the Canadian Broadcasting Corporation and he studied the charts of the NHL scoring leaders. But there were other important things in his life then. He averaged B grades in the Victory School, which he attended from first to sixth grade, and moved on to the Gibson School for the seventh and eighth grades. He attended Sunday School at the Parry Sound Baptist Church, and in his spare moments rode his bicycle down James Street, the town's main avenue, or tramped through the nearby woods with his grandfather, to whom he was very close.

Life was simple and too much fun for young Orr to comprehend that a major campaign was secretly being organized to obtain the right to his future services as a hockey player. The plan had to be secret because at any moment another hockey team could suddenly develop an interest in the lad and capture him first. It was also quite possible that the Orr family and their neighbors would not appreciate a big-league hockey team messing around in the affairs of their town or one of its junior citizens. Besides, Parry Sound traditionally rooted for the Toronto Maple Leafs although a vocal minority boosted the Montreal Canadiens. The Boston Bruins were from the United States, a foreign country, and besides, they were floundering down near the NHL cellar.

Obtaining Orr would require the guile and master planning that is normally associated with an international spy plot. The aim was to acquire Orr's signature on a Junior A "card" when he was fourteen years old. This entailed wooing his parents, who eventually would have to approve the lad's decision, and winning the hearts of Parry Sounders. The Bruins figured that the way to a Parry Sounder's heart was through his hockey program, so they proceeded accordingly.

The Boston hockey club decided to pay $1000 a year for three years to fund the Parry Sound minor hockey association. It was hoped this "philanthropic" effort would be appreciated, and it was. But the Bruins weren't about to take any chances. Blair, always an indefatigable ferret on the spoor of a good hockey player, extended himself beyond all reason to establish a rapport with the Orrs. While Parry Sound is a tourist haven in warm months it may be one of the last places on earth one would want to visit in midwinter. Yet, Blair was known to detour his entire Kingston hockey team into Parry Sound so that he could romance Bobby's family.

Although the Bruins had laid some significant groundwork, they soon discovered they were not alone on the trail of Orr. "Boston was first," allowed Doug Orr, "but soon there were others. Montreal sent Scotty Bowman [now general manager-coach of the St. Louis Blues], and Detroit and Chicago phoned."

The Maple Leafs, because of the natural rooting interest in Parry Sound, might have landed Orr except for a tactical error. Rather than dealing directly with Doug, the Leaf emissary mistakenly spoke with Bobby's school principal. This disenchanted Doug as far as the Toronto club was concerned, and the Leafs were immediately eliminated from consideration. That left Boston, Montreal, Detroit, and Chicago in the running. Boston won the prize mostly because of Blair's perseverance and grim determination. In August, 1962, on one of his frequent stopovers in Parry Sound, he persuaded Doug and Arva to permit Bobby to attend a junior tryout camp the Bruins would conduct at Niagara Falls, Ontario; no cost, no obligation. It was a reasonable enough offer. Bobby was on school vacation, and Terry Ainslie, another Parry Sound youngster, was going to make the trip. Doug Orr agreed to let Bobby make the journey, but from the trauma that followed one might have thought he was leaving to become a monk in the Himalayas.

On a Sunday night, the two youngsters walked along the railroad station platform. Doug Orr was fidgeting because Bobby had never taken a really long trip before, certainly not by train. The father finally collared a railway conductor and beseeched him to be sure the boys made the proper change for the Niagara Falls train. Arva Orr wept, and Doug told Bobby they'd be in touch by telephone to be sure everything was all right. As the train rumbled out of sight Doug wondered whether or not his son might be over his head.

At first, the big kids at camp laughed at the little guy, but they stopped laughing when Bobby started to play. By now the Bruins had seen enough of Bobby to realize that they might have one of the prizes of all time; nothing that young Orr did in those first few days of camp surprised them. If anything, Bobby exceeded their expectations and they became nervous; he was so good, they feared their prize might be nabbed by a competitor just when they seemed to have him.

After four days of watching him, they knew they had to make a move. On Thursday the phone jangled at 24 Great North Road in Parry Sound. It was an invitation for Doug to watch the Friday night game at Niagara Falls, which would bring the curtain down on the five days of hockey. Sure, Doug would make it. His shift at Canadian Industries ended at eight in the morning, and he and a friend drove to Niagara Falls. On the drive south the men talked about hockey, and Doug expressed his doubt about little Bobby playing against the bigger and older boys at Niagara Falls.

When he finally reached the rink he had prepared himself for a big disappointment.

"Instead," said Doug, "I was amazed. Bobby played a wonderful game. He was stick-handling very well, moving around the others like a bloody weasel. There was good reason for him to step lively when you consider the publicity he was beginning to get. A lot of players wanted to get a piece of him."

By now the Bruins were as impatient as a youngster on Christmas Eve. Getting his signature on the Junior A form was their Holy Grail. "He was obviously so good," wrote Frank Deford in *Sports Illustrated*, "that they began to implore the Orrs to let Bobby sign."

Doug, however, stoically refused to put a pen to anything, until he had a chance to talk to Arva. On Saturday, with Bobby and Terry Ainslie he headed back to Parry Sound. Unknown to them, Wren Blair was tooling his car in the same direction.

"We had about seventy players at the Niagara Falls camp," Blair recalled, "and the kid was a stickout. My wife, Elma, and I drove immediately to Parry Sound to convince the Orrs that Bobby ought to move to Oshawa, Ontario, and sign a Junior A card with the Oshawa Generals [a Bruins farm team in the powerful Ontario Junior A Hockey Association]. Then we'd have him, and my worries would be over."

Blair was well motivated for the task. Relatively new on the hockey scene and without any notable accomplishments as a player, he needed a coup such as signing Bobby Orr to really imprint himself in the minds of the NHL brass. Besides, he liked the boy and he liked the Orrs, and as a hockey man, he deplored the potential waste of talent if Bobby remained in Parry Sound.

For two days on Labor Day weekend, the rooms of the stucco house reverberated with hard hockey talk as Blair lobbied for the Bruins organization. He told Doug that Bobby would be more apt to reach the top with Boston because the team needed good young players as soon as possible, and he offered financial rewards. According to one report Blair came up with an estimated $800 in benefits, which included the cost of stuccoing the eight-room house. Another report put the figure at $2,800, some in cash, some to improve the house, and some to buy a second-hand car.

As an added fillip the Bruins mentioned purchasing some new clothes for Bobby. "But they kept forgetting about that," said Frank Deford.

Articulate and personable, Blair seemed to have bent Doug's ear by ninety degrees. The Orrs were ready to sign, except for one obstacle. They didn't like the idea of a four-teen-year-old boy being taken away from his home and moved to a boarding house 150 miles away.

"He's just too young," asserted Arva Orr, who can be downright dogmatic. "Next year, I promise you, he'll go. But not yet."

A less dedicated man would have quit right then, but Blair had a *riposte*. "I'll find a family for him to live with in Oshawa. He'll get the best of care. If he stays here another year he'll just deteriorate as a hockey player. He's too good for these boys. He'll just learn bad habits."

Then a pause, and like a good salesman who has his prospective client reeling, Blair added, "Just let him come on a four-game trial basis. You come with him. See the school. See the folks he'll live with. Watch him play. If you're not convinced after four games, we'll forget it."

Arva adamantly objected to his living in Oshawa. But Blair broke that impasse by suggesting that he commute to Oshawa from Parry Sound. That just about crumbled the opposition. Playing their last hand, the Orrs made two essential requests. They wanted the right to terminate the deal if Bobby appeared to be in over his head with the bigger players, and they wanted a similar pull-out clause for mid-season if his school grades or his health were suffering. Blair could feel the adrenaline flowing when Bobby signed the form. Although he may have suspected it, he never could have realized that with that stroke of the pen he had saved a hockey franchise.

Doug still had a smidgen of doubt. How would the boy stand up to the rigors of travel? And what about the brawlers and hatchet men in the Ontario Hockey Association? The father, who was familiar enough with the rough side of hockey, soon discovered that Bobby worked hard in school and pursued his hockey career with equal zeal. Doug would make the 300-mile round trip with him, sometimes accompanied by Bobby's chum, Bob Holmes, or his school principal, Ken Johnson, and others.

Doug suffered more from the regular grind than his son.

The return trip brought them home early in the morning, making it difficult to get up for work on time, although Bobby phlegmatically arose and went off to school as if it were a normal youngster's routine.

Inevitably, some Parry Sounders criticized the Orrs for permitting their son to leave home at the age of fifteen, and it was in its way a gamble. The Orrs took the gamble, and their son repaid their confidence to a point that silenced even the most critical neighbors.

What neither Doug nor Arva could know was how their prodigious son would comport himself in the high-pressure company of the OHA Junior A League. This would be the first genuine test of his superiority as a hockey player, and if he failed it would mean that all the expense and hard work of the Bruin Expeditionary Force had been for naught.

3. The Early Days in Oshawa

The hockey stepladder is so constructed in Canada that the Junior A divisions in Ontario, Quebec, and some of the western provinces are on a competitive level merely a cut or two below that of the professionals. Games are played by the same jungle law with bloodletting, coach-feuding, and all the trappings of the NHL pressure cookers. For that reason it has not been uncommon for the *crème de la crème* of the OHA Junior A Amateur League to make the jump to the NHL within a couple of seasons. A few gifted players have been known to make the jump directly without any minor professional experience and to succeed—but only a unique few. This is mentioned here to put in better perspective the situation into which fourteen-year-old Bobby Orr was entering.

His foes on the Toronto Marlboros, Peterborough Petes, and St. Catherines Teepees, to name a few opponents, would think nothing of shoving a butt end of lumber into his stomach or ramming a hard-fiber elbow pad into his mouth. And since they were, almost to a man, bigger and often stronger than Orr, the balance of power, at least for the present, was in their favor. Interestingly, several of those players who capitalized on their size and belabored Bobby in those formative OHA Junior A days became his targets when he joined the Bruins, and to this day many a score is still being settled, usually to Orr's advantage and satisfaction.

Circumstances were hardly in Orr's favor when he first pulled on the striped red-white-and-blue jersey of the Oshawa Generals. There was already a lot of locker-room talk, not all of it pleasant, about the kid with the special privileges: a kid who could travel back and forth from Parry Sound *and* do without the essential practices with the rest of the team. This was a bit much in the eyes of some of his teammates. There was only one way for Bobby to win them over and that was to play the brand of hockey that would win games for the Generals.

This, naturally, was a tailor-made situation for anxiety. Another lad might easily have found the combined strain of too much publicity too soon and the skepticism of his teammates too much to bear, perhaps either crumbling or giving up and returning home. But from the very start Bobby seemed oblivious to the whole troublesome business, betraying a special kind of courage explained in one of two ways: he either realized what was going on about him, and nevertheless forced himself to go on and excel; or he simply disengaged his mind from all the problems surrounding him, and carried on without concern as to whether or not he made it big with the Generals.

A well-decorated Royal Air Force pilot once described the men who fit in the first category as the braver. "They have a hell of a time," he explained, "but keep going. Usually they're not the spectacular types and they don't win the flash awards, but they're the bravest. The second group —the nonworriers—don't have the hard inward struggle and aren't in danger of being deflected by imagination."

Judging by all available evidence Orr falls into the second category, a man with a peculiar capacity for ignoring the probabilities of personal catastrophe, no doubt a fatalist without even realizing it. Certainly, he survived that first grueling year in an amazingly adult manner. He matched bodychecks with the big fellows, played his own extrasensory type of game, scored thirteen goals while playing a solid defense and, incredibly, was selected to the Second All-Star Team.

"Imagine," said Blair, delighted with his acquisition, "the kid never once practiced with the club and he made the Second Team."

Sudden fame had hardly dulled Orr's small-town charm. His penchant for work remained, and he found part-time jobs wherever the labor suited him. After the old Belvedere Hotel burned down, he took a job at the Victory Public School, a short walk from his home, where at age fourteen he was paid $10 a month as a furnace cleaner and general assistant to the caretaker.

Following his rookie season with Oshawa he was given a job in his Uncle Howard Orr's butcher shop in the center of town. He received $25 a week plus such fringe benefits as free meat for himself. Surprisingly, he displayed infinitely less dexterity with a meat cleaver than he did with a hockey stick and on several occasions nearly rendered himself a one-armed defenseman. In one nip-and-tuck battle with a slice of bacon, Bobby barely missed slicing off the knuckle on his left thumb, an encounter which later prompted Arva Orr to observe: "I think he cut his fingers more than he did the meat."

When he wasn't working, he was likely to be down at the Bay with his cronies, armed with a fishing rod. "He'd always loved to fish," Arva Orr once allowed. "He started like the rest of the kids in Parry Sound—with a line and hook on the end of a branch."

Bobby was scheduled to make his official break with the routine of traveling to Oshawa and back in his second year of OHA competition. By then it was generally agreed that it would be more practical for the fifteen-year-old to board throughout the year in Oshawa and attend school in the city.

This arrangement seemed to agree with everybody. By Canadian standards Oshawa (population 80,500) is a relatively big city, dominated by a General Motors plant, hence the team name Oshawa Generals. But since it is only thirty miles east of Toronto it is regarded as an adjunct of metropolitan Toronto, the largest English-speaking city in Canada.

NHL teams generally take great care about placing their junior prodigies in proper homes and enrolling them in suitable schools when they are playing away from home. It isn't very difficult for a fifteen-year-old to take a wrong turn, especially when he's far from his parents and close to a swinging metropolis like Toronto, so the Bruins were concerned that Orr enjoy all the benefits of an All-Canadian atmosphere not unlike that of Parry Sound.

He was boarded with the family of Bob and Bernie Elsmere and their three children and enrolled at the R. S. McLaughlin Collegiate, a public high school two miles from the Elsmeres' nine-room frame house. Bobby walked two blocks and then took a bus to school, where he majored in technology and specialized in refrigeration.

His grades, typically, were unspectacular but perfectly respectable B's and C's. This was not unusual for a junior

player who did quite a bit of traveling during a long season
much like a pro season. Nor was it unusual that Orr, never
a great intellect, was quite content to just pass while con-
centrating on what was to him more important—hockey
studies. Although he never dazzled his instructors with cere-
brations, Orr nevertheless made an impression with his personality.

One of his teachers observed, "There was an excitement
about him which was unusual, because on the whole he was
an unpretentious and reserved youngster. He had the knack
of impressing the teachers here as well as his fellow
students."

He also impressed his "foster" parents. They considered
him a fastidious gentleman with a hearty appetite but one
who paid strict attention to his diet. Occasionally he'd get
homesick for Parry Sound and, unknown to the Generals'
management, would hitchhike home for brief reunions.
Once in a while the team would phone to check on Orr but
the Elsmeres covered up, telling the brass he was sleeping.
The alibi usually worked, because rest is always a require-
ment for hockey players; it primes them for the next game
and keeps them out of trouble.

When Bobby couldn't get away he'd stay in touch with
the family by telephone. Once Trent Frayne, a Toronto
Daily Star reporter, questioned Bobby's sister, Pat, about
their conversations. The description went this way:

"We're a nutty family. We've all got wild tempers, but
we're soft as mush, too. Every time Bobby phones I cry and
I can hear him start to blubber, too. I always cry when I
see him. Dad thinks we're nuts; we'll all be watching a television program, and I look over to see if Mom's crying, and
she is, and she looks at me and we both look at Penny and
we're all sitting there blubbering. Dad looks at us and just
shakes his head."

There was no blubbering about Bobby Orr as a hockey
player, except for joy. And joy was boundless during his
second season with the Generals. He scored a three-goal hat
trick in the next-to-last game of a fifty-six-game schedule,
which gave him a total of thirty goals. This exceeded the
previous record set by Jacques Laperriere, a tall defenseman
who eventually graduated to the Montreal Canadiens. Sig-
nificantly, Laperriere was regarded as the best young defenseman in the NHL until Orr came along to eclipse him.

Also, Laperriere was nineteen when he set the OHA record, whereas Orr was four years younger. Bobby was also the unanimous choice of the OHA Junior A's eight coaches as All-Star defenseman on the first team. Even more arresting was the fact that he was eligible for another five seasons of junior play, that is, if the Bruins were willing to permit him to complete his development in the OHA.

That possibility, however, appeared more remote by the month. Firmly anchored in sixth place, the Bruins had become the joke of the NHL and appeared locked to the cellar unless help was promised, and soon. Since there were few skaters of promise on the parent team, the Boston management decided to focus on young Orr. It was a valid bit of strategy because the brass was now given a few years of grace to brag about the coming of the wonder boy. They made a point of telling people that Orr was almost certain to leap into their lineup the instant he turned eighteen— the league's legal minimum age—which for Bobby would be the night of March 20, 1966.

Conservative hockey critics were quick to suggest that the Bruins might be presumptuous in attributing such savior-like qualities to Orr. After all, he was only fifteen. There was still the possibility that injuries or even size—Bobby was still small by NHL standards—would militate against his professional development. But the Boston management had their best intelligence men on the spot in Oshawa, and according to all reports the not-so-secret weapon was progressing according to the timetable they had set. When key members of the BEF would fly to Oshawa to confirm the reports, they were never dismayed by what they saw.

"He amazes me every time I see him," said Lynn Patrick, then the general manager of the Bruins. "The way he can anticipate what's going to happen is sometimes uncanny; you know, sensing where the puck is going to be and moving there even before the puck does. I never saw a more promising player."

Patrick was, perhaps, more susceptible than any of the other Bruins bosses to criticism. As manager what else could he say about Orr except that he had Promethean powers, that Boston fans would be blessed by his coming? His opinion had to be confirmed by other Bruins observers and by more impartial critics.

Emile Francis, coach and manager of the Guelph Royals

and later a boss of the New York Rangers, toasted Orr to the heavens and cautioned that perhaps the OHA wasn't too good for him. The way Francis saw it, Orr had the head of a big-leaguer and would be even better as a pro than as an amateur.

The acclaim began snowballing to such an extent that on February 20, 1965, when Bobby was only sixteen, *Maclean's,* the national magazine of Canada, ran a cover color photo of him in action with an accompanying headline: "How hockey's hottest sixteen-year-old is groomed for stardom—has Boston captured the NHL's next superstar?" The evaluation inside the magazine answered the question with caution. "An outstanding star at sixteen has no guarantee that he will continue to develop and be still outstanding in five years when he is in against the Hulls and Hortons and the other one-in-a-hundred survivors of the junior leagues.

"Thus, at this stage in Orr's development, the Bruins can not allow themselves to be more than unusually hopeful that the fates have equipped Orr with an intangible urge to rise with fire in his eyes after some hulking oaf of an NHL defenseman has flattened him. And they must await nature's whim on whether his present slender five-foot-nine and hundred and sixty-six pounds spread up and out in maturity."

His coach at Oshawa, Jim Cherry, worked on improving Orr's fundamentals—the shooting, passing, positional play, and discipline. In each case he came through beautifully, as perfectly as the coach could expect. There were other intangibles, however, such as the matter of excess publicity. After his face appeared on the cover of *Maclean's* Bobby Orr became a household word in Canada. There was every possibility that he'd be overcome with swell-headedness, a malady that has ruined junior hockey players both before and since Orr. Somehow it never seemed to afflict Bobby.

"You've never seen a boy so polite," said Cora Wild, with whom Orr boarded in 1964–65 and 1965–66. Mrs. Wild and her husband Jack spoke of Orr as a person the way coaches and managers describe Orr as a hockey player. Only extravagant adjectives will do. "I remember telling a friend about him once, and she insisted no boy could be as perfect as I described. Then she met Bob—and agreed. So does anyone who knows Bob."

Wren Blair was concerned about what he once described as "the cause of the greatest casualty list of them all—

girls." He explained it this way, "They bug hockey players. They hang around the dressing-room door after a game, waiting for the players to come out, hoping for a pick-up. They'd like nothing better than to hook a guy, especially in junior where the kids are as big with the teen-age crowd as The Beatles.

"Hockey players are Canada's glamour boys. They get a kind of Hollywood adulation, particularly in the small- and medium-sized towns where junior hockey flourishes. In the smaller papers they get more space than the Prime Minister, particularly young Orr who, because of his extreme youth, has been getting incredible publicity for three years now. I mean, imagine playing Junior A hockey at fourteen—that alone is enough to attract wide attention. So I've drummed it into him over and over that it's his responsibility to be levelheaded enough to handle it."

How did Orr handle it? One day late in 1965 he was asked whether he was drowning in his printer's ink.

"I try not to read about myself," he replied. "So many people have told me not to get a swelled head that I'm scared to read the stuff."

Because of his role in Orr's hockey development and because he was respected by Bobby and his family, Blair was in a strategic position as general manager of the Oshawa Generals. He too had become a big name in Canadian hockey, although he had yet to reach the NHL. In 1958 he managed the Whitby, Ontario, Dunlops when they defeated the Russians to win the world's championship at Oslo. Blair's policy, as translated to the players by coach Cherry, accented strict discipline.

The Oshawa team had a 10:30 P.M. curfew; 9 P.M. on nights before games. Cherry would enforce the rule by making regular spot checks at the various boarding houses. If the boy didn't answer he was compelled to phone the coach when he did arrive home. The penalty for the first offense was a simple reprimand. The second offense resulted in a letter to the parents, explaining that their son was breaking the team rules. If he broke the regulation a third time he was automatically suspended and sent home.

Prior to final examinations at the local high schools Blair would insist on even tighter security. There was a practical side to this, since the Bruins were footing the bill for tuition, books, and room and board, as well as $10 a week spending money and up to $60 a week for hockey. The manager was also wary of the front-runners in town who encouraged a winner but departed with great speed when the team began losing. Orr was warned to beware of the rah-rah types.

"You'd be surprised how many hero worshipers there are," said Blair. "Even in big business in big cities there are guys who pander to name athletes just to be seen in their company. They wine and dine a good athlete, wanting to be seen by their friends with a celebrity. Sure, it's a free ride for the athlete, but he'll wind up a lush if he doesn't learn to handle these fair-weather friends."

Apparently Blair's persistent advice paid dividends. If it hadn't penetrated, Bobby would have been trouble, because he soon became the idol of Oshawa and its immediate vicinity. When word spread that he was living at the Wilds' three-bedroom brick ranch at 331 Walmer Road, youngsters were constantly at the doorstep pestering for autographs, and the parade of teen-age girls was unending. The Wilds recall the days of Orr with unmitigated affection. "He was wonderful in every way," said Mrs. Wild.

The same could be said of his hockey playing, which continued to improve immensely each year. By the end of the 1964–65 season he was again named to the First All-Star Team. One evaluation of his total excellence went this way:

"He is a swift, powerful skater with instant acceleration, instinctive anticipation, a quick accurate shot, remarkable composure, an unrelenting ambition, a solemn dedication, humility, modesty, and a fondness for his parents and his brothers and sisters that often turns his eyes moist."

One would be tempted to toss the entire paragraph into the wastepaper basket as just flak from the publicity man's typewriter, except that it was written by one of the most respected authors in Canada.

None of this praise apparently rubbed off on Bobby. Whenever he returned to Parry Sound he appeared to be the same regular guy he had been before. When he was sixteen he spent the summer as a $35-a-week clerk in Adams Men's Wear on James Street. "He lost money on that deal," said sister Pat. "He poured all his money on his back. What a Beau Brummell!"

To some friends of the family Bobby's sisters and brothers always seemed more naturally ebullient and gregarious than he. His mother explained that the burden of publicity and stardom at an early age was the cause of his reserve, and she considered it a natural and not at all bad reaction to the acclaim. But those who remember him in Oshawa will tell you that he possessed a whimsical streak and wasn't at all adverse to a practical joke, especially if he was on the detonating end of it.

Once when he was lounging around Joe Bolahood's sporting goods store on King Street East in Oshawa, Joe asked Bobby to get him a hamburger and a container of coffee. Bobby obliged and returned in what seemed to be record time, even for a hamburger and coffee. Joe, who had been distracted while fitting a customer, was hungry enough not to notice anything unusual about the hamburger. He took a big bite out of the roll, winced in a manner that would have pleased W.C. Fields, and discovered that the "meat" was nothing more than a rolled-up paper napkin. By this time Orr was outside, peeking in the front window with a broad grin on his face.

Other Oshawans remember what they considered hockey pranks, but which the Bruin management regarded as most serious business. Bobby would sometimes arrive at the Oshawa Civic Auditorium, home of the Generals, long before his teammates. He'd strap on the goaltender's equipment and surreptitiously work out with Jim Whittaker, his teammate and buddy from Parry Sound. They would stop before any of the brass arrived, fully aware that stern punitive measures would follow their discovery. The idea of Bobby Orr being injured *while playing goal* would probably have caused a collective stroke at Boston Garden in those days.

Such episodes merely underlined Orr's natural athletic versatility. He wanted to try everything. They say he played a solid shortstop in the Ontario Juvenile Softball Championships and was so successful a lacrosse player that the Oshawa Green Gaels offered him a tryout.

"Have you ever considered that the game of hockey is unique?" Blair said at the time. "A good hockey player can play all games well, but few stars of another sport can play hockey at all. Can you imagine Cassius Clay or Arnold Palmer or Johnny Unitas able to make even a school hockey team? Yet Gordie Howe used to work out regularly with the Detroit Tigers, and when Jim Norris promoted all the big fights and owned the Red Wings he'd look at Howe stripped down in the dressing room and he'd say, 'Gordie, with a build like that you could be heavyweight champion of the world.' Any number of hockey players can hit a golf ball as far as most pros; in fact, a lot of them *are* pros in the off-season.

"The point is, every hockey player must have the attributes of the top athletes in any game, except he must then add the encumbrance of skates. We grow up taking these things for granted in Canada, but the truth is that hockey is the most difficult of all games to master."

It had become clear to Blair that Orr had mastered hockey with a thoroughness that demanded he be imported to the NHL as soon as it was legally possible. In the meantime Bobby had to fortify only one aspect of his game, his toughness. It wasn't that he couldn't handle the rugged body play and in-fighting along the boards, but his physique was still slightly below the desirable NHL weight, so he did what he could to help himself. He worked on barbells twice a day for forty-five minutes, carried a set of handgrips to strengthen his wrists and forearms, and during the non-hockey months, he'd run around the Parry Sound harbor twice a day, a total of four miles.

The results, naturally, were positive, and Orr was now the total hockey player. So total, in fact, that Blair had the unmitigated gall, at least as one reporter interpreted it, to predict that Bobby Orr would be a better hockey player than either Gordie Howe or Bobby Hull. In fact, Blair suggested that the lad from Parry Sound could very well be the finest hockey player ever to lace on a pair of skates on this continent or in the Soviet Union.

But there was still another year of junior hockey to complete, and it remained for Orr to live up to what George Sullivan aptly described as "being a legend not only in his own time, but even before."

4. The "Greatest" Junior

If Orr wasn't a legend before his own time he certainly was orchestrating the most extensive symphony of adjectives ever heard for a young hockey player. Even searching through every paper in the Province of Ontario, one couldn't find any anti-Orr sentiment. Normally, the descriptions bordered on the outlandish, even among more conservative types such as Leighton "Hap" Emms, the veteran OHA manager whom Boston had imported as the new general manager of the Bruins. Emms made it clear that he would consider it a bad deal for Boston to trade Orr, the junior, for the *entire* Toronto Maple Leaf NHL team.

Naturally, the raves were no less stimulating in Oshawa. When he was sixteen, he broke his own scoring record with thirty-four goals and fifty-nine assists, and a year later he scored thirty-seven goals and sixty assists. That would be a remarkable feat even for a high-scoring forward; yet Bobby was still back on defense.

"His teammates would give him the puck," recalled Emile Francis, "then they'd stand around and watch him in amazement."

It was unanimously agreed that Bobby never required any assistance in hockey-playing, yet his family often chafed when they watched an opponent butt him into the boards or apply a bloodletting high stick. Arva Orr was probably more emotionally involved than any of her children.

"I try to let on I'm not with her," Bobby's sister, Pat, once said. "Let's say she's unrestrained."

To this, Mrs. Orr responded that she found it difficult sitting with her husband at a game. Her reasoning: "He sits me down too often!"

At that time Bobby's kid brother Doug was in the

schizophrenic position of being an ardent rooter for the Toronto Maple Leafs, though aware that his brother soon would be wearing the black, white, and gold colors of the Bruins. "I'll cheer for Toronto until Bobby turns pro," said ten-year-old Doug, "and then I guess I'll switch."

His older brother, Ron, who is taller and heavier than Bobby, remained in Parry Sound, where he played for the town's champion Junior C team; many observers insist, however, that he could have become an accomplished professional. Once Bobby's Oshawa Generals visited Parry Sound for a benefit game against the Parry Sounders, captained by Ron. At one point a fight developed, and Ron skated toward the battlers to pry them apart. To his surprise and later amusement, he suddenly found himself horizontal on the ice, encumbered by an Oshawa defenseman with a broad grin on his face. According to Ron, Bobby was smiling down at him "like a Cheshire cat."

Whenever possible the Orrs drove around the province to see Bobby play. The atmosphere was generally serene when they attended games at the Oshawa rink, but the fans were almost always hostile and often belligerent in visiting arenas such as St. Catherines, home of the Teepees. One night when Bobby's aunt, Marg Atherton, was in the stands at the St. Catherines' rink Chuck Kelly, a member of the Teepees, slugged her nephew. Kelly's aim was true but his positioning under the circumstances, was poor. He belted Orr directly in front of Aunt Marg. "You brute," she screamed, and then did what any good aunt would do, she let fly a punch at Kelly. "Don't you dare hit Bobby!"

If anything else about hockey perturbed Arva Orr besides the abuse of her son by opponents and a few jealous fans, it was that Bobby might not get a chance to complete his high-school education because of the demands of the Bruins management. When he was seventeen, completing what was to be his last year of junior hockey, Orr had reached his next-to-last semester of high school. Although Bobby wasn't setting any scholastic records, his mother was hopeful that somehow he would continue his education and receive his diploma.

Bobby himself then felt that despite the acclaim and attention he had received since joining the Oshawa team he still lacked the sophistication of an adult. "You should have seen me sometimes at Oshawa," he recalled after becoming a Bruin. "I'd go in to see somebody, and I knew what I wanted to say, but then they would start telling me things and turn it all around. They would tell me things that I knew were wrong—I *knew* they were—but I would just sit there and agree."

His sophistication on the ice had reached the penultimate degree by the close of the 1965–66 season. With Orr directing the attack *and* the defense, the Generals won the OHA Junior A championship and the Eastern Canada Junior championship, and qualified for the Memorial Cup finals against the Edmonton Oil Kings for the Junior championship of Canada.

While this was to be the high point in Orr's junior career, the 1966 playoffs were a traumatic experience for Oshawans who realized they soon would be losing their folk hero. The local newspapers underlined this feeling in their advertisements for Bobby's final games in a Generals' uniform.

"See Boston's $1,000,000 Prospect, Bobby Orr," shouted one ad.

"Probably Your Last Chance to See BOBBY ORR Play Junior Hockey," warned another.

The Memorial Cup finals meant many things to the people affiliated with Orr that spring. The natives were restless because Oshawa would return to virtual obscurity after Bobby left. The Generals' management was pulsating with the fervor that normally accompanies a shot at the Memorial Cup, and the Boston Bruins were wringing their hands with alternate glee and despair as the date of his signing loomed closer and closer.

The glee was the image of Orr wearing a Bruins uniform, at last satisfying those fans who were waiting for the day when he played in the NHL. The despair was the thought that, somehow, in his final game as a junior he might injure himself irreparably and thereby become lost to the Bruins. And in the backs of their minds, the Boston executives nurtured the fear that Bobby's contract demands just might be too staggering for their bankbooks. In many respects the fears were justified.

Of all the worriers the man who appeared most concerned was Hap Emms, the Bruins' manager. That spring the Bruins had finished out of the playoffs for the seventh consecutive season and, as usual, the loyal-beyond-reason

Bruins fans were clamoring for help. Emms realized that it would be his chore to sign Bobby. Then, he discovered that Orr was playing in the Memorial Cup finals with a groin injury. Emms envisioned that Orr might easily aggravate the condition to a point where it might affect his Bruins career. He was extremely vexed at the prospect of Bobby playing any additional games.

Needless to say, a crippled Orr was a better hockey player than most of his opponents who were in superb physical condition, and the Generals were most anxious for him to play. They were trailing, 3–2, in the best-of-seven series with the sixth game possibly the finale for Bobby and his team.

There was no question in Orr's mind. He was determined to put on a uniform and help the Generals, but he was willing to submit to a medical examination to satisfy the management and Emms, who was becoming more and more furious about the situation. On the day of the sixth game the doctor visited Orr at his Toronto hotel room before the team was to leave for Maple Leaf Gardens and the clash with Edmonton. According to the medical report Bobby could play the game if he wanted, and would probably not suffer any further damage to his groin. Doug Orr, who had motored down for the game, discussed the problem with Bobby after the doctor had left their suite. Ever since Bobby was old enough to sign a Junior A card Doug had made it a policy to permit his son to make his own decisions. All that mattered to Doug was whether Bobby believed he could withstand the inevitable pain that would accompany his movements on the ice. Doug knew he needn't bother to ask about that.

Meanwhile Emms had made up *his* mind that Bobby would *not* play, and the professorial Bruins executive went to Maple Leaf Gardens to lay down the law with the Orrs. Father and manager collided outside the dressing room, then walked into a nearby, empty press room. Suddenly, the decibel count in Maple Leaf Gardens mounted like the last aria in *Lohengrin*.

"I don't want that boy to play," Emms demanded.

"Bobby wants to play," his father countered, a few notes louder, "and that's good enough for me."

"He's *not* going to play," Emms insisted, his voice reverberating passionately across the room.

"Now, wait a minute, Mr. Emms," Orr replied, playing his trump card, "Bobby still doesn't belong to the Bruins. He's my son. Just remember that."

Emms could have—and many observers believe he should have—quit right there. But he felt obliged to launch a parting shot, and it was one heard for several years around the Orr household and the hockey world. To some, it was to be more damaging than anything else Emms did before or since.

"You know," Emms concluded, "when Bobby's in the NHL he won't be able to phone home every time he doesn't get things his way."

Fury engulfed Doug Orr and he was tempted to do something violent. But he contained himself and merely advised the bespectacled Emms that Bobby was still answerable to his father, and as far as his father was concerned he could play.

As things developed, the misgivings shared by Orr and Emms were inconsequential for either the game or Bobby's future. The young defenseman certainly suffered, as the pain knifed through his thighs, but his loyal followers empathized with him and shared his anguish.

"You never saw so many women crying in the stands," said Cora Wild. "We all knew how much pain Bob was in."

Nevertheless, Bobby clambered over the wooden boards as often as possible. Even when coach Bep Guidolin happened to turn the other way, he took to the ice, desperate to revive the Generals. But Edmonton prevailed and won the game and the Cup. When the game was over the fans stood as one and gave Orr a standing ovation. For Doug Orr, it was an unforgettable moment.

"Bob played his heart out," his father remembered fondly. "There were times in that game when he just couldn't get to his feet after somebody knocked him down, yet he kept trying. Bobby probably showed me more in that game than in any I've ever seen him play. I never saw a kid display more guts than he did that night."

Others contend that the *real* display of guts was that exhibited by Emms when he later conferred with the two Orrs about a Bruins contract. When the trio huddled at the Hotel Genosha in Oshawa, Emms opened negotiations with a figure that Doug Orr later described as unworthy of retelling, it was so absurd.

Obviously the Boston manager had recovered admirably from his earlier defeat at the hands of Doug Orr. It almost seemed as if he were trying to extract revenge by making a low offer. His logic was fascinating. Emms made the point that Gilles Marotte, a burly French-Canadian defenseman, gladly permitted the manager to fill in the blank spaces on a contract and that numerous NHL players had signed for less than $10,000. Even Gordie Howe was quite satisfied to accept a Detroit Red Wing jacket as a bonus for joining the NHL organization.

Emms' empirical reasoning made all the impression on Doug Orr of a bullet on a tank. When Hap realized his offers were being deflected rather harshly right back in his face he upped his ante to what he suggested would be the absolute maximum—a $5,000 bonus and an $8,000 salary. Doug Orr thought to himself, surely this man isn't serious. Negotiations temporarily broke down at this point with Emms unaware that once again Doug Orr was holding a trump card. This time it was R. Alan Eagleson, a bright young Toronto lawyer, former athlete, and a man who later became prominent in the Progressive-Conservative Party of Ontario.

Eagleson had already made a name for himself in the NHL; Carl Brewer had obtained his counsel in 1963 when the All-Star defenseman clashed with the Toronto Maple Leaf management. With Eagleson calling the shots, Brewer won his case and, in time, Eagleson represented other Toronto players including Bob Pulford and Mike Walton. As the lawyer piled success upon success, word spread through the hockey leagues, from the NHL down, that this was the man to see if you had a problem with management.

Thus, it was not surprising that Doug Orr had heard about Eagleson. He had heard him speak at a sports banquet, liked what he heard and saw, and decided to obtain his advice as Brewer had a few years earlier. The barrister actually was doing very well before he ever met young Orr. A member of the Bay Street, Toronto, firm of Blaney, Pasternak, Smela, Eagleson and Watson, Barristers and Solicitors, Eagleson was overflowing with work. But the Orr case intrigued him and he agreed to assist Doug if he ever called.

On the day that Doug, Bobby, and Emms were conferring at the Hotel Genosha, Eagleson was strategically waiting at Joe Bolahood's house for the signal, like any good reinforcement regiment. When Emms offered his "final" figure, Doug decided it was time to get into some serious negotiating, so he advised the manager that hereafter they would be represented by Eagleson.

The name Eagleson impressed Emms the way the name Moshe Dayan would impress President Nasser. Eagleson? Why, there was absolutely no way that Emms would talk to that Toronto lawyer. He didn't realize that young Bobby had already grown to respect Eagleson and was now furious with Emms. Bobby interrupted the dialogue between Emms and his father and laid it on the line with the Bruins manager. Either he would talk with Eagleson or Bobby wouldn't play for the Boston hockey club. It was as simple as that.

Emms realized he had plenty of time to negotiate. There were still the summer months, and maybe a little more thought would put some sense into the heads of those Orrs. He was not going to talk with Eagleson, and that was that. The talks ended in an impasse, and each faction went his own way, wondering who would make the next move.

Anyone with a little insight would have realized that the Orr contingent would prevail. It was only a question of how long Emms would hold out and how much he would eventually pay. He couldn't possibly win, because thousands of Boston hockey fans and hockey writers were waiting for Orr. After hearing the Bruins brass eulogize Orr for four years—Emms was one of his most emphatic boosters—the fans felt that the Boston team had a moral obligation to sign the lad as partial reparation for their extraordinary support during the cellar-dwelling days.

Eagleson had a ploy of his own; the NHL, he reasoned, wasn't the only place where Bobby could improve his hockey playing. Canada's National Hockey Team was on the look-out for outstanding young talent. The rewards, perhaps, were more modest than the NHL contract Eagleson was seeking, but they were attractive in their way. In a more relaxed atmosphere than would be possible in the NHL, Orr could play hockey for his country while completing his high-school education and could possibly even continue on to college, with the government footing the bill. It was a prospect that must have appealed to Arva Orr if not to Hap Emms.

Some preliminary soundings were conducted, with the

aim of signing Orr with the Nationals. This information reached the press and of course, put Emms on notice that time was running out on him. August was rapidly coming to a close and soon the hockey training camps would open. Without Orr the Bruins might as well close Boston Garden, because the natives would be furious if he didn't show up in a hockey uniform.

In the interim Emms discussed the financial situation with the Bruins hierarchy to which he was answerable. After all, it was the owners, not Emms, who would ultimately have to pay the tab, and they had to make clear just how high he could go.

By August Emms had made up his mind that Eagleson was a fact of life with which he had to deal. He eventually notified the lawyer that he would talk with him. Eagleson, in turn, put in a call to Parry Sound alerting the Orrs that Emms was ready to talk. Negotiations were to be conducted aboard Emms' forty-two-foot cabin cruiser, *Barbara Lynn,* anchored in the harbor of Barrie, Ontario, a relatively short drive from Parry Sound.

The talks had all the august overtones of the signing of a peace treaty, as the group sat down that Friday evening, September 2, 1966. Included in the entourage were Bobby, Doug, Eagleson, Emms, and Alex Eagar, manager of the Brunswick Motor Hotel in Parry Sound and the man who had helped launch the lad on a hockey career by buying him his first pair of gloves and shoulder pads.

Unlike previous Emms-Orr conversations this one was more like mediation among virtual allies. They went over the various points in the Eagleson-inspired contract and appeared to have reached an agreement at last. Emms excused himself, clambered off the boat, and walked to a telephone to phone Boston. Shortly after 2 A.M., Saturday morning, September 3, the Boston Bruins had signed the eighteen-year-old who was to become hockey's greatest star.

The most intelligent estimates, supported by not-so-oblique observations by Doug Orr, place Bobby's two-year contract at somewhere between $50,000 and $70,000. Emms had signed Orr for more than four times his original "top" offer, including bonuses.

"And," said Eagleson later, "he was worth every dime. Boston hockey writers told me that by Christmas the kid had increased Bruins attendance by $100,000."

Ironically, Emms scored one triumph in the signing ceremony. He finally achieved a measure of one-up-manship with Eagleson by calling a photographer aboard the boat for the historic photo of the signing—but he refused to pose with the lawyer.

The photograph, which might someday be mounted in Hockey's Hall of Fame in Toronto, depicts a smiling but obviously tired Emms on the left, holding his cigar in one hand, with his other clenched in a fist. Bobby is in the middle, pen in right hand, grinning with his mouth open. On the right his dad is resting his left hand on the table as if to keep it from tilting while his right hand is invisible behind Bobby's back. He is obviously patting him for a job well done. As well he might, for his son, by the stroke of a pen, had revolutionized the economics of NHL hockey. Orr had thoroughly routed the NHL establishment.

Emm's omission of Eagleson from the photograph may have been more symbolic than the Bruins manager realized. For it was the lawyer, then thirty-three years old, who, while apparently out of the picture, had actually executed the *coup* that overthrew Emms' plans.

"Al's done more for hockey in two years," said Chicago's Bobby Hull, "than anybody else had done in twenty."

"L'Affaire Orr" catapulted Eagleson into the hockey limelight for good. Players sought him out for legal help, and almost always he came through with a significant victory. He helped the Springfield Indians of the American Hockey League defeat owner Eddie Shore whose policies, by comparison with Emms', seemed medieval. Later the NHL players inevitably came to him for help in organizing their union. Despite an unsuccessful attempt by the owners to torpedo the movement, Eagleson and the players led by Orr formed the NHL Players' Association and "Good Old Eag," as he became known, was voted its first Executive Director.

But players such as Bobby Hull, Gordie Howe, and Stan Mikita didn't need a Players' Association to realize that a rookie named Bobby Orr, who hadn't played a single NHL game, was making a fat five-figure salary and that they, as record-breakers, certainly deserved more. They demanded more money and they got it. Two years after Orr signed aboard the *Barbara Lynn,* Hull had lifted his pay to an estimated $100,000, the highest hockey has known, and others had won substantial increases as well.

Perhaps it was also noteworthy that when Bobby put pen to contract Emms heralded the event by popping open several bottles of Teem, a fruit-flavored soft drink that in no way resembles champagne. Having slurped down the soda, the Orr negotiating team retreated from Emms' boat and returned north to Parry Sound with their prize. Historians have noted that they made one significant stop en route. A short detour was effected at Orillia, one-time home of Canadian humorist Stephen Leacock who would have been amused by the proceedings. There they dropped in at Eagleson's summer home where they opened a bottle of champagne and gave each other a warm and well-deserved toast.

Now for the first time, Orr was receiving international recognition. Sure, he was renowned throughout Canada and had even been hailed by the Soviets for his extraordinary performance against the Russian National Team when Bobby led an OHA Junior A All-Star Team against the talented visitors. But not until he signed with the Bruins was he truly recognized in the United States, where it really counted. Then, and only then, did he achieve real athletic manhood—*Sports Illustrated* acknowledged his existence with a by-lined story called "A High Price For Fresh Northern Ice."

"Orr comes to the NHL," *Sports Illustrated* commented, "as the most ballyhooed and highest-paid rookie in hockey history. The Bruins have not made the playoffs since 1959, so they have promised the fans, more and more, that Bobby Orr would be there soon. Then the Bruins would lose another game, and the crowds, grumbling, would fall out of the Boston Garden into the dark of Causeway Street and stand there under the el and talk of Bobby Orr and the day when he would be there."

Meanwhile, Bobby returned home and began packing his belongings for the trip to training camp. He vowed to himself that he would buy his folks a new home, although Arva Orr later pooh-poohed the suggestion simply because she preferred the simplicity and warmth of their comfortable stucco. He also had time to think about the machinations that had taken place ever since the Memorial Cup playoffs, which had left him a wiser if less idealistic young man.

"I learned more in the last five months about people and life than I ever did all before," he revealed. "I learned a lot of things I never knew."

Then he pondered training camp and the season ahead. The Bruins veterans would be waiting to test him in the intrasquad games, and the big-league opponents also wanted to see what he was all about; they had heard so much about the junior that they were getting sick of it.

"I think I know what to expect," Bobby said early in September, 1966. "There will be some players—probably not the real good ones—who'll be right after me. But I expect that most of the others feel like a lot of people I know do, and I think I did something that will be good for all the players someday. I just stood up, eh? I don't think they can mind that."

What the opponents really wanted to know was just how good he really was. Could he lead a rush as well as Doug Harvey could when Harvey played for the Montreal Canadiens? Could he shoot the puck as hard as Chicago's Golden Jet, Bobby Hull? And was he as strong as the strongest player of all, the already-immortalized Detroit Red Wing, Gordie Howe? Would it be possible for Bobby Orr to dominate the NHL the way he had manipulated the OHA Junior A League?

No, nobody believed it was humanly possible, least of all Bobby Orr. "I know," he said, "I know I can't do all the things I've done." Then, a pause. "I guess there'll be a lot of sleepless nights for me if I don't live up."

5. At Last, the NHL

If Orr was revered in Boston even before he put on a Bruins uniform, as many Boston writers have suggested, this affectionate sentiment was not shared by his new teammates. When he arrived at training camp early in September, 1966, Bobby was introduced almost immediately to one of the Bruins' more primitive rituals, the Shave.

"It is a complete operation," observed Chris Lydon of the Boston *Globe*. "Yes, Virginia, they shave the whole man—not, mercifully, with a straight razor. But, as Eddie Johnston of the Bruins explains, 'the idea is to loosen the blade of a safety razor enough so that it scrapes. Some guys have had fifteen or twenty stitches after it's over.' "

Orr did not escape unscathed, which would have been impossible. He was duped, however, by a simple ruse that shouldn't have fooled a schoolboy. Some Boston players in the locker room suggested he test drive a "magic blanket" that they had obtained. They led him to an ordinary blanket spread out on the floor and recommended that the standard flying position was horizontal. Bobby obliged. In a trice his teammates jumped him; the razor was out, the Shave was on.

"I fell into it," Orr recalled, "like a real country huckleberry. It was awful."

The episode apparently traumatized listeners who later heard about it more than it did Orr. "The Mafia tradition, as Joe Valachi described it, of making new members sign an oath of secrecy in their own blood sounds kiddish by comparison," noted Lydon. "It is hard to image a rite like the Shave surviving in any other corner of the modern world, but then it would be hard to find another group of men like hockey players."

Once Orr stepped on the ice his teammates knew at once that their savior had, in fact, arrived, as the brass had anticipated all along. "Every thing Bobby does so beautifully now," said Milt Schmidt, "he was doing about the same when we first saw him."

Veteran defenseman Ted Green, who had suffered through Boston's most abysmal hockey years, studied Orr's moves a few times and then remarked, "Kid, I don't know what you're getting, but it ain't enough!"

Bobby started the season for the Bruins on defense, and in his first game he received a vivid lesson in what to expect. Teammate Joe Watson went into the corner for the puck and emerged with his head in his hands.

"Joe came over to the bench," Bobby recalled, "with his mouth bleeding like he'd been shot. Danny, the trainer, said: 'It'll be okay, Joe. Just rinse it out.' So Joe rinsed his mouth all right, and eight or nine teeth came out with the water."

Orr didn't suffer quite so gory an injury in his early games, but he was undoubtedly the most desirable new target the bully boys had seen in years. Roughnecks like Reg Fleming of the Rangers would attempt to nail him from the "blind side," when Orr, with his eyes riveted on the puck, would be in a position where he'd be unable to see an opponent rushing at him, hellbent to destroy. He was flattened often enough to become acutely aware of the problem, but not enough to become battle shy. If anything he responded with even more determination and fight. In time he was doling out considerably more punishment than he received, and his original tormentors were wishing fervently that they had left him alone in the first place.

Bruins fans immediately adopted him as their very special baby boy and anyone who dared attack him was regarded with a special contempt. Once when a Detroit player was penalized two minutes for hooking Orr, an annoyed fan shouted, "Make that a two-and-a-half-minute penalty—two minutes for hooking and an extra thirty seconds for hooking Bobby Orr!!"

Within a month of his debut he was being lavishly compared with Hall-of-Famer Eddie Shore and, even more surprising, the people one would expect to extol Shore's virtues were siding with Bobby.

"He's as good as Shore," pronounced Milt Schmidt, himself a Hall-of-Famer and an old teammate of Shore's. "In the old days there was no forechecking. Shore could wind up without interference behind his net and start a big rush. Now there is excellent forechecking, and the modern defenseman has to think faster. Bobby does just that."

When it was suggested that Shore was a better skater Schmidt promptly issued a denial. "No, he wasn't. Shore could perform a lot of steps on skates but he wasn't a better skater. Bobby is deceptive; he has two speeds. And it doesn't take him the usual three, four, or five strides to accelerate from one speed to another. One stride and he's away."

His speed was a constant source of analysis and fascination to his players and bosses. "You may have noticed," said coach Harry Sinden, "that Bobby skates with his feet fairly far apart. Most sound skaters are a little bowlegged, which is good because it gives them better balance."

Eventually, Schmidt reappraised his position and said Orr possessed three skating speeds. Sinden put it at four, while Green commented that the kid had "eighteen speeds of fast."

His talents were so diverse and his behavior so unique—he insisted upon calling his teammates "Mister" and "Sir" in his early days as a Bruin—it was difficult to fit Orr into a specific category. Although at first he was neither articulate nor a humorist, he later began to take on these characteristics.

There were some who detected a parallel between Orr of the Bruins and Joe DiMaggio of the Yankees. He was also favorably compared with Ted Williams, Carl Yastrzemski, and Vince Lombardi for variously similar traits. In time he inevitably was described as a "mild Canadian version of Joe Namath."

"Were he an American," said Bill Marshall, a former Oshawa *Times* writer and now Toronto producer-publicist, "he would have been exposed to so much more publicity than a Canadian athlete could, so he developed as not nearly as extroverted as an American counterpart like Namath. Were Bobby in any other American sport than hockey he would have been internationally known by the time he was seventeen. In Canada we don't have a Broadway as in Broadway Joe Namath; so how can you have a Broadway Bobby? But in another few years he'll come out of this."

There were those, such as author Bill Surface writing in *The New York Times Magazine,* who suggested that Bobby *had* "come out of this." Like Bobby Hull, Orr has become a sex symbol for the female hockey fan. But Hull is balding, getting old, and talking of retirement. Orr's features may not be Adonislike in their perfection but they have a certain arresting appeal. Orr's *joie de vivre* had developed rapidly by his third NHL season. For laughs he'd phone a teammate—who just happened to be recovering from an injured jaw—and feign a journalist's voice. Bobby would maintain a reporterlike decorum throughout the dialogue, sprinkling sugary compliments here and there to inspire the player to continue talking although he was in obvious pain.

Another time coach Sinden was cautioning his players to beware of the Hong Kong flu. "I'm already fighting it off," Orr replied, displaying the third pint container of orange juice he had gulped down in ten minutes.

"Does that stuff fight it off?" Bobby was asked.

Orr looked at his coach with a bemused expression, "I don't *have* the flu, do I?"

While all this was going on Doug Orr was sitting back proudly, having the last laugh at those Parry Sounders who were skeptical when he permitted Bobby to leave town at the age of fifteen. When Bobby scored his first goal in Boston, Doug was there and decided to engrave the puck in gold. He watched his son score his sixth goal of the season at Maple Leaf Gardens and told Stan Obodiac of the Gardens staff that he might have that one engraved, too.

He also betrayed a growing disenchantment with certain journalists, a skepticism that was to be shared by Arva Orr and, in time, by Bobby himself. This time Doug was peevish over some allegedly faulty observations about Parry Sound weather conditions made by the *Sports Illustrated* reporter who so enthusiastically described Bobby in that first major feature in an American magazine.

"In that article," Doug Orr told Obodiac, "he thought the guys in Parry Sound were boobs when he wrote that ice froze on Parry Sound in September. Why, today, almost December, I drove up in the rain."

It wasn't long before newsmen discovered that Bobby's father was just as good copy as his son, and infinitely more outspoken. He criticized Emms publicly, while defending all the other Bruins officials, and even spanked the Toronto Maple Leafs for not taking a keener interest in Bobby when he was a Junior C player.

"Bob Davidson [The Leafs' chief scout] said Bobby was too small," Doug Orr observed, "yet he scouted Dave Keon who is smaller. But I'm satisfied he's at Boston. Maybe he wouldn't have been given the chance in Toronto."

Superficially at least, Orr appeared to have all the equipment to personally lift the Bruins to a playoff berth. There was something intrinsically wrong with the team, however, something that was not apparent to the casual observer or the regular fan, but was detected by alert newsmen who penetrated the Bruins locker room. The team was riddled with dissension; everybody appeared contaminated by the infection except Orr.

"The rest of the players," said *Newsweek* sports editor Pete Axthelm, "seemed to be coming to the rink just to stand around and watch him. The Bruins desperately needed changes in personnel, in morale, and in the front office. Sometimes the Bruins felt as if Emms was treating them like captive bush leaguers."

Some of the veterans were disgusted enough to complain for the record; others complained privately. But the feeling, as goalie Ed Johnston would eventually put it, was that Emms was not enthusiastically received by all the Bruins. "He could probably handle kids," said Johnston, "but he sure didn't know how to work with guys who earn $20,000 at this game."

Boston writers mentioned that Emms had surrounded himself with yes men and had begun alienating his players. The low point of the Emms-Bruins relationship was plumbed in January, 1967, when Ted Green was selected to play in the All-Star Game by Detroit coach Sid Abel. Emms promptly endeared himself to Green by stating that Green did not deserve to play in the All-Star Game. This infuriated the defenseman and he decided not to attend the contest.

Cherished in hockey circles as a spectacle exceeded only by the Stanley Cup matches, the All-Star Game attracted writers from coast to coast, from Canada and the United States. For a player to shun the "classic" was the height of insult, and Green was acutely aware of what he was doing. However, this in no way diminished Abel's fury when he learned about the AWOL Bruin. The All-Star coach vented his anger on Emms when the two met in the lobby of Montreal's Queen Elizabeth Hotel prior to the game.

"Why in hell didn't you tell me Green wasn't coming?"

Abel demanded of Emms. "I would have had time to get a replacement. Now I'm stuck."

If Green had worked out a blueprint for humiliating Emms he couldn't have succeeded better than by staying away from the All-Star Game. Abel was livid with anger at Emms. The press, respecting Green as a veteran who had often played though hampered by injuries, was not enthused about Emms. The general sentiment was that by charging that "Green doesn't deserve to be on the All-Star Team," Emms rather than Green had emerged as the goat of the fooferaw.

"Eventually," wrote D. Leo Monahan in the Boston *Sunday Advertiser*, "Emms cut his own throat."

The time was spring, of 1967. Emms, who had nearly lost Bobby Orr and who had allegedly alienated some of his best players, returned to the OHA Junior A League, and Milt Schmidt succeeded him as manager. The rank and file of the hockey club greeted the change with jubilation. Nor was Bobby Orr noticeably depressed. Despite the Bruins' malaise Bobby's rookie season was eminently successful even when judged against the astronomical standards set for him by newsmen, opponents, coaches and, most significant of all, by Bobby himself.

6. Instant Success

No rookie who ever graced an NHL rink—not Gordie Howe, Bobby Hull, Jean Beliveau, Eddie Shore, Maurice Richard, Frank Boucher, Milt Schmidt, or any of the other members of the Hall of Fame—ever overwhelmed the league the way Orr did in 1966–67. Beliveau came close in 1953–54, but the Montreal Canadiens center didn't even win the Calder Trophy as rookie of the year nor did he win a position on the First or Second All-Star Teams. From Orr's collection of prizes an outsider might have accused him of being downright greedy if he didn't realize the awards had been made by distinguished judges. Bobby was a landslide choice for the rookie award and was picked to the Second All-Star Team. Several writers contend that he would easily have made it to the First Team if he hadn't suffered a knee injury, the first of many debilitating accidents that were to haunt him from then on.

His scoring feats were an embarrassment to his teammates; thirteen goals, twenty-eight assists, for forty-one points in sixty-one games. That placed him third highest on the team, and he was a defenseman. The fans were fully cognizant of his contribution, and late in the season one subscriber assailed the manager. "Hey, Emms, why don't you trade Orr? He's making the rest of the Bruins look bad."

Bobby started performing that way right from the opening face-off of his premiere. The Bruins defeated the Detroit Red Wings, 6—2, and Orr contributed to the victory with an assist and some alert defensive play. In the second game of the season, Montreal at Boston Garden, fans saw for the first time his alarmingly fast slap shot at its best. It was a blur from the blue line, and before Montreal's goalie could move, Bobby had his first NHL goal—and Doug Orr was to have his first NHL souvenir.

The venerable Boston Garden trembled with noise as if

in the midst of an earthquake. First one by one and then almost *en masse* the crowd moved to its feet and tendered the eighteen-year-old a standing ovation. It was only a goal, but the applause lasted for several minutes and amazed even Montreal's veteran coach Toe Blake. "I never heard anything like it," Blake said.

At that moment it became apparent that Orr, no matter what would follow, had been placed on a very special plateau by the fans. "He is a sweetheart, isn't he?" a middle-aged woman said the following day, while waiting on line at the ticket window. "He brings out the mother instinct in me."

No parent likes to admit that his son has done wrong, and when *their* Bobby made a mistake the Bruin fans merely shut their eyes to the culprit's number and shouted their criticism at someone else. Once Montreal's John Ferguson fooled Orr with a rudimentary between-the-legs feint and then went around Bobby for a solid shot on goal. The fans hurled their insults.

"Westfall," they shouted at the team's excellent utility player, "you're a big bum." What did it matter that Westfall hadn't even dressed for the game?

But if the fans were blind to his *faux pas*, Bobby certainly wasn't. He remembered the time he organized a rush against the New York Rangers, crossed the opponent's blue line and heard a voice yelling "drop it, drop it." He figured it was a teammate suggesting a drop pass. Bobby slipped the puck behind him and cruised ahead to screen the Ranger goalie. By this time Vic Hadfield, the Rangers left wing, who had yelled for the puck, had swerved around with the disk and skated in for a New York goal. Another time Orr scored a spectacular goal against the Chicago Black Hawks on an end-to-end rush. Yet a minute later Bobby and Dennis Hull outwitted Orr and tied the game for Chicago.

A few onlookers noticed that when Orr, raging, was ordered from the ice he began weeping and ultimately hid his head behind the side of the rink. To some viewers it was the tantrum of a spoiled child who didn't get his way. To others it was the reaction of a bitter loser who suffered excruciatingly when a goal is scored against him.

"There was a time," a Bruin season-ticketholder bitterly recalled, "when you got the impression that nobody gave a damn about the team. But Bobby has helped change that."

Zealous might be the best description of Orr's attitude toward the game, and pity the poor opponent who got in his way. The hatchet men who Bobby knew would be after his scalp were put on notice early in the season that he would brook no foolishness on their part. What is more, he went up against Ted Harris of Montreal and Orland Kurtenbach of New York and emerged with victories against two of the best boxers in or out of the NHL. He knocked Harris down twice in one bout, which was to be the beginning of an energetic rivalry; and he fought Kurtenbach to an admirable draw. "The kid's got good balance," the Ranger slugger explained. "He's hard to knock off his pins."

Wren Blair and Emile Francis, the two men who were among the first to see Orr play junior hockey, watched the development of the defenseman with mixed emotions. Blair, of course, was thoroughly delighted and unabashedly predicted, "Orr will be bigger in Boston than Ted Williams ever was."

Francis, who had moved on to become general manager and coach of the Rangers, eyed Orr with a mixture of unbounded appreciation and professional jealousy. As Francis' right wing Rod Gilbert put it, "I wish he was on our team." Francis had said all along that Orr would be a better pro then a junior, and now his prophecy was proving true.

"In the pros," Francis explained, "I figured they'd throw the puck up to him and then set themselves up for a return pass. That's what happened. I figured that since he's a defenseman maybe he should spend more time defending. But I try to think how many times we've caught him for a goal and I can't find it happening too often. Kids that age aren't supposed to have that poise. I see veterans panic in a tough spot and most of the time you can't blame them. Orr? He's standing there as if he owns the place. He's some meal ticket, isn't he?"

There was always some question about how the lower-paid Bruins would accept Orr in the dressing room. Bobby was supersensitive at first, and it soon became known that he didn't want any special attention. "He's always worried about how the other guys on the club will be affected by it," said Coach Sinden.

In a matter of weeks, though, the uptight feeling wore off, and, with the help of some of the more loosey-goosey

Bruins, Orr truly became one of the boys. One of the pivotal incidents occurred one afternoon when a rather large package addressed to Orr arrived in the Bruins dressing room. "What's that," inquired Ron Stewart, "your weekly bag of money?"

It got a laugh from Bobby, which is what the players wanted to see. That was by no means the end of the gags, and eventually Orr was organizing pranks himself. One time he and teammate Marotte thought they noticed that coach Sinden was losing some hair. Their antidote to Sinden's potential baldness was the purchase of a comb almost as long as a hockey stick.

With young Sinden in command the team could generally stay on the light side. He still was feeling his way around the league—1966–67 was also his NHL rookie year—and he was young enough to enjoy a friendly jape.

Emms, who was still boss in those days, theorized that since Orr was such an adroit and powerful skater maybe he shouldn't be anchored to a defense post; perhaps it would be more useful to have him play forward—center, for example. The idea has since been ridiculed but it was not without precedent. The Rangers in the past decade had done the same thing with their hard-skating defenseman Jim Neilson, and Punch Imlach, when he was coaching the Maple Leafs, would often throw a defenseman up front. Usually, however, the strategy is born out of panic or desperation, and so it was with the Orr experiment.

"I did what I was told," was Orr's comment, "but I didn't really like it. What I enjoy most about playing defense is that you're facing the play all the time. You can't do that in any of the other positions. A forward loses the puck, he has to turn and lose sight of what's happening."

Sinden, who had to apply the directive for Orr to play center, looked back at the idea after the 1966–67 season and also indicated it had been bad both for the Bruins and for Orr. "We stopped using him as a centerman," said Sinden, "because we decided in a hurry that there's no sense taking the game's best defenseman and playing him in another position. It makes as much sense as playing Elizabeth Taylor in a boy's role."

That feeling was confirmed at the 1966–67 awards ceremonies at the conclusion of the season: Orr received the Calder Trophy, but Harry Howell of the Rangers was given the James Norris Trophy as the NHL's best defenseman. Howell embraced the silver trophy and turned to the audience: "I might as well enjoy it now," he said, "because I expect it's going to belong to Bobby for the next ten years."

Howell's good-humored attitude was consistant with everything else said about the crew-cut kid from Parry Sound. It was hard not to like Orr, both as a person and as a player. Knocking him was like putting down the flag; you just didn't do it. At least you didn't unless you were in an unassailable position, and few in the realm of hockey ever enjoyed such an exalted role. One who did was Bobby Hull, the almighty left wing from Chicago who had broken the goal-scoring record so many times that he was in a position to speak his mind. Often Hull would do just that in a syndicated column he wrote for the Toronto *Daily Star*. On November 4, 1967, one of the first genuine bits of criticism zeroed in on Orr.

"Last year," wrote Hull, "Bobby was often caught out of position defensively because he rushed so deep into the other end that he couldn't get back to his own zone in time. When one defenseman is out of position it places a heavier burden on his partner. That's why Gilles Marotte, who played beside Orr last winter, was beaten for so many goals —he was left alone too often to handle two- and three-man rushes."

Powerful words, but not the last to be heard against Orr. Even Harry Howell detected a flaw or two in Bobby's armor. "Sometimes," Howell pointed out after Orr's rookie season, "I've seen him look down at the puck instead of keeping his eyes on a guy's chest when he's coming at you. I'd say that right now he's got 75 per cent of his defense worked out. The rest will come in two or three years."

Sinden indicated that Orr's shots were soaring too high when they reached the goaltender and suggested a change in stick size. Bobby countered that the reason was that he was not following through properly. He worked at it, and eventually the shots improved. "In those areas where he's weak," Sinden added, "he knows it himself."

At no time did Orr ever claim to have a copyright on hockey perfection. He generally was his own worst critic, but nobody but himself would listen. He blasted himself for dropping too far back when opponents moved into his own zone and criticized his own attentiveness in the Bruins defensive area. But it was all relative; by comparison to other players he was, as acclaimed, much closer to perfection than any other defenseman.

"Nobody is a perfect hockey player," said Jean Beliveau, the Montreal Canadiens' captain. "The important thing is to correct your mistakes. Orr, he does that. He is always there. He blocks the shots. He can skate. He can shoot. Is there anything more?"

Well, yes, there was. It was the matter of self-assertion. In the hockey jungle it is axiomatic that the player who runs from trouble too often gets run right out of the hockey league. By the same token, the more celebrated the player, the more attention he will get from the woodchoppers and spear carriers. In spite of boxing triumphs over Harris and one or two others Orr unfortunately could not expect a hockey version of diplomatic immunity. No, he had to keep asserting himself until he had established an invisible bumper around him, so that the tormentors would realize the challenge of Orr wasn't really worth the price. It was a process that would take years of battling and, perhaps, a display of meanness beyond Orr's normal potential.

In any event, his original mentor, Wren Blair, put the advice in very real terms when he told Bobby, "Don't back up. There's gonna be players who'll resent you. When that happens, throw off your gloves and go at them. Let them know right away where you stand. There are damn few players who really want to fight. If you show them you want to fight, they'll get the message in a hurry. Get it over with so that you're not hampered by that nonsense too long. Then let your hockey ability take over."

A few purists were prepared to challenge Blair's philosophy on the grounds that violence of any kind was unnecessary for true-blue Bobby. But Blair did not want to see Orr succumb to the doctrine of posthumous self-defense. Quick self-assertion was the only course.

"If those low-grade players are holding a gun to Bobby's head," one observer explained, "he has to ask himself when he's entitled to hit them. According to some people's definition he'd have to wait until they pulled the trigger. He'd never survive that way." No, posthumous self-defense was not for Orr, especially since injuries were quickly becoming the bugaboo of his playing life, making him a perfect target for opponents.

His first major mishap occurred during the benefit game at Winnipeg in August, 1967. "It was a pure accident," said Bobby. "A guy steered me into the boards and another guy, who was on my side, hit me. I wore a cast on my knee for five weeks." His subsequent injuries were enough to provide fodder for newsmen. It didn't take very long for Orr to be labeled "brittle," nor did it take long for the Bruins to deny the allegation.

"Bobby's a guy who plays hard and takes chances," said one member of the Bruins official family. "Hell, Milt Schmidt never played a full season for us and you couldn't have asked for a finer player."

Nevertheless, the feeling persisted that Orr would be tested more severely than ever in his sophomore year, 1967–68, and his reactions to the assaults would be a good indicator of his survival quotient for future years.

7. Bobby's Other Side

The tip-off to the path Orr would follow came less than a month after the 1967–68 season began. The Toronto Maple Leafs were visiting Boston Garden early in November, when a collision occurred between Orr and Brian Conacher of the Leafs. Some contradictory evidence remains as to whether Conacher broke Orr's nose with his stick or with his elbow. In such crack-ups it's often difficult to determine which came first, the stick or the elbow, since much of what happens is a product of a normal defense reflex.

There was no question that Orr was flamboyantly, if not seriously, injured. He was bleeding, as he later put it, "like a stuck pig," and there was little opportunity to bring Conacher to the witness stand in an effort to determine whether he *meant* to maim Orr or whether it merely was one of those wrong-side-of-the-road accidents that do happen every season.

Had the situation taken place in more tranquil surroundings than Boston Garden, Orr might have considered that in the last NHL season—it had been Orr's rookie season too —Conacher was regarded as a rugged but relatively clean-checking forward, the scion of a distinguished hockey family, a veteran of the Canadian National Team, and a chap who acquired only 47 penalty minutes in 66 games, compared with Orr's 102 minutes in 61 games. But it was no time for cerebration. Orr clambered to his skates and pursued Conacher the way a storekeeper chases a thief. By this time John McKenzie of the Bruins had already intercepted the Leaf, who wasn't fleeing, but merely returning to play, and trapped him for Orr, who was not far behind. Bobby then attacked Conacher and proceeded to pummel the living daylights out of him. It looked as if Orr was determined to piledrive him right through the ice.

Like all hockey brouhahas, this one was quelled before

anyone was actually murdered, but the sight of Orr atop Conacher, his arms thumping like a pneumatic drill, was too much even for some of the writers. Kevin Walsh, a reporter for the Boston *Globe*, was so appalled he wrote a four-column open letter to Orr that appeared on November 7. The headline blazed: "Chasing Conacher Error—Hurt Bs." Then Walsh went on to rip into Orr as few have before or since. The scathing letter read:

Bobby, what did you prove Sunday night? That you are tough? That you have a low boiling point? That you're not going to be pushed around on the ice?

It was a mistake—chasing after Brian Conacher and getting into a fight with him after he hit you in the face with his stick. It hurt your team. It led to a series of events that marred an excellent hockey game.

Instead of Conacher going to the penalty box with a five-minute major, you got involved in a fight and erased the Bruins' advantage.

At that point in the game the Bruins might have scored a goal or two and broken the game wide open.

You lost your temper and it may have cost the Bruins a victory.

I am sure you are aware of it now. The Bruins are paying you to play hockey.

Hockey is an emotional game. At times it's rough and players get injured. A player's boiling point can be low when his nose is broken and blood is rushing from a cut. But the superstars have self-control.

They don't lose their temper. It's rare when Gordie Howe or Bobby Hull is put off the ice for fighting. They are too valuable to be off the ice. The stamp of a great player is self-control.

You were involved in a couple of fights in an exhibition game against Montreal and were put out of the game. Sunday you were able to take one turn after the Conacher affair. You couldn't continue playing because you injured your thumb fighting, not because of the broken nose.

When you arrived in the league the only "unknown" concerning your chances of making the jump from junior hockey to the pros was how tough you were.

You don't have to prove you're tough now. Everyone

in the league knows you won't step away from anyone.

That is why it was a mistake to go after Conacher. He was gone for five minutes.

If you lose your temper and go after everyone it's going to hurt the Bruins. Every team in the league is going to send its hatchet man after you. They are going to attempt to draw you into the penalty box. The opposition will lose a fixture from the end of the bench. The Bruins lose an All-Star defenseman.

It isn't a fair trade in any market.

You don't belong in the penalty box or in the trainer's room having your injured thumb treated, Bobby. You belong on the ice playing hockey, the way only you can play.

Conacher isn't being absolved for his high stick that hit you in the face. It's a long season, seventy-four games, and Conacher will have to skate up and down his wing all season. Brian probably won't be too anxious to carry the puck along the boards or go into the corners against Boston.

You're lucky the X-ray proved negative and your thumb isn't broken. You were able to practice with the team Monday. You could have been out of action for six or seven games.

At nineteen, you are on the threshold of being a superstar. Don't let a low boiling point overshadow your ability.

Others took Orr to task, including Milt Dunnell, the respected sports editor of the Toronto *Daily Star,* who suggested that the Bruins start hurting when Orr the hockey player becomes Orr the fighter.

"With Orr enjoying good health," said Dunnell, "the Bruins are liable to take any team apart on any given night. An Orr with a fractured hand or a crack in his collarbone could mean the difference between second and sixth place. In dollars that's enough to buy a shipload of pucks. So, Milt Schmidt was greatly disturbed the other night when Orr commenced flailing Conacher with both hands."

While Schmidt certainly did not want to see the Leaf forward sent to the hospital with a concussion, his primary concern was that Orr remain as free of injury as possible.

"After the Conacher incident," said Schmidt, "I had a talk with Bobby. I told him he could avoid such things as that. I can understand his feelings. He had been cut for three stitches by Conacher's stick. If a penalty had been called immediately, the thing might have ended there. It was called later."

Questioned later about the incident, Orr made it clear that Blair's philosophy was his prime motivation. "Conacher got me in the nose," Bobby explained, "and frankly, I didn't want to fight. But if they see you backing up in this league, it's no good. So, if they want to fight, I'll fight."

What apparently galled him most of all was the fact that Conacher brought him down with the stick rather than with his body. "I don't like that," he said with as much intensity as you'll ever get from Bobby. "A guy can beat hell outa me with his fists and I won't complain, but not with the stick. I hate sticks."

In his second NHL season Bobby was learning with great speed that life wasn't exactly the proverbial bowl of cherries, but he was also finding the brighter side. The departure of Hap Emms didn't hurt one bit. His replacement, Schmidt, suited Orr fine because "Uncle Miltie," as they affectionately called him, was a more relaxed type who didn't demand to be addressed as "Mister."

Schmidt wasn't naive either. He knew there was a morale problem to be dealt with and he started dealing. "I spoke to each guy," said Schmidt, "and told him what I wanted from him. I think morale and spirit have to begin in the front office."

He also was distressed with the size of the Bruins. "We have too many little guys on this team," Schmidt added. "The first thing I have to do is get two or three big forwards. I got to thinking of guys who played for the Bruins in the days when we were winning. I thought of Dit Clapper, Eddie Shore, Johnny Crawford, and Ray Getliffe. At one time, you know, they used to say that if you could get through the door, you couldn't play for the Bruins."

One of his early moves at first made Schmidt look like a schoolboy. He traded the hard-hitting Marotte to the Chicago Black Hawks. But on closer examination the move was quite defensible. Marotte was one of Emms' boys, which might have been cause for dropping him. More important though, was the fact that along with Marotte went smallish center Hubert "Pit" Martin and Jack Norris, an undistinguished minor-league goaltender. In return, the Bruins received a cornucopia of talent—centers Phil Esposito and Fred Stanfield and wingman Ken Hodge. At first Schmidt was somewhat dubious about the deal, but in a matter of months it turned out to be one of the most one-sided hockey trades the NHL has known, all on the side of the Bruins.

"Well, I was gambling," Schmidt allowed. "I took a big chance letting Marotte go, but things have worked out just fine."

That may have been hockey's understatement of the half-century. The Bruins moved right up to the top of the NHL's East Division, and the Black Hawks began a dive that dropped them to fourth place in 1967–68 and last in 1968–69. Orr appeared unaffected by the loss of his former defensemate, Marotte. Both Dallas Smith and Gary Doak worked well with the prodigy and he was well on his way to his initial First All-Star Team selection.

All of this was taking place in an atmosphere that suggested a hockey version of *Laugh-In*. By now Orr had shed whatever feelings of self-consciousness he might have harbored in his rookie year and was a full participant in the revelry orchestrated usually by goalie Gerry Cheevers or Esposito.

A typical vignette unfolded one afternoon early in December, 1967. Esposito was sitting on the sidelines nursing a minor knee injury, while his colleagues sprinted up and down the ice in a pre-game workout. When it was over Tom Williams walked by and needled, "What do you have to do to get a day off around here? Be Italian?"

Esposito was well aware that Williams was one of the few American-born players in the NHL. He wasted no time retorting. "You can be anything," snapped Esposito, "except American. You Americans need all the work you can get."

Not to be outdone, Orr remembered that Esposito had been Bobby Hull's linemate the previous season when Hull broke the fifty-goal mark. "Hey," snapped Orr. "Hull practiced every day, didn't he? Didn't he make you practice with him?"

Teetering on the brink of a verbal defeat, Esposito rallied with a final *riposte:* "You're right—but there are no Hulls on this team."

By this time, however, an Orr was regarded as dearly on

the hockey exchange as a Hull. And Orr had youth on his side. At nineteen, he was still eligible to play in the OHA Junior A League, but instead he was gracing the cover of *Sports Illustrated*.

"Bobby," said author Pete Axthelm, "seems to improve all the time. His reflexes and anticipating allow him to block many opponents' shots before they ever reach the goal. It is not unusual to see him block a hard shot with his legs, knock down the shooter, and skate forward with the puck. Offensively, he still has the heavy, accurate shot that excited the fans last year, and now he can set up more plays because he has more scorers playing with him. More and more he is becoming their leader."

Orr told Axthelm he could see the difference in training camp. "After one practice," Bobby confessed, "a few of us went out, and the whole team ended up in the same place. It's been that way all year. We go to the same places, we hang around together as a group."

To nobody's surprise, Orr was unanimously voted to the First-All-Star defense berth in the midseason (1967–68) poll of the twelve NHL coaches. He was acclaimed the best defenseman in the world. In a manner that had previously been reserved for Gordie Howe, hockey people began making little jokes about Orr. "He plays the funny kind of game, he doesn't let anybody touch the puck."

Said Howe, in answer to a question: "What's Orr's best move? I'd say his best move is putting on those skates!"

Coach Sinden had another version: "Bobby was a star when they played the national anthem in his first game!"

"How does he fit in with the team?" a Bruin said, mulling the question. "What do you mean—with the team? He *is* the team!"

Orr reinforced the extravagant claims by playing in the All-Star Game at Maple Leaf Gardens in Toronto in January, 1968, and outplaying every one of the great ones— Howe, Hull, Stan Mikita, and Norm Ullman—and by a wide margin. The fact that he injured his shoulder in the game and could have begged off at any time never prevented him from stopping. No, he was on the ice right down to the final buzzer.

"I never knew of a single player who could lift a team as Orr has done with Boston," said Mikita, the league's only two-time Triple Crown winner (Art Ross, Lady Byng, and All-Star trophies).

Montreal *Star* sports columnist Elmer Ferguson is the oldest active hockey writer on the beat. He has covered the NHL since its inception and especially remembers the wizardry of Eddie Shore. Normally, such veteran critics tend to side with the old timers in evaluating the qualities of the contemporaries in terms of All-Stars of the twenties, thirties, and forties.

"Orr," concluded Ferguson, "is a better hockey player in practically every way than the great Shore. Eddie was great. He exuded drama with his powerful rushes and he was courageous, but in the mechanics of polished hockey, Orr is a greater player than Shore. Orr is a brilliant stickhandler. He's adept at getting the puck away from attackers and wheeling off on a sortie of his own.

"He is a better puck-carrier than Shore. And Orr can whip away a wrist shot at lightning speed. He has speed afoot, hits the ice with such power he uses up four pairs of skates per season. Orr may, indeed, be creating a new concept of defense play. The day of huge, slow-footed defense players passed with the era of such as the late Harry Mummery, the Rangers' Taffy Abel, and Ching Johnson, among others.

"There has been a steady swing toward puck-carrying defense players, and Orr has added a new dimension to this trend. He may become a model for defense players of the hockey future, featuring speed, fine stick-handling, and scoring ability."

Model for defense players of the future? Indeed! Orr already had become a model for superstars of the present. Howe, the magnificent, the impresario himself, was studying the Orr technique for new ideas and wasn't the least embarrassed about admitting it.

"When other players start watching one guy, trying to figure out what he's doing and imitate it," said Howe, "he's got to be pretty good."

One of Orr's most unique traits is what's known in hockey as "puck sense." Translated roughly it means the knack of following the puck to the right places on the ice the way a bloodhound instinctively finds his quarry.

"Bobby is at his best," said coach Sinden, "when he anticipates where the puck will go. Sure you can be a guesser and make a few lucky steals of the puck and have the crowd cheering like you're a hero. Then you guess wrong and get burned enough times and you'll be back in Saskatchewan looking for a job. But when Orr goes for a pass, he has the uncanny knack of being there and gone with the puck."

In diagnosing Orr's style it is difficult to isolate his special forte because he does everything so well. Certainly, he stick-handles and skates as well as any All-Star forward, hits as hard and poke-checks the puck as well as any defenseman, and can block shots with some of the best goaltenders.

"Most defensemen can't do much with the puck even when they take it away from you," pointed out Phil Goyette, the veteran New York Ranger center. "And that's why they're playing defense. But Orr handles the puck well enough to be a forward, and if he gets a chance to shoot he's extremely accurate."

Apart from the threat of recurring knee ailments and his temporary shoulder problem, Orr approached the January-February home stretch of the 1967–68 season with equanimity. The Bruins had unassailably established themselves as contenders for a playoff berth, for the first time in *nine* years. What's more, they were given a fair-to-middling shot at first place. Naturally, this was all contingent on Bobby remaining in good condition.

He himself could see no reason why he would not. His junior hockey career was relatively free of major damage, and his broken nose total was six—about super-par for the course. His stitch count was a mere twenty-two from five gashes. "Stitches like mine," he admitted, "are just Band-Aid stuff so far. You know I've still got all my teeth. But I don't want anybody to think I'm bragging about it."

All in all, life was just fine for Bobby Orr as he emerged from the All-Star Game ready to lead his Bruins into the essential two months of the season. And then it happened.

Agonizingly but relentlessly, Orr's left knee began tormenting him with pain early in February. As always, he attempted to ignore the difficulty until it became obvious to everyone connected with the team that he was partially immobilized.

"The knee locks up on him," said Schmidt. "It's been getting worse. When he lifts his leg and tries to skate, the joint sticks and won't come back easily."

Bobby returned to Boston on February 10, 1968, a dour, almost melancholy figure. His traditional beaming facade was gone and, to reporters, he was almost as mute as the sphinx. Reporters who greeted him at Logan Airport heard him repeat, "I just don't know. Please, I just don't want to talk about it."

The Boston *Globe* reporter at the scene observed, "The All-Star defenseman, who faces possible knee surgery, got off the plane and didn't look up once as he made his way through the airport."

Dr. Ronald Adams, the club physician, realized that surgery was imperative. A few days later the operation for removal of a cartilage in the left knee was performed at Newton Wellesley Hospital. "The operation was completely successful," said Dr. Adams, "and badly needed."

When he was finally presented to the press after the operation, Orr, from his wheelchair, pontificated to his constituents and then allowed them to speculate about his future. John Ahern of the *Globe* took due note of the cast on Bobby's left knee and predicted, "That means forget the rest of this season and keep your fingers crossed for the playoffs."

Such ominous pronouncements apparently did nothing to diminish Orr's optimism. He began a therapeutic course that involved riding a stationary bicycle and lifting weights with his leg. "I feel super," he commented on February 21.

Bostonians, remembering that Red Sox pitcher Jim Lonborg had been sidelined for a considerably longer time after his ski injury, speculated that Orr might be in for an equally long recuperation. But, day by day the reports from Boston Garden appeared brighter. "Orr," it was said, "has everything going for him. He's only nineteen and he isn't that big. He also has time on his side. Compared to Lonborg, Orr has a minor knee injury."

A typical late-season surge lifted the Montreal Canadiens into first place, leaving the Bruins, Rangers, and Black Hawks to battle for the remaining playoff positions in the East Division. In early March it seemed that the Bruins and Rangers would be vying for second place and the Black Hawks settling in fourth. More than ever, the Bruins felt a need for Orr in the lineup, and on March 12, 1968, he laced on a pair of skates and took his first strides on the ice since his operation. It was a particularly important experience because if the knee failed in any way this might be the end of the line for Bobby.

He moved gingerly across the ice, his blades hardly crunching the surface, but the movements were not awkward, just slow. It seemed that only time was necessary for Bobby to recover his typical tempo.

"I was anxious," he said later. "I was also a little worried about how I'd feel. It's like going into your first game. You just turn, easy and slow. It feels all right."

The Bruins could have adamantly refused to play Orr either in the remaining games or in the playoffs and thereby insured a healthy player for the following season. But the pressures to use him were great, and it was obvious that they would capitulate.

"It would be nice if we could play him in a game or two before the playoffs," said Sinden. "But we'll have to play it by ear."

He returned to the lineup on March 24, 1968, at Detroit's Olympia Stadium. The Red Wings defeated the Bruins 5—3, and Orr's comeback after a seventeen-game absence could hardly be termed auspicious. He received two ten-minute misconduct penalties from referee Bill Friday and was verbally spanked by the Boston press.

"The occasion," said Tom Fitzgerald of the *Globe,* "was marred . . . by a couple of developments. . . . Bobby seemed to make a gesture toward his throat which Friday interpreted as criticism of his work . . . the other misconduct was attributable to a rather forceful slamming of the Boston bench gate by Orr."

Bobby's hasty return backfired on the Bruins almost as if it were preordained by the gods. In the next game, on March 28 at Boston Garden, the Bruins faced the Rangers for a contest which would determine the occupant of second place. New York won the match, 5—4, and did finish in the runner-up spot. Boston wound up third, and Chicago fourth.

The Bruins then faced Montreal in the opening round of the East Division playoffs and were humiliated with four straight losses. Orr's contribution was a measly two assists and some singularly undistinguished defensive play. It appeared in retrospect that the Bruin front office had perhaps acted hastily in permitting Orr to return. But the gravity of his physical condition was not realized until June.

Early in June, 1968, it became clear that Bobby's hockey career could only continue if he submitted to additional surgery. On June 11, Dr. John Palmer of Toronto performed the operation for a cartilage chip in his previously injured left knee.

"Bobby won't have any problem with the knee in the future," assured Dr. Palmer.

The statement did not seem all that reassuring, as similar words had been heard at Newton Wellesley Hospital earlier in the year. How did Dr. Palmer reconcile that with his enthusiastic comments?

"Bobby simply aggravated his condition," explained Dr. Palmer. "The first operation was to remove a piece already torn. Today's surgery was simply to remove a small chip."

The optimistic medical report was hardly as substantial as a remark made by former Bruins defenseman Bill Quackenbush. "Remember," said Quackenbush, "Gordie Howe had cartilage operations on both knees, and it doesn't look as if it ever bothered him, does it?"

Nevertheless, it would be four months before Bobby would have an opportunity to test the rehabilitated limb in a hard scrimmage. All he could do now was rest and wait and think about the two seasons past. Along the way he would confer with lawyer Eagleson because there was a new contract to negotiate with the Bruins.

8. The $400,000 Controversy

By now it was not uncommon for a reporter from a major publication to venture north to explore the town of Parry Sound and its environs. Bobby Orr had never needed a newspaperman to make him, and no journalist would ever be able to break the defenseman in print. So the Orrs felt no obligation to throw out a red carpet whenever a member of the Fourth Estate dropped over to the Brunswick Motor Hotel on James Street, where Arva Orr continued to work and chat with the townspeople.

Those who think they know Arva report that she loses her tranquility when she watches her son play hockey. They have also observed that she is less than enthusiastic when reporters she doesn't know come to visit Parry Sound or contact her on the telephone. Whenever possible she refers them to Alan Eagleson, the Toronto attorney who counsels Bobby.

Bobby was difficult to interview at first, not because he didn't want to talk, but because he just wasn't loquacious enough to suit some writers. By 1969, however, he had developed into an often pleasant conversationalist after and between games. From time to time, he confessed that he felt singed by some of the copy written about him, which was only natural. As he matured as an unchallengeable star, he also began to assert his independence from management. There was to begin with, his reliance on Eagleson, who was not a team official, as his contact in any major involvement, from an advertising contract to an interview with a major publication. Then there was also Orr's realization that he was a very, very big man in Boston.

From the start, the image that the Bruins hierarchy had of Orr ranged from a self-reliant star to a naive kid just dying to get into the big time. It merely depended on the day and the individuals with whom he was dealing. Few would doubt that Bobby realized his importance as the prime spoke in the Hub team's scheme of things. He knew he was badly needed by the Bruins and, all things considered, he managed to maintain a modest decorum in his early confrontations. But the Emms episode had given him a new dimension of life, and a few encounters with the press exacerbated these feelings.

All these factors were manifest in the hullabaloo surrounding his knee operation and again as the Bruins ignominiously lost four straight games to Montreal in the 1968 playoffs. The Bruins dressed two goaltenders, young Gerry Cheevers and Ed Johnston, a veteran who had suffered through the long sixth-place era with the team. Both were adequate, if not spectacular, goalies who had almost identical goals against averages during the regular 1967–68 season.

On the basis of his extensive experience alone, Johnston appeared to be the choice to start the series against Montreal. If he failed, coach Sinden could always call in Cheevers to finish the playoff. But Sinden started the younger goalie, who allowed seven goals in the first two games that Boston lost at Montreal. Still, Sinden chose to use Cheevers in the third game—the first to be played at Boston Garden—and this time, Cheevers played horribly as Boston lost, 5—2.

If Sinden had ever wanted good reason to switch goaltenders, Cheevers' three straight losses gave it to him. But the Boston brass was not terribly enthused about playing Johnston. There were reports that Johnston had offended a Bruin official, and they weren't particularly happy about the fact that Johnston and Orr were such close friends.

But Orr liked Johnston, and the behavior of the brass toward the goaltender only strengthened his resolve to maintain this friendship. On top of that was the foolishness about not playing Johnston in the Montreal series. At some point, a report bubbled forth in a Boston paper that Orr and a few other Bruins were disenchanted with Sinden's refusal to use Johnston, although this was later denied by all concerned. It didn't take long for the rumor to catch fire, and when the series had concluded a very definite picture had taken shape—some of the Bruins were behind their beleaguered goalie, Johnston, and were resentful of management.

Time is a great healer and it wouldn't have taken many weeks for "L'Affaire Johnston" to have disappeared from everyone's mind. But early in June, just before Orr's operation in Toronto, another episode involving Orr and management occurred.

On June 8, 1968, the citizens of Parry Sound celebrated "Bobby Orr Day" in honor of their local hero. It was a jubilant occasion, a real old-time small-town celebration with brass bands, flower-bedecked floats and speeches. Everybody in the immediate vicinity showed up for the occasion; Detroit goaltender Roger Crozier drove over from his home in Bracebridge, fifty miles away, and Parry Sounders, Gary Sabourin and Terry Crisp of the St. Louis Blues were also there.

More significant was the appearance of Bobby's teammates, including Johnston, Eddie Shack, Derek Sanderson, Gary Doak and assistant trainer John Forrestall, each of whom traveled long distances to honor their friend. It was significant that not one member of the Bruins front office was there: not President Weston Adams, not manager Milt Schmidt, not coach Sinden. Bobby Orr took note of their absence.

"One fella came all the way up from Florida for the day," said Orr, applying a gratuitous boot to management. "It would have been nice if they [members of management] came but maybe they were too busy, I don't know."

Management may have missed Bobby Orr Day but it was impossible for the brass to avoid the more important confrontation with the *wunderkind* later in the summer. There was a new contract to be negotiated and, frankly, the Bruins negotiators were not in a very comfortable position because Orr presented them with an enigma. By gaining a First-All-Star berth and winning the Norris Trophy as the best defenseman in the 1967–68 season he had unequivocally established himself as one hell of an athlete—at age twenty. However, he had just come through a very questionable knee operation and it was possible that he might be a crippled, or at least a brittle, athlete in seasons to come.

If the Bruins had their doubts Eagleson certainly did not. "Bobby proved in just two years that he is now the greatest player in the Bruins' history," the lawyer asserted.

All hands appeared ready for a titanic battle that would dwarf the summer-long negotiations with Emms in 1966.

The 1968 bargaining also took a long time but that's where the comparison ended. With Emms gone, Eagleson found the Bruins infinitely more reasonable and by late August a bountiful three-year six-figure contract was hammered out.

It is possible that the exact terms of the contract will never be known; the circus of claims, denials, and counter-denials that followed the completion of the Orr-Bruins talks was enough to confuse the most lucid mind.

The furor started when the Toronto *Daily Star* reported that Orr had signed for $400,000 which, if correct, would make him the highest-priced player in hockey. According to many insiders, the $400,000 figure is reasonably accurate when one takes into consideration various tax gimmicks and other bonuses the Bruins tossed in that could later be translated into hard cash.

Whether it was accurate or not, the $400,000 report affected the NHL owners the way an earthquake stimulates a seismograph. There was alarm, rapidly followed by panic. A Toronto writer who was unusually close to the Orr-Eagleson scene reported that the star's figure was accurate and that the league was alarmed that Orr's alleged contract figure would cause a dangerous inflationary run on other team treasuries. Something had to be done—and fast!

The result was a news conference at which Orr's *true* contract figure would be revealed, except that it really wasn't. The $400,000 tab was unanimously denied, and, as a result, the newsmen achieved a consensus that $200,000 was more like the real price.

As expected, Orr remained tight-lipped about the contract and bridled when some reporters pressed him for specifics. It was then that a touch of naiveté betrayed itself.

"I never said what I signed for," he told Mark Mulvoy of *Sports Illustrated*, "and I don't think it's right for anybody to write what they think I signed for. I don't know or even want to know how much writers make. I don't know why they should know what I make.

"I just know I wasn't making any money at all two years ago—oh, I was clearing about $10 a week after paying my expenses while playing in Oshawa—and now Alan Eagleson has made me a lot of money. They all wrote about endorsements and life insurance and education. They said all those things were in my contract. Well, they weren't. Sure, I'd like to finish high school, and I'll probably do it this year in Boston. But all I ever really want to do is play hockey. I don't care about anything else."

A month later Tom Fitzgerald of the Boston *Globe* asked him about the contract and, this time, Bobby appeared more resigned to the speculation that swirled around him. "I guess I understand it. Writers have a job to get stories, and fans are interested in what players make; I am myself when I read about ball players or golfers. Sometimes it bothers me a little. I wouldn't go up to another fellow and ask him what he makes. And I think I'm entitled to the same thing. Actually I am sure there are only six people who really know my salary."

Perhaps, but every player in every professional league *thought* he knew what Orr was making, and that figure was $400,000. Word spread fast, and within a day, the superstars and the lesser stars were consulting their logarithm tables to determine where they would fit on the salary scale based on Bobby's presumed figure.

"I think I'm half as good as Bobby Orr," said Ed Westfall, the Bruin who plays both defense and forward. "Maybe I can get half as much money."

Management kept pointing to the declaration that $400,-000 was the *wrong* figure but it made absolutely no impression on the players.

"I don't care if the story was wrong," Henri Richard of the Canadiens insisted, "it should help us all. I don't see why we don't get paid as much as the baseball and football players anyway. I'm almost through, but I wish I'd had somebody like Eagleson to talk for me when I broke into the league."

Eagleson had now become a household word in hockey. For the players the adjectives were coated with sweetness, but for the owners, obscenities. "Good Old Eag," as Mike Walton of the Leafs called him, couldn't have cared less what the owners thought of him.

"You just let me know when the players don't like me," he'd tell critics.

Eagleson's success with Orr had a two-pronged effect because it also strengthened his position as head of the Players' Association. Membership leaped to just short of 100 per cent in 1968–69, with only a few players on Punch Imlach's Maple Leafs holding out. Eagleson also was pleased with the relative ease he had in handling the Orr negotiations this second time around.

"The negotiations," he recalled, "were long but fairly easy. The Bruins knew what Bobby was worth and they were quite reasonable."

That couldn't be said for contract talks involving other stars on other teams. A stalemate developed in meetings between the Black Hawks and Bobby Hull. After a series of verbal sallies, Hull stunned the hockey world by announcing his retirement shortly before the season started, a decision he later rescinded when Chicago produced a six-figure sum not unlike Orr's.

At least one player fooled himself, after thinking he had outwitted the team. Phil Esposito of the Bruins anticipated Orr's figure and negotiated with the team right away. "I beat them to it," said Esposito. "I knew what Bobby was going to get all the time, so I went in before him and told them to give me my figure or else. They gave it to me."

Esposito's mistake was in settling for a multi-year contract. In 1968–69 he broke several league scoring records; he would have been wiser to limit himself to a single-season deal that could be altered for 1969–70.

Others, such as Detroit's Gordie Howe, found themselves stranded in the middle of a two-year contract when Orr's deal was proclaimed. "I don't think he's actually getting all that kind of money," said Howe. "Still, the bad thing about those figures is that the wives all get talking and pretty soon you're back in there with the general manager talking about rewrites. Don't kid yourself; a lot of guys will have clippings of Orr's contract when they talk to the boss this year. I'm going to mention it.

"I'm in the second year of a two-year contract now, but I think my contract is renegotiable. We play more games and the prices are going up. I still go in there by myself. I'm too far along to have a guy like Eagleson negotiating for me. But if he had been around when I was twenty, I'd have made a lot more money in my career."

Howe's contract was renegotiated and he received an estimated $80,000, by far the highest figure in his twenty-three-year career.

The most mathematical explanation of the significance of Orr's deal was offered by Wayne Maki, an unobtrusive forward in the Black Hawk system. "I hope Bobby gets one million a year," said Maki. "Every ten thousand more he gets means another thousand or two for the rest of us."

The bountiful Orr money package proved to be dynamite for one member of the Bruins. When defenseman Ted Green attempted to renegotiate the second year of his two-year contract, management refused, and Green walked out of the Bruins' training camp in London, Ontario, on September 18.

The episode was a very delicate one for the Bruins, for Eagleson, and for Orr. Green had been playing a superior brand of hockey for Boston and deserved a raise. In fact, a few observers believed he meant more to the Bruins than Orr. Management would have a difficult time justifying his low salary. Meanwhile, Eagleson found himself in the position of being Orr's private negotiator while also, as Executive Director of the Players' Association, being Green's confidant.

Eagleson correctly informed Green that he had to fulfill the second year of his contract, which further complicated matters. Orr, himself, could do little.

"I'd rather give those players my money," he said, "than have any of that unhappiness; that is, if there is any. I don't know if there is or was any. If there is, I'd just as soon not know about it. But I haven't seen any evidence of it; in fact all the guys on the team have been super to me."

For three weeks Green remained at his Transcona, Manitoba home, off and on threatening to quit hockey. The first week in October went by, and he still hadn't come back to the fold. Finally, on October 10, one day before the Bruins' season opened, he changed his mind and returned to Boston.

It was assumed that Orr was the cause of Green's pout, but the truculent defenseman insisted that it was nothing of the kind.

"I know there were a lot of second-guessers who claimed what I did was because I was mad over the super contract Bobby got," Green argued. "They couldn't be more wrong. That had nothing to do with it. Bobby is worth every cent he gets."

Green insisted that his retreat from training camp had nothing to do with being upstaged by Orr. "You know," added Green in an insightful moment, "for five years or so I had most of the limelight. When Orr came along, he stole a lot of it, and it wouldn't be intelligent if I said I didn't notice it. But he deserves it, and the way this team is going, everything is good for us."

During Green's AWOL period only two members of the Bruins cared enough to phone him with encouragement. One of them was goalie Johnston; the other was Orr. But the man who needed the most encouragement of all was Bobby himself, who reported to training camp with no guarantee that his rehabilitated knee would hold up for the 1968–69 season.

9. Bobby at Home

By sheer coincidence I had the good reportorial fortune to spend two days with Orr during those desperately uncertain days before the opening of training camp in September, 1968. Early in the summer I had been assigned by a national magazine to write a full-length article about Bobby and had negotiated, as most magazine writers do, for an interview through Eagleson. We had finally agreed upon a date immediately after Labor Day.

The site would be Toronto; the meeting place, the Royal York Hotel, where Bobby, Mike Walton of the Maple Leafs, and Bobby Haggert, once the Leaf trainer but now an associate of Eagleson, would announce plans for a summer hockey camp. I was to interview Orr after the press conference.

As personality X-rays go, the experience with Bobby provided as much in the way of off-the-ice insights as I could want from an athlete. In some cases my preconceived notions about him turned out to be wrong; he certainly was more voluble than Chris Lydon of the *Globe* had suggested. On the whole, he emerged as a friendlier person than I had anticipated. I had expected a diffident young man, not particularly willing to cooperate with a New York writer, and perhaps with a smidgen of doltishness. On the contrary, he was amusing, candid—although he was careful to note that some of his remarks were off the record—and delightfully pleasant. I considered this all the more remarkable since he still had no idea whether or not his knee would be strong enough to permit him to play in 1968–69.

The press conference was attended by about a hundred radio, television, and newspaper men from the Toronto area. Except for myself, the only out-of-town hockey writer present was D. Leo Monahan of the Boston *Record-American* and *Sunday Advertiser*. Orr chatted with several of the

men and appeared singularly comfortable, although he told
me several months later at the NHL All-Star Dinner in
Montreal that he still feels somewhat embarrassed by the
crowds and prefers to talk quietly with friends in a corner.

Toward the end of the conference Haggert introduced me
to Orr. Apparently he had been misinformed about our
interview and thought we were to repair to Parry Sound,
where I would stay overnight. Bobby suggested I drive up
with him, and we agreed to meet later in the afternoon at
Maple Leaf Gardens, where he was to undergo therapy on
his repaired knee.

It was about 3 P.M. when we left the Gardens for Parry
Sound. As we stepped into Toronto's Church Street the
blinding sunlight made him blink, and he quickly flipped on
his mod sunglasses. For the moment he looked thoroughly
show biz. The glistening blond hair, no longer defaced
by an old-fashioned crew cut, curved slightly down his
brow.

He opened the doors of his Meteor Rideau, a Canadian-
made Ford product, almost identical to the American-made
Mercury. His gait appeared normal, which pleased him.
"Y'know," he said, "the knee feels real good."

Two pieces of yellow paper were tucked under the wind-
shield wiper on the left side of the car. He got out, looked at
them, and stuck them in his left pocket. "Bad luck on
tickets, today, by George!" he said, and we were off for
Parry Sound.

The opening minutes of conversation were difficult, as
they are between strangers at a cocktail party. Bobby talked
about his new real-estate purchase near Route 401 in Toronto and marveled at the growth of the city. We discussed
our mutual friend, Carl Brewer, the former Leaf defenseman then with Detroit, and Bobby closed the subject by calling Brewer "a real gentleman," with a fervor that bordered
on idolatry.

He wended his way through the maze of traffic on Yonge
Street, found some room as he reached the suburbs, and
rolled on to the superhighway that threaded its way north
from the metropolis. He seemed relieved to get out of the
city and said as much.

"I just like to get away and relax," he observed. "I really
hate the city."

I asked whether he'd feel uncomfortable if I took notes

during our ride. He said, no, he wouldn't mind, and to go right ahead. It was a delightful late summer day, and the southern Ontario countryside was still overflowing with green. All this seemed to open Bobby up as Toronto fell behind us.

There were a few things I had wondered about, stories I had read about Orr, and now seemed a good time to find out about them. For one, there was that item on the Orr family being a bunch of criers.

"Oh," Bobby said, smiling, "it's mostly my mother and my older sister. More likely they're apt to do it at Christmas Eve." Then he suddenly changed the subject, remembering that his sister, Pat, was going to be married on the weekend. "Cripes," he blurted, "do we have a lotta confusion around the house."

It wasn't difficult to get him back on hockey, and soon we were talking about the early days and the old cliché, "pressure." He granted its existence but explained that it varied with the geography and the game.

"To begin with," he said, "I'm always nervous in any game, but once I get hit, or hit somebody, it's not bad anymore. In juniors it was easy, almost like playing at home. When I came to the Bruins I was scared. I mean a lot of crap had been written about me and I didn't know if I could play or I couldn't play in the NHL. As soon as I got to camp I went straight up to my room; then the players came to get me. I was lucky in a way. In some training camps the rookies go here and the veterans go there. In our camp everybody was together; the rookies, the vets, the married guys, and the single guys. Every one of them was just super to me." That was the first time I had heard him use the word "super." I later discovered it was not only one of Orr's favorite expressions but was on the tongues of almost all the Bruins.

Bobby, chewing lightly on the tip of his tie, suddenly resembled a grown-up Charlie Brown. He talked about how Al Eagleson had become virtually a father-figure in his hockey life, and I wondered how the two had met.

"Al was a guest speaker at an affair up near Parry Sound and my parents spoke to him," he explained. "Soon, my dad got to talking to him and started to ask questions and that's how it all started."

As we drove past the gleaming green lakes and white clapboard cottages it became obvious that Bobby was near home; the tie came off, he broke into a soft whistle, and leaned back comfortably in his seat. "I just can't wait to see those bass bite," he said. "Plenty of bass, pike, and pickerel, right on Georgian Bay. It's unreal!"

The car swerved left at the junction of Routes 69 and 69B. "Be careful," he warned. "Don't blink your eyes or you'll miss it." The big, black Parry Sound railway trestle loomed ahead and behind it, the vast expanse of Georgian Bay. "Here ya are. Parry Sound—small but she's powerful!"

He spun up James Street and stopped at the corner of Sequin, honking his horn at somebody in the store across the street. There was a sign across the top of the window, "Ron and Bobby Orr's Clothing and Sporting Goods." Bobby's older brother Ron operates the shop. There are those in Parry Sound who will tell you that it's mildly unfortunate how Bobby has overshadowed his brother, who was a darn good hockey player himself. Some Parry Sounders insist that Ron gave up competitive hockey during his late teens, a young player's most formative years, because of the pressure created by his kid brother's overdose of publicity.

They say that Ron has been needled on the ice because he *is* Bobby's brother, and some insensitive types have made it clear to Ron that he never came up to Bobby's standard of play. Others have suggested that Ron could have made it if he had paid more attention to his "big" brother, when actually, Ron is Bobby's older brother. Just how successful and how wealthy a hockey player Ron might have been under different circumstances is a question that never will be answered.

The Orrs' house in Parry Sound, today, appears paradoxical for a "Million-Dollar Hockey Player," as Red Fisher, the new sports editor of the Montreal *Star,* described Bobby. I expected to see a sprawling ranch home on top of Belvedere Hill, with a swimming pool in the rear. Instead, Bobby's family was still living in their old house nestled by the harbor cove.

Although her eminently successful son had insisted on buying a new home, Arva told him she preferred their comfortable old house. Not only that but she had no intentions of forsaking her job as a waitress at the Brunswick Motor

Hotel, simply because she likes it. She did allow, however, that advanced years might eventually persuade her to both permit Bobby to buy her a home and to give up her job at the hotel.

The Orrs are self-reliant and stubborn in the venerable tradition of rugged individualism. Bobby's earnings are his own, they insist. To tacitly prove the point Doug continued working at Canadian Industries Ltd. as an explosives handler for $125 a week and wouldn't even buy himself a car.

As Bobby drove me to a motel, we talked about his ability in terms of his personal aspirations. "I made a lot of mistakes in my first two seasons," he admitted, "as many or more than the next guy, I'll tell ya."

He turned past the Victory Cafe and, interestingly, didn't point out sites to me, just people—not important people, but people who were important to him. Finally, he parked the car in front of the Kitchener Motel.

A town constable approached. At first Bobby pretended not to see him, then he suddenly began ducking and throwing fake punches. The constable roared appreciatively. Later, he introduced me to his cronies, Neil Clairmont and Bob "Homer" Holmes. The three of them give the impression of having leaped right out of the pages of *Archie* comics.

Parry Sound unofficially adopted the Bruins as its favorite team when Orr signed his first contract with the NHL team. Today its sporting goods stores sell out Bruin jerseys almost as fast as they are delivered, but when Bobby was a kid it wasn't that way.

"Actually," he reminisced, "we liked all the teams; it just seemed that Montreal and Toronto were the ones that always got into the playoffs."

The following day Bobby gave me a walking tour of James Street, the main drag. We walked into Adam's Men's Shop and chatted with Doug Gignac, the proprietor, who reminded Bobby that it was getting late if he intended to rent a tuxedo for his sister's wedding. Then, we walked to the bus-terminal restaurant and kidded with Sara Mahaffy, an older but most amusing waitress, who traded gags with Orr. "I don't like that shirt on you," she said in a brief moment of seriousness, commenting on the loud, tight outfit he was wearing.

We talked about life in Parry Sound, and I asked him about marriage. Unlike some mothers, Arva Orr has made it a policy not to nudge Bobby about matrimony. She is in no hurry to see him march to Mendelssohn's "Wedding March." Nor is Bobby.

"Maybe when I'm thirty-five," he said. "That's a good age for it. By that time you've done all the things you want to do that you couldn't when you're married."

Bobby had to remain in Parry Sound to prepare for the big wedding, and I was going to take the bus back to Toronto. As we waited for the bus to arrive, Orr noticed a lanky eighteen-year-old boy sitting in the terminal. It was Ray Reid, who had played defense for the Parry Sound Junior C team and was now heading south to try out with the Kitchener Rangers in the OHA Junior A League.

"I'm goin' to take a shot with the big fellas," said Reid after we were introduced.

"Just a minute," Bobby turned to me, excusing himself. He walked over to the side of the terminal and talked alone with the youngster.

"It's a funny thing," Reid mentioned later on the bus to Toronto. "I went to a hockey school a few weeks ago, and they had this big guy from the NHL. He could hardly make the Detroit Red Wings but he acted like he was the greatest, y'know, the biggest big shot in the world. And here's Bobby, who *is* the greatest, and he'll think nothin' of helping me whenever he can."

When I mentioned this to Orr some months later, he dismissed the matter with a sense of embarrassment. "I like kids," he said simply. "I just get a big kick outa kids. Once I was up at a hockey school in Sault Sainte Marie, Ontario, and there was one little kid there. He was working real hard. Finally, I took him aside and taught him for a half hour. Next day the little bugger didn't come back and it bothered me. Two days later he showed up and I asked him why he missed the two days. 'Oh,' he said, 'I was just tired.'" Then, Bobby burst out laughing, amused by a seemingly prosaic episode.

Before the bus arrived we talked about his failure to finish high school. "I was a little lazy in school," he admitted, "and never a number one student or anything like that; but I'm sure I'll finish high school someday. I know if a kid asked me whether he should play hockey or go to school I'll tell him to go to school—it's the wise thing to do. My mother always tells me I should finish.

"Funny thing is, I once went to a banquet near my mother's home in Callendar. It was a question-and-answer thing, and the first kid to ask me a question wanted to know how far I went in school!"

The bus finally pulled into the station and as we said good-bye I wished him well, wondering whether he would survive the training-camp ordeal and continue his conquest of the NHL. It was a question that puzzled the Bruins management and the press and became more perplexing later when doctors ordered him off the ice, after the knee acted up and began paining him again.

10. The Off-Side of Orr

Much as they might have liked to, the Bruins officials couldn't censor the news that Orr was not practicing regularly with the club. Word rapidly got to the office of every general manager in the league, with a mixture of sorrow and jealous satisfaction. Automatically, the question was raised: "Is Bobby Orr washed up?" Only time would tell.

Boston newsmen did their best to ferret out the facts, and *Globe* reporter Tom Fitzgerald, who then was president of the National Hockey Writers Association, managed to corner Bobby on September 21, 1968. He prodded him about the injury question and elicited this response:

"I know there are some people who say that I am injury prone. The way some of these things happen, though, the result would have been the same for anyone. Heck, Gordie Howe had things happen to him when he was a young player and he's going into his twenty-third season. I was on crutches for eight weeks after the operation on my left knee this summer but now it really feels good. I feel super. I'm skating well, but I'm just waiting until they let me get some contact work."

But Bobby remembered that for a brief but scary period during training camp there was a fear that his knee would hamper him. There was pain and anxiety. "It just acted up," he said, "so I just decided to quit for a week."

With each day the outlook became more pessimistic. Meanwhile, Bobby exercised the leg with weights, hoping to strengthen the muscles. Finally, another test run was ordered. "This time, touch lumber," he said, rapping his knuckles on a wooden table, "it felt good." On October 7, 1968, less than a week before the opening of the season, Bobby was pronounced fit to practice and managed to work himself into condition in less than half the time it takes an average player.

"He amazed me," said Phil Esposito. "He looked like he'd been playing for twenty practices."

All the scare stories were thrown into the waste basket after the season opened. Orr was manning the Bruins blue line with more efficiency, flamboyance, and total dominance than ever before. There was absolutely no evidence that his knee was hampering his play. If anything, he appeared to be playing more violently than ever.

His first test of 1968–69 was the Bruins' opening game against the Red Wings. Gordie Howe skated past him and swiped at his knee. "He whacked me good," Orr remembered. "I can't forget that one." Bobby shrugged off the blow and later in the game led a rush at center ice, when a linesman whistled an offside. Just as Orr relaxed his body he was tripped by Pete Stemkowski. As Bobby collapsed to his knee, coach Sinden rushed to the edge of the boards and railed at Stemkowski.

"It was a cheap shot," Sinden said later, "by a cheap-shot artist."

Orr slowly climbed back on his skates and resumed his defensive position. He was not going to be stopped. He played more than twenty-five minutes, killing penalties, taking his regular turn, and working the power play. Boston won the game, 4—2, and Bobby scored the winning goal on an end-to-end rush.

Wasn't he furious with Howe and Stembowski? Well, not really. "Listen," he said breathing realism into the question, "we all indulge in a bit of sneaky play, the little things. Those guys have a job: they have to get me. But they're good guys. In fact you don't find many bad apples in this game."

His second and most severe test for the knee developed at Madison Square Garden early in December, 1968. By now a running feud had developed between Orr and Reg Fleming of the Rangers, a player whose hockey ethics are open to debate. The first time they had clashed Fleming shoved the butt of his stick into Orr's stomach—another of those rookie tests. Bobby had replied by dumping Fleming to the ice with a devastating bodycheck.

This time Fleming ran at Orr as Bobby dropped his head to locate the puck behind the Bruins net. Before Orr could sidestep the check Fleming had careened into him with a legal but nonetheless crushing blow that collapsed Bobby to the ice. If the knee was going to fail him, this was the time. He rolled over, planted the razor-sharp blades into the ice, and strained forward. There were no problems; he shook the snow off his yellow-and-black jersey and etched in his mind the number of the truck that hit him.

"I'm not going to go skating right after a guy," he explained later, "but eventually I'll let him know I remember him."

For half an hour Orr remembered and then, midway in the game, Fleming cut diagonally to the left at center ice. Bobby spotted him and galloped at the Ranger, lifting his stick above his chest so that it crashed into Fleming's head as they collided. Later he admitted, "I got my stick up *too high.*"

Fleming was unhurt and Orr had been given an obvious penalty. But he "got even" in the Howe eye-for-an-eye tradition. Fleming had been taught his lesson and commended Bobby for it.

"He's learned to be mean," said Reggie. "He's learned that he has to stand up for his rights in this league; I can't blame him for that."

Like most big-leaguers, Fleming nurses a quiet admiration for Orr. Until Bobby arrived, hockey players were the lowest-paid serfs in professional sports.

"I hope I can put money in everybody's pocket," said Orr. "For that matter, I hope everyone gets twice as much as I'm getting."

What he meant was that he hoped the run-of-the-ice stick-handlers could get some good out of the new inflation. They did, but it was because of Orr in a different way. It was Bobby's role in molding the NHL Players' Association that really lifted the standings of hockey players out of the Middle Ages.

It happened in December, 1966, when Orr and Eagleson were dining in a Montreal hotel. Suddenly, two Bruins players appeared at the table and invited Eagleson up to Orr's room. To the lawyer's surprise he discovered that the entire Bruins team had assembled there to see him.

"What about helping us form a players' association?" one of them asked. Eagleson agreed, and before the season was over more than 100 NHL players had signed a pledge authorizing him to act as their agent "in pursuing the formation of a Players' Association for professional hockey." To-day, all but a few of the more than 200 NHL players are members of the union.

"Al is a friend as well as my lawyer," said Bobby. "We have a nice arrangement. If he comes up with something good for me, he makes the deal and then phones me up and I tell him, 'Yeah, Al, it's okay, Al' and that's it. He's made a lot of money for me."

Just off the top of his head Orr mentioned a few of the ventures: a carwash, an apartment development, city and country acreage, and, most recently, the summer hockey camp that he owns with Mike Walton and Bobby Haggert. No fools they; whenever a youngster writes Orr or Walton for an autographed photo they send the request to their secretary, who obliges with the photograph and also inserts an attractive brochure describing the wonders of the summer camp.

In its own disturbing way the $400,000 contract has boomeranged slightly on Orr, and he knows it. The stories, the speculation—and the criticism—have touched one of his more sensitive nerves, and he has occasionally blown his cool when the questions got too personal about the finances.

Jim Proudfoot, the Toronto *Daily Star* columnist, won-dered whether Orr's summer-camp involvement with Maple Leaf forward Walton might produce a credibility gap of sorts. Old-timers consider fraternization of opponents singu-larly unacceptable and believe it smells of conflict of inter-est.

Haggert, an articulate young man, rejected the suggestion that fans would lose confidence in hockey if a Leaf and a Bruin teamed up in business. "That argument," said Hag-gert, "was first used against the [Players'] Association and was proven ridiculous. People who talk that way are either engaging in management propaganda, are simply jealous, or they are people who have let the world pass them by. I've been around hockey too long to think for a minute that Bobby is going to do less than his best to stop Mike just because they happen to be in business together. And if Bobby ever thought it was a possibility, he'd be out of this deal in a minute."

If it were only the reporters he wouldn't mind so much, but the fans have needled him right from the start. "I've gotten letters from people asking who the hell I was, getting this kind of money. One girl had enough guts to put her name and address on a letter like that. I wrote her back that I don't pay my bills with love."

What happens when they needle him face to face after a bad game?

"It's better to get the hell out of there," he said. "You never know when a wise guy's goin' to come along. You can't hit him 'cause that'll just get you in trouble. But I try to sign as many autographs as I can; I mean these people are paying my salary and most of them have been super to me. Just su-per."

Tom Capucci is one of these people. Once during the 1967–68 season Capucci was trying to start his car in the Boston Garden parking lot. It was an hour after the end of the game on a miserable sleety night, and every time Capucci gunned the engine the wheels skidded on the ice.

"Then," said Capucci, "this fellow came over to give me a hand. He spent about twenty minutes helping. He really got soaked. At first I didn't recognize him and even offered something for his trouble. Finally, I realized it was Bobby Orr."

Reminding Orr of the episode produced a simple answer: "What the hell, he would've done the same for me."

He doesn't shed the good guy role when he leaves Boston. In December, 1968, he granted an interview to the editor of a high-school paper late on a Saturday afternoon before one of those uptight games with the Canadiens. "Why not?" he countered, dismissing the question. "She had written me in advance and I wasn't doing anything."

On the ice, however, he was doing things that arrested the imagination of even veteran stars.

11. A Record Year

"That Orr," marveled Rod Gilbert of the Rangers after the opening Boston-New York game of 1968–69, "he seems to skate faster now than he did before. And he has got a few new moves."

Billy Hicke, the Oakland Seals' forward, who has been around the NHL long enough to be listened to seriously, was as amazed as Gilbert. "I don't believe there is a Bobby Orr," said Hicke. "He's really a committee of about nine guys. He just does so many things at once."

Bobby's chum, Ed Johnston, viewed the third-year defenseman from the unique vantage point of the goaltender's crease. "He whittles a sixty-minute game down to about forty minutes," Johnston explained, "by controlling the puck so long. And his blocked shots alone should earn him about half our salary—as if he needed it."

Experience had not tempered Orr's urge to lead the grand assault on the enemy's fortress, but it didn't seem to matter, because his return speed was as fast as his attacking speed. "Just as you think you've got him," said Toronto Maple Leaf center Bob Pulford with a suitable measure of awe, "and you're closing in, suddenly there he is."

At this time in a young athlete's life an overdose of praise can produce an irrevocably inflated ego. The jury isn't unanimous in Orr's favor, but the majority opinion is that he's still basically "a good fellow." At least, Lynn Patrick, his former boss and now managing director of the St. Louis Blues, can see no change.

"I bumped into him accidentally in the corridor outside the dressing room," Patrick said, early in the 1968–69 season. "He walked up to me, stuck out his hand and said, 'Hello, Mr. Patrick.' We had a nice chat. The kid hasn't changed from the day I first met him."

Gordie Howe likes to tell about the time he visited

Parry Sound during the summer of 1968 with his two sons. Orr led a welcoming committee of citizens, and when the formalities were over Orr and the Howes repaired to Bobby's house. Orr excused himself for a moment. When he returned he was wearing an old sweatshirt with the letters "GORDIE HOWE" spelled out across the chest.

Late in November, 1968, Kevin Mannix, a reporter for the Boston *Record-American,* was mistaken for Orr at Boston Garden and beseeched for autographs. Mannix ran a story in his paper, pointing out that he was *not* the real Bobby Orr but he would be pleased to have Orr sign autographs for all those who desired them. And, of course, Orr obliged.

A few weeks later he attended a caddy dinner at the Myopia Hunt Club near Boston along with Bruins vice president Charles Mulcahy. He charmed the youngsters with quips and advice. "Youngsters shouldn't fight on the ice," he warned. "When we professionals play it's different. We're playing for our living and if we get beaten it's money out of our pockets, so sometimes fights get started in our games."

That was a colossal understatement. The chain of injuries over the first two years appeared to have grated Orr's temper. There were many times during the season when he appeared spoiling for a fight, and sometimes he'd get it. Rarely did he lose. But win or lose, his reputation for unequivocally clean hard play was rapidly being challenged by his mounting penalty minutes. Referees were noticing it, too. He occasionally clashed with officials, and when his language became too spicy he would be directed to the penalty box with a misconduct.

Because his image as a clean-cut, energetic, but clearly above-board player had been clearly established, many critics found it difficult to reconcile the miscreant Orr with his lily-white reputation. They could expect such enthusiastic conduct from, say, Ted Green or Derek Sanderson, but not from Bobby.

However, those who remembered the Brian Conacher incident and those who studied his subtle "in-fighting" realized that his IQ (infraction quotient) was as high as some of his other less dainty teammates on the Bruins. Following a stoppage in play in a game at Madison Square Garden he boxed Ranger Rod Seiling's ears with his stick when the

New York defenseman was without his own stick. A few seconds later, after linesmen had intervened, Orr hurled a punch over a linesman's shoulder, catching Seiling hard on the jaw. He was no less gentle with some of his other opponents.

A few hockey students suggested that Bobby could be as rugged as the situation demanded. Others rallied to his defense, citing the ubiquitous NHL jungle law, clause one, which indicates that the strongest survive. Orr was compared with Gordie Howe, who early in his career established himself as such a ruthless attacker—he once nearly chopped off Ranger defenseman Lou Fontinato's ear with his stick—that most players became wary of disturbing him.

Bob Pennington, sports columnist of the Toronto *Telegram,* noted that Orr's new aggressiveness was enough "to chill Boston more than any blizzard." He then mentioned an episode in a game with the Rangers. "Orr dropped stick and glove to slam his fist into the face of Dennis Hextall. The blow was delivered so swiftly that no penalty was involved. . . . League rivals who blast the Bruins for overtoughness, suggest Orr, the shy, gentle Canadian boy of yesteryear, has become 'Bostonized,' meaning brutalized. Where once a fight involving Orr was headline news, the Orr of 1969 seems eager to lead the charge into battle."

Pennington found the change depressing, especially since the Bruins' traditional policeman, Ted Green, appeared to have mellowed somewhat. "Is it possible," Pennington concluded, "the mellow, wiser Green of this day will also exert restraint on the prodigy of the decade? My hope and my guess is he will."

By midseason the Bruins high command seemed almost paranoid about the spate of stories citing their violent behavior. National magazines featured Boston's All-Star defenseman, Orr, with accompanying descriptions of his exuberant teammates. Gerald Eskenazi, the *New York Times* hockey writer, railed about the "gutter language" and vulgar deportment of the Bruin fans as well as the fact that the Garden herded fans out of the rink with two huge dogs. *Newsweek* headlined Boston's "Fire on Ice."

At Bruins headquarters in the depths of Boston Garden, the hockey officials countered that Orr's behavior was nothing more than self-defense and that, all violence considered, he was consummately decorous. Yes, sir, Lady Byng would have been proud of the lad.

"I am surprised at Bobby," said manager Schmidt. "Surprised that he has been so level-headed and controlled his temper despite great provocation. Every time he goes out on the ice, he has the same problem as Gordie Howe or Bobby Hull. Players like these have the puck 70 per cent of the time and everyone is taking a run at them. I'm delighted to see Orr standing up for his rights.

"It's much the same with his injuries. Having the puck so much, he is more liable to get hurt. But you won't see him giving away any silly penalties."

Coach Sinden didn't seem to mind Orr's bullying behavior either. Late in January, 1969, the Bruins installed a speed boxing bag in their dressing room. "You should have seen Bobby," Sinden said with obvious enthusiasm. "He'd never used one before, so he asked how it worked. Within two minutes he had it going—rat-tat-tat-tat—like Sugar Ray Robinson."

The theory, "As Orr goes, so go the Bruins," was still holding as the 1968–69 season passed the halfway point. Bobby played in the All-Star Game for the second consecutive year and for the second consecutive year he stole the show from Bobby Hull, Frank Mahovlich, Stan Mikita, and the rest of the older veterans. One of the players on the West Team was Doug Harvey, who has been regarded as the best defenseman of the fifties and by some as the most accomplished defenseman of all time. Comparisons with Orr were obvious, and today most observers agree that Orr has the harder shot and the better skating and attacking ability, but that Harvey played a more intelligent game in his own defensive zone. On the whole, though, the sentiment appears to be leaning in Orr's favor.

Said Chicago Black Hawk coach Billy Reay, who played with Harvey in his prime on the Canadiens, "Doug was one of the three greatest hockey players to come out of Canada. But Doug was twenty-two before he made this league. By the time Bobby Orr is twenty-two, he'll hold ten records."

The ovations Orr received from the Montreal fans at the Forum during the All-Star Game were compared with the explosive reactions to goals made by the old French-Cana-

dian favorite, Maurice Richard. Others noted that while
most of the All-Star players seemed to be going through the
motions, Orr was moving at full speed and hitting with all
the strength at his command. His superior play inspired observers to predict great things for the Bruins in the remaining weeks of the season.

"While the Bruins win and win," commented *Sports
Illustrated*, "Montreal and the rest of the East Division
seem to be groping."

Boston had a substantial first-place lead over Montreal
late in January, and the Bruins seemed destined to annex
their first pennant since 1941. Sinden was playing Orr on a
regular shift, on the power play, and as a penalty killer.
He felt there was no other way.

"I know I use him a lot," the coach rationalized. "But
every time we're in trouble and I see him sitting on the
bench, I throw him out there. I'd be crazy not to."

Sinden led his team into the Los Angeles Forum for a
seemingly simple game against the West Division Kings on
Thursday night, January 30, 1969. Of all the expansion
teams the Los Angeles entry had some of the lightest
players and the softest hitters. The game figured to be a
romp for Boston and certainly no problem for Orr. But
during a rudimentary play in the game Bobby was skating
backward as a Los Angeles formation moved in on the
Bruins zone. Suddenly, his skate blade became trapped in a
rut on the ice. He felt a twist in the knee, and when he
limped off to the bench the soreness persisted. "I was
worried," he admitted.

The Bruins, who have a history of being less than candid
about their athletes' injuries, at first announced that Orr
would miss a game or two and everything would be all
right. But the games passed, and Orr remained sidelined.

"We thought a forty-eight-hour rest would be all Bobby
needed," said Coach Sinden, "but the knee still is sore and
we don't want to take any chances."

Team officials went to great pains insisting that the injury
was minor, but some of the Boston writers refused to believe
the Bruins flak and publicly challenged the team to give the
details about Orr's condition. When D. Leo Monahan ex-
clusively reported from Chicago that the Bruins were
"deeply concerned" about Orr's health, denials flew at the

writer. But as each day passed and Bobby remained inactive, Monahan's claim appeared more and more accurate.

"The management's handling of Orr's latest ailment," wrote Monahan on February 9, "has been, to put it mildly, curious."

Then without forewarning, Bobby disappeared.

Newsmen failed to locate him at his Boston home, nor were there any signs of him around the Bruins. The plot thickened when rumors began circulating that Bobby was suffering from mononucleosis, the same disease that earlier in the season had sidelined Orr's roommate, Gary Doak.

Before any general panic could set in Orr emerged from seclusion in Toronto. He had flown to Canada to consult with Dr. John Palmer, who had performed the operation on his left knee in June, 1968. Bobby wanted Palmer's interpretation of the condition of his ailing limb.

While Boston's hockey fans held their breath, Dr. Palmer probed Orr's joints thoroughly. When the examination was over the surgeon revealed that Bobby had irritated the knee lining but had not damaged the ligaments. The defenseman was ordered to remain inactive for another week to ten days.

As for the reports of mononucleosis, Schmidt snapped, "Hogwash, pure hogwash. . . . not a word of truth in it. If this was the case we certainly would have no reason to hide such a thing because he would not be playing any more this season."

Orr's sabbatical, combined with injuries to other Bruins, sent the team into a desperate tailspin. By the time they had righted themselves the Canadiens had pulled ahead and were hellbent for their second straight first-place finish. Only a healthy Orr could stop them.

"A lot depends on Orr," commented Milt Dunnell in the Toronto *Daily Star*. "He's the Bruin who provides the thrust that puts the spaceship in orbit. Without him, the Bruins would be like a soggy Fourth of July skyrocket."

On Sunday night, February 23, 1969, Bobby returned to the Bruins lineup for a match against the Rangers at Madison Square Garden. Once again his return seemed premature, and his performance in New York was as dismal as that of the entire Bruins team. Boston was defeated 9—0, and Orr was on the ice for five goals. Whether the embarrassment had any permanent psychological effect on the Bruins in the homestretch is debatable. Superficially at least, they seemed unperturbed.

Coach Sinden predicted the battle for first place wouldn't be decided until the final weekend of the season when his Bruins met the Canadiens head on in a home-and-home series opening in Montreal on Saturday, March 29, and concluding in Boston on Sunday, March 30. He was right.

Meanwhile, Orr began cranking himself back to his normal speed. He required a few games to shake off the sloth induced by his nine-game absence from the Bruin lineup, but that accomplished, he was the Orr of old.

His reputation was so uniquely established by the latter stages of his third season, that Orr's play—at the age of twenty-one—was the standard by which others measured defensive excellence. When the Rangers rookie defenseman Brad Park began pacing the New York club, Ranger writers asked, "Is he another Bobby Orr?"

When Serge Savard, the gifted Montreal Canadiens defenseman, executed a deft scoring play a headline appeared in a Montreal paper: "SAVARD PULLS AN ORR FOR WINNER AS HABS BEAT HAWKS."

Asked about his maneuver after the game, Savard explained his thrust in terms of his Boston counterpart. "Let's say I took a chance like Bobby Orr does and gets so many goals."

The surprisingly frank and seemingly bland explanation touched a few Orr watchers on a sensitive nerve. "One thing you have to say about Serge Savard," commented D. Leo Monahan in the *Record-American,* "is that modesty is not his bag. If Serge Savard lives to be 100, he couldn't carry Bobby Orr's, er, ditty bag."

Yet it was Savard who had all the money in *his* ditty bag when the season had finally ended. Montreal defeated the Bruins on March 29 at the Forum to clinch first place in the East Division and defeated Boston in six games in the East Final. Eventually the Canadiens won the Stanley Cup, and Savard was voted the Conn Smythe Trophy as the outstanding player in the playoffs.

But few except the most partisan Montreal supporters would dare suggest that Savard has attained Orr's level of proficiency. As expected, Bobby was voted to the First All-Star Team in May, 1969, his second straight First Team.

He received the highest vote of all the players nominated and won the Norris Trophy as the best defenseman.

He scored 21 goals and 43 assists for 64 points in sixty-seven games, thus breaking two NHL defensemen's records. His 64 points surpassed the record for defensemen (59) previously held by Pierre Pilote of the Black Hawks. His 21 goals exceeded by one the record held by Flash Hollett of the Red Wings. His 43 assists came within three of the record set by Bill Gadsby of the Rangers in 1959 and tied by Pilote in 1965.

The figures tell only a fraction of the story. Bobby Orr's supremacy really must be seen on the ice. He is all things to all players. "Just when you think that you've got about every move he makes figured out," said teammate Gerry Cheevers, "he'll show you a new one. I've never seen anybody like him."

Opponents view him from a different angle, but the reactions are equally laden with superlatives. "You find out how good this Orr is when the three of us (Phil Goyette, Bob Nevin, Don Marshall) would go in on two defensemen," said ex-Ranger center Goyette. "I'd go in with the puck and then suddenly leave it behind me for either Nevin or Marshall and continue skating into the defenseman to block him out of the play. This left two guys against one defenseman. You might eliminate yourself from the play, but you don't eliminate Orr too often. He's so fast that he's almost never too far away to block a shot."

When coach Sinden says, in answer to a question, "No, I wouldn't want to say that Orr played an unusually great game, I don't recall that Bobby ever played anything but a great game," he leaves little room for challenge.

Perhaps the definitive explanation of Orr's meaning to a hockey game—and to the Bruins—can be capsulized in a rather insignificant two minutes of action against the Rangers.

It started when Sinden sent Bobby over the boards right into the midst of the play. He immediately launched an attack by skimming the puck to teammate Glen Sather, who pushed the puck ahead of him into the corner behind the Ranger net. The New York defense got there first and counterattacked. First the Rangers passed the Bruins forwards and then moved around Boston defenseman Dallas Smith, leaving only Orr behind to protect the goalie. Rod

Gilbert had the puck for New York. He tried to circle Orr, but Bobby rammed him into the wooden sideboards with his shoulder, at once relieved him of the puck, and transferred it to teammate Derek Sanderson.

But Sanderson got nowhere, and again the Rangers had penetrated the perimeter of Boston's defenses. Dennis Hextall tried to bypass Orr, with the same result that Gilbert had had earlier. Again the puck went toward the Rangers end, and again, the Rangers recovered. Gilbert had another chance to dupe Orr. This time Orr, instead of using his body, thrust his stick along the ice and ladled the puck onto his own black-taped blade. Rather than pass the puck forward, Orr carried the disk forward himself. When Larry Jeffrey of the Rangers charged at him, he bounced off Bobby's body the way a handball rebounds from a concrete wall.

Shaken by the blow, Orr managed to regain his equilibrium and continue moving into the Rangers zone. He was challenged by defenseman Brad Park who thumped Orr to the ice. But as he fell, Bobby nudged the puck to teammate Sanderson, whose shot was stopped by the Rangers goalie.

Breathing heavily, Orr climbed back on the Boston bench and inhaled deeply to prepare for his next assignment. It came within twenty-five seconds, because the Bruins received two consecutive minor penalties and would be playing short-handed—five Rangers skaters to three Boston players—for the next two minutes.

The face-off was deep in Bruin territory. There was a scramble and, almost instinctively, the puck rolled to Orr, who kicked it away. The Rangers recovered and tried another shot. Again Bobby stopped the puck and proceeded to control it with a series of pirouettes that suggested a solo in the Ice Capades. He picked up speed, faked to go to the left, and passed to a teammate on the right. The return pass was crisp, and Orr then frustrated the Rangers by hurling the puck off the boards and down the ice. Seconds after the New Yorkers recovered the rubber disk, Orr was on top of them and in command again.

Often his manipulation of the stick has all the precision of a skilled surgeon's scalpel, but such artistry appeals only to the minority of purists with a special "hockey eye" for such subtlety. Mostly, Orr appeals to the masses, whose grasp of the game is simplistic. A hurricane rush up the ice, a crashing bodycheck, or a crisp slap shot stimulates them most, and in this area, Bobby has rarely let them down.

Orr's classic dénouement for the 1968–69 season was executed on Sunday afternoon, April 20, 1969, at Boston Garden, appropriately. The ancient rink was overflowing with 14,659 fanatics on this nippy spring day to see the Bruins and Canadiens at each other's throats in the fourth game of the East Division's Stanley Cup final.

In a moment of youthful impetuosity—and braggadocio —Orr had predicted at the start of the series that Boston would sweep the defending champion Canadiens in four straight games. Montreal then proceeded to win the opening two games at the Forum, besmirching Bobby's crystal ball. The Bruins, however, won the third game of the series in Boston, 5—0, thereby creating a dramatic setting for the fourth contest. Apparently disdainful of the embarrassment that Orr's prediction had brought him, Bruins coach Sinden had gone on record that Montreal unequivocally would not win another game in the series. The win in Boston had given Bruins fans the illusion that maybe he was right.

Boston nursed a 2—1 lead through the end of the first period and throughout a scoreless second period. By the middle of the third period the Canadiens had revved up their attack and were harassing goalie Gerry Cheevers with devastating slap shots. With less than three minutes remaining in regulation time, Yvan Cournoyer, the fleet Montreal right wing, captured a pass twenty-five feet in front of the Bruins goal. A split second later his stick cracked against the puck and it was winging its way to an open corner to the left of Cheevers.

"I got my glove up pretty late," the goalie admitted, "but I just did get a piece of it."

On the counterthrust, Orr set Bruins captain John Bucyk in motion with a short pass.

"Then," Bobby remembered, "he gave it back to me and we were off."

The puck bounced off the sticks of Orr, Ed Westfall, and Orr again like a pinball bouncing off a spring. At last, Westfall's pass brought Orr almost to the lip of the Montreal goal crease guarded by tiny Rogatien Vachon.

"I just jammed it under him," Bobby explained.

The flash of the red light signaled a cacophonous wave of applause throughout the Garden, for this was still another special goal for Orr. It represented his first score in Stanley Cup competition, leaving the twenty-one-year-old with very few peaks to conquer in the hockey world.

12. Orr in Perspective

"The worst thing that can happen
in show business is to have
a buildup to a letdown."
                                    —Anon.

Late in the 1968–69 season, when it had become apparent
that Bobby Orr would win every award available for an
NHL defenseman, a reporter asked Doug Harvey of the
St. Louis Blues to evaluate Orr. The newspaperman expected the obvious. It had become almost axiomatic to dis-
cuss the young defenseman in reverential terms, only the
metaphors varied.

But Harvey, a long-time All-Star defenseman himself,
was always the iconoclast. He commended Orr, to be sure,
but he underlined the fact that three seasons were hardly
enough to warrant definitive appraisals of Bobby's potential
sainthood. Certainly, Harvey pointed out, more evidence
was required.

Whether Harvey was protecting his own interests in the
defenseman's corner of Hockey's Hall of Fame is irrelevant.
What is pertinent, however, in any evaluation of the young
Bobby Orr—and he will remain "young" in hockey at least
until he reaches the age of twenty-five—is that he has not
earned any right to immortality, because he has not played
long enough to qualify for that claim.

Conceivably, and very likely, Orr is the best total hockey
player in the world today. Conceivably, he has been for the
past two years, but two years are nothing, compared with
the achievements of a Harvey, a Richard, or a Howe.
Harvey was named a First All-Star defenseman for *seven*
consecutive seasons, from 1951–52 through 1957–58, and
was a First All-Star in ten out of eleven years. Using that
as a standard, Orr has a long way to go before earning a
comparison with Harvey; at least on defensive abilities.
But, offensively, Orr seems to be without a peer. Late in the
1968–69 season he was detected practicing his shooting and
stick-handling from the right side and then from the left.
Only one other player, Gordie Howe, can play ambidex-

trously, and no defenseman in hockey ever did that—not even Eddie Shore.

"It's like anything else," Orr said one afternoon, cracking his knuckles, "if you practice you'll be able to do it."

His stick-handling legerdemain is equaled by his less delicate but no less valuable bodychecking. Few players in the league would dare challenge the herculean Bobby Hull of the Black Hawks in muscle-against-muscle combat, but Orr seemed to relish the challenge.

"The thing to do with Hull is to have some surprises for him," Bobby explained. "But mainly the trick is tight checking. I have to make him realize that he's got to shoot from the blue line or else.

"That 'else' is me. Hull's shot rises so fast that, if you're ten feet away and try to block it with your knees, it'll rise up and take your head off. You better believe it'll kill you. Eddie Johnston, our goaltender, got hit in the head with a puck that wasn't going nearly as fast as Hull's shot. He got a blood clot on his brain and didn't even remember the first few days in the hospital. You can't be bashful about checking Hull."

Hull, on the other hand, never suspected Orr of being bashful about walloping him. "Running into Orr," Hull noted with due respect, "is like getting hit by a pickup truck."

Unfortunately Orr's long and highly-publicized Junior career has both embellished and distorted an accurate evaluation of his playing. A great emphasis has been placed on the fact that he jumped directly from the Juniors to the NHL with so little difficulty and under such extreme pressure, which is truly commendable. But other players have encountered the glare of the spotlight with as many of the attendant difficulties as Orr faced.

Certainly, nobody met as much attention as Henri Richard, the younger brother of Maurice Richard, when Henri bridged the gap between the Juniors and the majors. Not only was Henri burdened with the fact that he was "The Rocket's kid brother," alias "The Pocket Rocket," but he also had to contend with problems of playing on a line with his older brother. Then, too, Henri came up from Juniors as one of the tiniest rookies in the NHL.

When Harvey recommends patience in defining Orr for posterity. he also must be thinking, as so many objective critics have, that recurring injuries could permanently disable Bobby at any time, still so early in his professional career. The sudden and unexpected accident in Los Angeles in January, 1969, was an excellent example of the threat of injury that must be Orr's sword of Damocles.

As for his records, they too have the tinge of chrome, quick to rust, as they have been accomplished in the "expansion era" of the NHL. His opponents in nearly half the games played by the Bruins have been West Division teams which, despite heavy NHL propaganda, are essentially minor-league teams wearing major-league uniforms. The mind boggles at the thought of what a Rocket Richard or a Doug Harvey in his prime would do against the Los Angeles Kings or the Pittsburgh Penguins. For the inescapable fact is, that the overall standard of hockey play has deteriorated appreciably since 1967, when Orr was a rookie.

The proof of this is in the NHL roster. During Harvey's halcyon days a big-league hockey player usually was washed up at thirty-five. Some, like Toronto's superb captain Ted Kennedy, have quit before reaching thirty. Others realized they couldn't keep up with the rest when they were thirty-one or two. But quality has ebbed so markedly and the production of good players has been so slow that ancients such as Gordie Howe, Allan Stanley, Johnny Bower, and Harvey have continued to excel long after their fortieth birthdays. In fact, at forty-four, Harvey played in the 1969 All-Star Game against Orr. What this signifies is that Orr's acclaim must be examined from a different perspective: hockey is not the same today as it was a decade ago.

What remains unchallenged is Orr's right to distinction in the hockey of the late sixties and early seventies.

"Only one great hockey player comes along every ten or twenty years," Ranger defenseman Harry Howell observed. "Orr is that man for these ten years."

PART II

The Bruins,
an Informal History
of Hockey's Gashouse Gang

1. The Roots of the Bruins

Of all the big cities in the United States, Boston unequivocally has the first claim to the title, "Hotbed of Hockey." Pinpointing the exact date of hockey's birth in Boston is as difficult as naming the date that Neanderthal man first whacked a stone with a tree branch to play the first hockey game.

The best estimates of the origin of first-rate organized hockey in Boston point to 1912, when a group of young men strolled into the year-old Boston Arena. They said they represented the Brae Burn Hockey Club, and they wanted to play at the Arena. The Brae Burns did play, but their opponents and the results remain a mystery to this day.

A year later, in the 1912–13 season, hockey caught on as a participant sport. Three teams—the Boston Athletic Association, The Irish-Americans, and the Intercolonials—competed. The BAA drew its talent from ex-Harvard and Dartmouth players. The Intercolonials obtained their aces from Canada, and the Irish-Americans scoured the Boston ponds for their skaters. By the end of the season the BAA and the Intercolonials agreed to play a City Series.

"It was a three-out-of-five affair," wrote Howie McHugh in his history of Boston hockey, "and produced some really brutal bodychecking. In fact, Ralph Winsor hung one on Rollie Molyneau, a Sherbrooke, Quebec citizen, that knocked Molyneau out of hockey for life. Winsor went on from there to become one of America's foremost hockey coaches at Harvard."

A year later the Boston Arena organized its own team, naming it "the Arenas." The team sponsors made one vital mistake; they imported players from Nova Scotia, which annoyed loyal Bostonians. The result was that Arena promotors booked games with the New York St. Nicholas Club and the Brooklyn Crescents, and later, teams from Pittsburgh and St. Paul.

Boston's reputation as a hockey center burgeoned, and more teams visited the Hub for competition. Soon such renowned outfits as the Toronto Aura Leas, Sherbrooke Red Raiders, Quebec City Sons of Ireland, and others played at the St. Botolph Street Rink.

The now-mature BAA team entered the 1916 National championships at St. Paul and discovered they were rather naive. The Hub sextet went up against a St. Paul team and was soundly trounced; only later did the Bostonians discover that nearly all of the St. Paul players were Canadians.

At the same time, college hockey was also booming. Harvard and Princeton became powers and great rivals. Princeton was led by Hobey Baker, regarded by many as the greatest American player in history, while Harvard boasted good balance more than individual stardom. Usually a Baker-led team defeated Harvard, but on one occasion the teams battled for ninety-six minutes before a third-string Harvard forward beat the Tiger goalie and won the game. The shot was fired by Leverett Saltonstall, who later became governor of the Commonwealth of Massachusetts.

"In that game," noted McHugh, "Baker received the only penalty of his life in Boston, and to this day old-timers insist that referee Junie Foster made a mistake."

After graduation, Baker joined the famed St. Nicholas team of New York and returned to Boston Arena to compete against Hub teams.

"A true amateur from start to finish," McHugh noted. "Hobey's exit from Boston hockey was interesting. In those days the regular fee for bringing a team to Boston from New York was $250. When Boston went to New York they received the same amount. A game between the St. Nicks and the BAA sold out the Arena, and an enterprising promotor, who thought he saw a chance to put over another big house on the following weekend, called Baker aside and offered him $3,000 to bring over a team. Baker turned the offer down and never returned to Boston as a player again."

Shortly after World War I, in which Baker was killed, a joint American-Canadian hockey team competed in the Olympics at Antwerp, Belgium, as United States representatives. They were defeated in the finals, 1—0, by the Toronto Granites. Between 1921 and 1924 the BAA, the Père Marquettes, and the Westminsters dominated Boston hockey. The outstanding line in Beantown consisted of Duke Garen, Tubber Cronin, and Hago Harrington, who eventually became coach and manager of the Boston Olympics, the Bruins farm team in the Eastern League.

Meanwhile, the sinister hands of professionalism were intruding into Boston's amateur hockey scene—a factor that was to lead directly to the formation of the Bruins—and hockey purists were becoming more and more disenchanted by the stick-handling scene.

"In those days," concluded McHugh, "it was an open joke that the 'simon pures' were gathering in the back office each weekend to get their envelopes out of a now famous cigar box. Threats and counterthreats flew back and forth. And when one of the players brought the issue out into the open, the amateur game suffered a black eye which took years to live down. The professional game moved in during the lull and a new saga of hockey was about to be written."

Enter, the Boston Bruins!

2. The Eddie Shore Era

Technically speaking, the Boston Bruins were born in a Montreal hotel room in 1924, when the National Hockey League governors voted to grant the first American franchise to New England grocery magnate Charles F. Adams. But from a practical point of view, the Bruins were really born in the wheatfields of Saskatchewan, for it was there that Eddie Shore grew up and learned to play hockey. In truth, it was Eddie Shore who gave the Bruins life, when they were struggling for existence in those uncertain early days in the NHL. Without Shore, the Bruins might well have collapsed.

Adams had become enamored of hockey after watching amateur games around Boston. He sponsored a team, but soon became disenchanted upon discovering that some of his rivals were spreading rather large gratuities among their players, even going so far as to lure several lads down from Canada. This breach of the good-fellowship code didn't wear well with Adams, and he seemed ripe as well as ready to switch his interest to professional hockey.

A group headed by Tom Duggan, Frank Sullivan, and Russ Layton began hammering away at Adams to obtain a big-league franchise. When the millionaire discovered that he was being duped by the amateur teams he decided to further investigate the world of pro hockey.

"In 1924," Adams' son, Weston, explained, "he went to Montreal to attend the Stanley Cup final. That did it. When he returned home, he told us this was the greatest hockey he ever had seen. He wouldn't be happy until he had a franchise. . . . Shore made hockey in Boston, but Montreal got us started."

Adams wasted little time organizing his new enterprise. During his Canadian excursion he had met a crusty, dour Scot by the name of Art Ross who had once enjoyed a successful career as a player. He liked the man and promptly named him coach, general manager, and scout of the new team. Shore, meanwhile, was playing defense in the old Western Canada League, where he already had earned the nickname "The Edmonton Express." But he was still a year away from Boston; Ross had heard of Shore, but was dubious about his talents. He decided to ignore "The Edmonton Express," at least for the time being, and signed a number of qualified players, including goalie Alex Connell and Clarence "Hap" Day, who was later to be a star defenseman with Toronto and one of the NHL's most successful coaches. Other first-year Bruins were Carson Cooper, Hooley Smith, Ed Gorman, and Bert McCaffrey.

When the 1924–25 season ended, the Bruins' only claim to fame was that they were America's first NHL team. They barely held up the bottom of the six-team league; with a feeble record of six wins and twenty-four losses, the Boston group lagged far behind the Maroons, Ottawa, the Canadiens, Toronto, and Hamilton.

"We had three teams that year," said Adams, "one coming, one going, and one playing."

As things developed, though, someone else's misfortune developed into Boston's hockey turnabout after the 1925–26 season. The old Pacific Coast Hockey League, directed by Frank and Lester Patrick, had run aground and the Patricks were auctioning off some excellent players at reduced prices, including Eddie Shore, Harry Oliver, and Perk Galbraith. Adams had the money, and for $50,000, half of it in cash, purchased Shore, Duke Keats, and Frank Boucher in a seven-man package. Boucher, in turn, was sold to the newly-organized Rangers. Others were dealt to the new Detroit team that had also joined the league.

During the summer of 1926 the NHL once and for all shed its Canadian provincialism and emerged as a truly inter-American organization. An American Division, composed of the Rangers, Boston, Chicago, Pittsburgh, and Detroit was formed to compete with Canadian Division, made up of Ottawa, the Canadiens, Maroons, New York Americans, and Toronto Maple Leafs.

Nobody really knew it that summer, but the first Boston hockey dynasty had begun to form, and Eddie Shore was to be its general. Until Shore came along the Bruins lacked a definitive image. They were both amusing and pathetic, effervescent and fumbling, but if you tried to find an adjective that would adequately describe them, you wound up with nothing.

Shore changed that! From the moment he tugged on the gold, white, and black jersey the Bruin adjective was "tough." With very rare exceptions it was to remain the most singular characteristic of the team, even in the days when it appeared to be loaded with lightweights. And, obviously, it is true today.

What speed has been to the Montreal Canadiens, unadulterated roughness has been to the Bruins. In some ways this characteristic is an anomaly. After all, Boston is America's seat of culture, the home of Harvard, the acme of gentility, the place where books were banned for their purple prose. One would expect the Boston hockey team to represent all that is pure and artistic in the sport. But it didn't quite attain that level, partly because of Shore and, strangely enough, partly because of Boston. The best explanation of the phenomenon was supplied by the incisive Canadian author and editor Peter Gzowski, who once diagnosed the Bruin psyche.

"There are really two cities in Boston," Gzowski explained. "On the one hand there is the old, Puritanistic headquarters of the Cabots and the Lowells, the Boston of Beacon Hill and Back Bay and John Phillips Marquand, of Harvard Yard and bone china and the Isabella Stewart Garner museum. On the other hand there is the lusty, saloon-tough seaport of the shanty Irish, of Mayor James Curley—and before him of "Honey Fitz" Fitzgerald, whose descendants have crossed the tracks to the side of lace curtains and high success—of gay wakes and oyster bars and Rocky Marciano, the shoemaker's son from suburban Brockton, and of Boston Garden, or, as Bostonians of both persuasions say, Gaaden.

"There is no confusion about which Boston is reflected by the Boston Bruins. Although *every* team in the NHL (East Division) has come to personify its home city, none has held more consistently to a single style, over the years, than the Bruins. They are as delicate as stevedores . . . at a poker table they are the burly boisterous redhead in the corner, ready to give the first man who says he's misplayed a hand a good rap in the mouth. They seem to take as much pleasure out of knocking someone down as in scoring a goal.

The Bruins have played the game with a joy-through-brawling that is as Boston Irish as a last hurrah."

None of this would have been possible were it not for Shore. Consider, for a moment, what the Bruin character might have been like if Frank Boucher, the champion Lady Byng (good conduct) trophy winner, had come to Boston, and Shore had been dispatched to New York. The Bruins then would have belonged to the Cabots and Lodges.

Ironically, manager Art Ross wasn't convinced that Shore belonged on the Bruins when Eddie reported to training camp in the autumn of 1926. This was surprising because Shore, at twenty-four, had already created a Bunyanesque aura about himself in western Canada.

Sure, Eddie had demonstrated his toughness in the minor leagues out West, but Ross wasn't so sure the big fellow with the slicked-back hair could make it with the big leaguers. The answer was supplied in a training-camp scrimmage. The Bruins had a hard-hitting veteran named Billy Coutu who wasn't particularly enamored of Shore's behavior. During practice one day Coutu punched Shore in the mouth. The rookie returned the blow, and it seemed a truce was declared. A few minutes later Coutu lumbered along the ice like a rhinoceros, picking up speed with every step. Everybody in the rink knew he was bearing down on Shore, and not because he wanted to score a goal; he was after Eddie's head.

Shore instinctively realized that Coutu had him lined up for a pulverizing bodycheck so he dug his skates into the ice and crouched for the blow. Coutu hit him amidships but Shore was the immovable object this time. He held his ground as the veteran crashed to the ice, stunned and embarrassed. When Shore returned to the bench he discovered that he hadn't escaped without injury. His ear was soaked with blood and hanging loose as if it had been sliced with a razor.

The Bruins' trainer rushed Shore to a physician, who stopped the bleeding and stopped Shore—the ear would have to be amputated! Eddie, who had accumulated a wealth of questionable medical "knowledge," challenged the diagnosis. "I want to see another doctor," he demanded.

One after another, the physicians reiterated the original diagnosis: the ear would have to go. But Shore persisted until he at last discovered a doctor who would stitch the ear together. It was not a simple procedure, and with the aid of a mirror, Eddie instructed the physician just how he wanted the job done, almost like a customer telling the barber how to part his hair.

Rarely did a rookie skate in the NHL with such impudence. Shore was brash beyond belief and just as mayhem oriented.

Al Silverman, editor of *Sport Magazine,* observed, "It has been written that man is the cruelest of the animals, and also the most maligned; that man is capable of dealing out merciless, inhuman punishment, and yet is just as capable of absorbing such punishment. Man endures all, say the philosophers. Well, in real life this is true only of certain extraordinary men. Men like Eddie Shore."

In his second NHL season Shore set a league penalty record with 166 minutes worth of fouls. The boisterousness that personified Shore was immediately translated to the Boston crowd, until it was impossible to determine which was the catalyst for mania, the frenetic Bruins audience or the player, Shore. To this day visiting managers, coaches, and players denounce the ferocious behavior of Bruins fans as if it were a contemporary phenomenon; in 1969 Ranger forward Reg Fleming titled a magazine article, "Boston Fans Are Animals." Actually, this behavior was manifest the night Shore made his debut and was magnified to hysterical proportions when the new Boston Garden was opened on November 20, 1928.

Like most other aspects of Boston, the new home of the Bruins played second fiddle to its New York City counterpart. It was smaller and considerably uglier than Madison Square Garden in Manhattan. And in a burst of originality it was named "Boston Madison Square Garden." Because it was integrated with North Station and hidden behind elevated tracks, the new arena's architectural features were practically hidden from view. Always ugly, it has somehow managed to deteriorate in appearance and hospitality, which wasn't easy. Some of those present suggested that the behavior of Bruins fans on opening night set humanity back several centuries, establishing the tone for Boston hockey forever. Others insist Bruins fans are delightfully ebullient and the most faithful in captivity. In any event, columnist Stanley Woodward recreated the scene on the pages of the Boston *Herald* in horrified tones. "It was a riot, a mob scene, reenaction of the assault on the Bastille," wrote Woodward. "It is estimated that 17,500 persons, 3,000 in excess of the supposed capacity of the Garden, saw the game."

One might have expected the crowd to behave itself once it obtained entrance to the rink. After all, this *was* the premiere of the "Gaaden." But good manners were forgotten in that frenetic atmosphere. When referee George Mallinson ruled a Bruins foray offside, the fans bombarded the ice with garbage; or at least they tried to reach the rink with their missiles.

The game itself carved the mold for future developments decades later. Boston played host to the Montreal Canadiens and, despite harassment from the crowd and some lusty bodychecks by Shore and Company, the visitors won the game, 1—0. Tall, dark, and handsome Sylvio Mantha sent the 17,500 rooters home depressed when he outwitted Bruin captain Lionel Hitchman and scored with only two seconds remaining in the second period. Reviews of the game sounded almost as if they had been written about the classic 1969 Montreal—Boston playoff round at the Garden.

"A constant stream of fresh Boston skaters, three and four to a position, emanated from the players' box and carried the game interminably to the Canadien end of the rink," said Woodward, "but the most virulent attacks were fruitless against the sturdy checking of the Canadien defense and the matchless goaltending of George Hainsworth."

As if the general air of exuberance generated by Boston fans wasn't enough, Shore was also galvanized to fury by Ross's machinations. "He played up the villain in Shore by various stunts," wrote Silverman.

One of the best—or worst, depending on one's sense of the dramatic—kept Eddie off the ice when his teammates appeared for the opening face-off. When the ploy was first executed fans wondered if Shore had been injured, so they wouldn't be getting their money's worth for the night. Precisely at that moment, the band would break into a chorus of "Hail To The Chief," and Shore would trot out in a matador's cloak, followed by a valet, who would remove Eddie's outer garment, allowing him to play.

Boston fans interpreted the episode as the height of

drama—and humor—but opponents took a dim view of the shenanigans. Some foes griped about it and at least one decided on a countermeasure that in its symbolism was a deft put-down of Ross, Shore, and the entire Bruins contingent.

One night the obstreperous New York Americans were visiting Boston Garden. They silently observed the now-boring Shore ritual to its conclusion. Then, before the referee had an opportunity to drop the puck for the opening face-off, the Americans departed *en masse* to their dressing room. A minute later they returned with a rolled-up carpet, which they proceeded to unroll before the incredulous fans. When they reached the end of the rug who should crawl out but the noted Americans player, Rabbit McVeigh. He got to his feet and promptly blew kisses to the audience, and with special attention, to Shore in the fashion more recently adopted by night club and television performer Tiny Tim.

Shore was embarrassed to the point of humiliation by the Americans' act and immediately decided he would no longer endure the cape routine, Ross or no Ross. But hockey promotors have been known to permit their intelligence to lag behind the masses, and Ross wrongly thought the absurd behavior was essential to the game. Actually, the Bruins hardly required boisterousness from their fans or cheap promotion from their management. They could have done without both and succeeded admirably, while creating a more positive image for themselves, because they had the quality team with which to draw fans. As the Montreal Canadiens have proven over the decades, that's all that really matters.

The Bruins certainly could have eschewed all the nonsense because, by the 1927–28 season they had finished in first place, repeated in 1928–29, and won the Stanley Cup in 1929 with a three-straight sweep over the Canadiens in a best-of-five series.* Shore had refined his playing style to a point at which his offensive ability matched his brutal defensive play, and he was regarded as one of the best all-around players in the NHL, if not the most fearless. En-

---

* It should be noted here that the NHL used various forms of play-offs through the years. At times a best-of-three series was employed and on other occasions a total-goals series. Sometimes the first- and second-place teams met in the opening round and sometimes not. The best-of-seven playoff became standard in the mid-forties.

counters with Rabbit McVeigh, the Montreal Maroons team, and a New York goalpost put him on a pedestal of durability that he shared with no one else.

The McVeigh incident was innocent enough. Shore had been checked to the ice by an Americans defenseman and lifted himself to his skates just as McVeigh approached head on. It was too late for the Americans forward to sidestep Shore so he leaped over the kneeling Bruin. McVeigh's razor-sharp blade didn't quite clear Eddie and sliced him between the eyes, knocking him back to the ice and out cold.

As the blood gushed from the wound, it appeared that Ross's prophecy about Shore's ultimate doom was to be fulfilled. He looked as if he were dead. The Boston trainer and a doctor skidded out to the fallen player in an attempt to pump some life back into his inert, blood-smeared body. They got Shore to move and eventually he regained his feet, skated to the bench, and had the trainer put a piece of tape on the gash. He resumed playing immediately and performed as if the accident had happened to some other player.

His clash with the Maroons was even more severe. Several of the Montreal players had decided that Shore was too liberal in his manhandling of them. During one game, one of them tore open Eddie's cheek with his stick blade, and another sliced his chin. With trip-hammer consistency, the Maroons clobbered Shore, and in the waning minutes of the game Shore was felled by a clout in the mouth tossed by a Maroon which removed several teeth and knocked him so cold he had to be carried from the rink after lying unconscious on the ice for fourteen minutes. In that one game Shore had accumulated wounds that many players avoid in a lifetime. He had a broken nose, three broken teeth, two black eyes, a gashed cheekbone, and a two-inch cut over the left eye.

He returned to action in the next Bruins game. And when friends tried to commiserate with him, he dismissed their platitudes abruptly. "This is all part of hockey," he replied. "I'll pay off."

His high-speed collision with a goal post at Madison Square Garden left the steel upright intact but cost Shore three broken ribs. The damage was so severe the Bruins left Shore in the care of a physician and entrained for a game in

Montreal. The doctor eventually escorted Eddie to a nearby hotel and left momentarily to register Shore at a hospital.

"Now, Eddie," the doctor cautioned, "I want you to stay in your room until I can come back and take you over to the hospital."

The doctor, who should have known better, assumed that Shore's lack of response indicated compliance. He left the hotel, signed up for a hospital room, and returned to Shore's room to escort the wounded player to the infirmary. But he found the door wide open and no trace of the player or his baggage. Eddie had stumbled to the lobby and had hailed a cab for Grand Central Station, where he purchased a ticket for the late train to Montreal. He arrived in time for the game with the Canadiens and scored two goals and an assist.

Shore's exploits were almost an insult to the Frank Merriwell legend and did much to erase Eddie's image as a ruthless, insensitive player. Were it not for an incident in the 1933–34 season, Eddie might well have completed his long NHL career completely on the positive side, at least in the eyes of his fans. But as Shakespeare has noted, "there's much virtue in if."

If the Boston–Toronto bitterness had not exploded in such intensity, perhaps Shore might have averted the fate that befell him, and if he had realized who his tormentor was, the episode might have been minimized. But it didn't happen that way.

In the early thirties Ross and Conn Smythe, the Toronto Maple Leaf manager, had ignited what was to be a long and bitter feud. The intercity hockey rivalry—which, incidentally, was never more evident than in the 1969 playoffs —hit a new high in hostility early in December, 1933, and for good reason. The Leafs and the Bruins were the two best teams in hockey during the 1932–33 season and proved it by finishing first in their respective divisions.

They then collided in the first round of a best-of-five Stanley Cup playoff. Four of the five games went into sudden-death overtime. Boston led the series, 2—1, but lost the next game, and the teams battled without a score through the regulation three periods in the deciding game. They then played 100 minutes of overtime without a decision, at which point Smythe and Ross enjoyed one of their few moments of agreement. The two managers asked NHL

President Frank Calder for permission to stop the game and resume it the following night. "Nothing doing," said Calder. Other proposals were rejected and the game resumed.

Early in the sixth overtime Shore attempted a clearing pass that was intercepted by Andy Blair of Toronto. Blair spotted Ken Doraty and slipped a pass to the little forward, who raced in and scored the winning goal at 4:46 of the sixth overtime, or 164:46 of the game.

Shore was the goat of the longest game played in the NHL up until that time* and he was reminded of this several times by the Toronto players. The animosity spilled over into the 1933–34 season and was quite evident on the night of December 12, 1933, when the Leafs and Bruins met at Boston Garden.

Exactly what inflamed Shore to detonate one of the most widely-discussed episodes in hockey history remains debatable to this day. However, most observers agree that the incident started when the Leafs were killing a pair of overlapping penalties and simultaneously nursing a lead. Toronto coach Dick Irvin dispatched defensemen Red Horner and King Clancy on defense and inserted Ace Bailey up front as his lone penalty-killing forward. George Hainsworth was in the nets.

Bailey was a splendid stick-handler and tantalized the Bruins on this occasion with some uncanny bobs and weaves until the referee whistled a stoppage in play. At that point Ross summoned Shore to the bench and whispered some advice to him. When Shore returned to the face-off circle, Bailey won the draw and continued to dazzle the Bruins with his footwork. Exhausted at last, Bailey skimmed the puck down the ice into the Bruin end of the rink. Shore retrieved it and began picking up speed in his inimitable locomotive fashion.

Confusion regarding subsequent events arises at this point in the play. Frank Selke, Sr., who was at the time of the incident assistant general manager of the Leafs, contends

---

* The longest NHL game on record was played on March 24 and 25, 1936, at the Forum in Montreal between the Detroit Red Wings and the Montreal Maroons. Detroit defeated Montreal, 1–0, on a goal by Modere "Mud" Bruneteau after a total of 176 minutes and 30 seconds, of which 116 minutes and 30 seconds was overtime play. The winning goal resulted from a pass by Hec Kilrea at 16:30 of the sixth overtime period. The game ended at two-twenty-five A.M.

that Shore tried to round Clancy, was tripped by the minis-
cule Toronto defenseman, and lost the puck to the Leaf.
Selke assumes that Shore was intent on retribution and
charged at a player who he *thought* was Clancy. Actually
it was Bailey, who had dropped back to Clancy's vacated
defensive position and whose back was turned to Shore.

Sport Magazine editor Al Silverman in an extensive
article about Shore asserted that Shore was bodychecked by
Horner and went after the Toronto ruffian after he recovered from the fall.

"Raging," said Silverman, "Shore went after Horner, mis-
taking Ace Bailey for Horner."

"Whether he mistook Bailey for Clancy," wrote Selke in
his book *Behind The Cheering*, "or whether he was annoyed by his own futility and everything in general, nobody
will ever know."

But this much is known. Shore gained momentum as he
moved back toward the play in Boston territory and soon
was skating at full speed as he approached Bailey from behind. According to Selke, he struck Bailey across the kidneys
with his right shoulder. The impact of the blow was so
severe that Bailey described a backward somersault resem-
bling a gymnast's trick; but he landed on his head with such
force that onlookers could hear the crack all over the vast
arena.

Selke, who was sitting in the front row of the press box,
had one of the best vantage points in the building. He described the incident this way: "Shore kept right on going
to his place at the Boston blue line. . . . Bailey was lying on
the blue line, with his head turned sideways, as though his
neck were broken. His knees were raised, legs twitching
ominously. Suddenly an awesome hush fell over the arena.
Everyone realized Bailey was badly hurt. Horner tried to
straighten Bailey's head, but his neck appeared to be locked.
Red skated over to Shore, saying, 'Why the hell did you do
that, Eddie?'

"Shore, little realizing how badly Bailey had been hurt,
merely smiled. His seeming callousness infuriated Horner,
who then hit Shore a punch on the jaw. It was a right upper-
cut which stiffened the big defense star like an axed steer.
As he fell, with his body rigid and straight as a board,
Shore's head struck the ice, splitting open. In an instant, he
was circled by a pool of blood about three feet in diameter."

At that moment the Bruins, as one, vaulted the boards and charged at Horner, but teammate Charlie Conacher rushed to Horner's side and the two held their sticks in bayonet position. "Which one of you guys is going to be the first to get it?" Conacher demanded. The Bruins suddenly conducted an orderly retreat to assist Shore and see if Bailey was still alive.

For nineteen minutes Bailey lay unconscious while doctors worked frantically over him. An ambulance was summoned to rush him to the hospital, where he teetered precariously on the brink of death. He had suffered a cerebral concussion with convulsions, and appeared incapable of recovery. Before he was removed to the hospital Bailey looked up at Selke from the dressing-room table and pleaded, "Put me back in the game; they need me."

As Selke and others suspected, Bailey was in danger of dying at the time, and only immediate surgery would save him. A day after the injury two brain surgeons familiar with that type of damage were found in Boston. They operated on Bailey, thinking he had suffered only one concussion. After the initial surgery, however, they discovered he had suffered two, and a week later, another operation was performed.

Few held out hope for the player, and the Toronto management made plans to have Bailey's body shipped back to Canada. Two weeks after the injury Ace appeared to be slipping into an irretrievable condition, but he was attended by two unflaggingly spirited nurses who kept urging him to "keep fighting."

Suddenly, Ace took a turn for the better, and he was released from the hospital two weeks later. Shore, meanwhile, had taken a turn for the worse in the eyes of hockey fans and officials. He was suspended by the NHL, and cries for his permanent suspension were heard from New York to Chicago.

When he was sufficiently recovered, Bailey graciously minimized Shore's dilemma by saying, "We didn't see each other coming."

When Eddie heard that, he replied, "I wish we had. I'd have slugged him—and nobody ever got hurt that way but Shore."

The Bruins sent Shore on a recuperative vacation, and a month later the NHL concluded that since Eddie had

never before suffered a match penalty for injuring an opponent, he would be reinstated. He returned to the Bruins
lineup in January, 1934, neither penitent nor restricted in
his play because of the furor.

Shore played fourteen seasons in the NHL, thirteen and
a half with the Bruins. Four times he was voted the Hart
Trophy as the league's most valuable player and was named
to the All-Star Team seven times. The best estimates place
Shore's total number of stitches in excess of 970. His nose
was broken fourteen times, his jaw shattered five times, and
all his teeth had been knocked out before his career had
ended. He barely missed being blinded in both eyes and
nearly lost an ear.

The Bruins finished in last place in the American Division
during the season of the Shore-Bailey incident, but they
recovered admirably to recapture first place the following
year. Those opponents who suspected—and, one imagines,
hoped—that Shore would become more temperate were unquestionably dismayed when he returned. Old feuds were
reopened and new ones, especially with younger players,
started.

Because of Shore, the Bruins cultivated keen disputes with
several teams, but the Leafs and Rangers remained at the
top of the hate parade. Over the years the New Yorkers
were a more purist, more skilled, but smaller club than the
Bruins and generally absorbed more abuse than they dis-
tributed. But when former Canadian heavyweight champion
Murray Patrick joined the Rangers in 1937, the New
Yorkers temporarily gained the balance of power. Patrick
was the Rangers' policeman and he objected to Shore's
abuse of Phil Watson, New York's young and rather small
center. Shore once cracked Watson in the head, sending him
to the hospital with a concussion.

"He was tough," Patrick recalled. "You had to be sure
to get him first."

Frustrated to the point of paranoia by the Bruins' physical
superiority over the Rangers, New York hockey fans waited
impatiently for the day when Shore would get his come-
uppance at the hands of Patrick. Oddly enough it happpened
because of a confrontation involving Watson and Jack Portland, a Bruin defenseman. Murray Patrick was observing the
two-man battle without interfering when he noticed Shore
stealthily move in on Watson from behind. "He started

massaging the back of Phil's neck with his stick," wrote Al Silverman in his Shore chronicle. Disturbed by the two-to-one odds against his teammate, Patrick rushed Shore and attempted to wrest him away from Watson. Shore wheeled around and swung at Patrick, hitting him on the shoulder. In a trice, Patrick let his two leather gauntlets slip off his hands. He retracted his fists and then—bomb-bomb-bomb— he smashed Shore three times in the face. "I could feel his head squash when I hit him," Patrick admitted later.

After game officials intervened Shore left the ice with a cut eye and lip and a nose broken in two places. He headed straight for the medical room, received stitches, and was back on the ice less than ten minutes after the fight had started.

Every so often Eddie would have an off year, and critics would charge that the law of diminishing returns was taking its toll on the aging star, but he had a knack, irritating to opponents, of bouncing back with even more élan the following year. He did it the season after his suspension and repeated the feat in 1937–38, after what most Shore watchers regarded as his worst season. Eddie played only eighteen games in 1936–37, and the Bruins finished second in the American Division, but were quickly dispatched from the playoffs by the Maroons. A broken vertebrae had sidelined Eddie, but he was A-one when he returned in the fall of 1937. He won a spot on the First All-Star Team as well as the Hart Trophy.

As the Bruins began rebuilding around a youth movement, Shore began searching for a new home. He was temporarily delayed, however, by his own surprising rejuvenation as well as by the Bruin renaissance. The dual bonanzas occurred in the 1938–39 season when Shore reached his thirty-seventh birthday.

It has been said, and with some substantial evidence, that the Bruins that season comprised the greatest hockey team of all time. This, of course, is debatable. But it was certainly *one* of hockey's finest squads.

3. Boston's Best Team

The 1938–39 Bruins were such a glorious squad that even a complaining Shore could exult in its success, which he did while contributing substantially to its eminence. Certainly, Bostonians were unanimous that it ranked with the best teams that ever wore the Bruins' colors, and Art Ross was the first to second that motion.

"Every player was a major leaguer," said Ross, underscoring his point. "We had a great goalkeeper in Frank Brimsek, a fine offense, and defensively we were very strong with Shore, Jack Portland, Dit Clapper, and Jack Crawford. In fact, our defense was so strong we used to do something that would be suicidal in later years. I used to order my forwards to play outside when backchecking against the opposing wings.

"In other words, instead of driving the play to the outside, which is normal, I had them driving it inside, *toward* the goal and not away from it. That way my forwards could be looking at their defensemen at all times and be ready for a pass or loose puck. You had to have a great defense to play like that, and we had it. They were the best team I ever saw in my life."

Like their foes in New York, the Bruins had come to understand the importance of a farm system. The Rangers began developing players in Winnipeg, Manitoba, and the Bruins discovered a mother lode of talent in Kitchener, Ontario, home of a local team known as The Greenshirts. Woody Dumart, Bobby Bauer, and Milt Schmidt, three boyhood chums from the Kitchener-Waterloo Germanic Canadian community, were linemates for the Greenshirts—so swift and adroit they were promoted directly to the Bruins in 1936.

Their accomplishments were virtually nonexistent in the 1936–37 season, and Dumart and Schmidt played adequately but not sensationally the following year. Bauer, however, scored twenty goals, third highest in the American Division. Everybody knew the kids were on their way to the top.

Depending on the writer, the trio was known as the Kraut Line, the Sauerkraut Line, and the Kitchener Kids. The first two nicknames were eschewed during World War II because of the German association, and the name Kitchener Kids lasted until the line broke up in the late forties.

The Krauts were as fraternal a threesome as Shore was an independent cuss. They not only played together, traveled together, and relaxed together, they also presented a united front when it came to contract-signing time.

"We felt if we went in together, asked for exactly the same salary for each, and took a stand in our dealings we'd be better off," Schmidt once explained.

The Krauts, as they well knew, were only cogs in the total Bruin machine. Their scoring feats were matched and often surpassed by Bill Cowley, an unimposing-looking center who dribbled the puck with uncanny imagination. The line of Cowley, Charlie Sands, a smooth-skating wing, and Ray Getliffe was regarded as the premier scoring unit at the start of the 1938–39 season while the Krauts were listed as the second line. The third line—one that slightly downgraded the Bruins in any comparison with other great hockey clubs—was solid but not especially threatening. It consisted of Conacher, Gordie Pettinger, and Mel Hill.

For years Ross had received excellent service out of goalie Tiny Thompson and there was no surprise in Boston when Tiny started the 1938–39 campaign in the nets again. But Ross was unhappy, not so much about Thompson as about a young goalkeeper, Frank Brimsek, who was impressing scouts at nearby Providence in the International-American League. Ross believed Brimsek was ready for the NHL and felt there were several good reasons why he should act on his supposition. Brimsek was not only a good hockey player, he was that rare breed—a good American-born, American-developed player, who had learned the game in the cold wastes of Eveleth, Minnesota. Also, the Detroit Red Wings had revealed their willingness to spend $15,000, at that time a respectable sum, for Thompson.

Ross put one and one together. Thompson was aging; Brimsek was ready. Late in November, 1938, the Bruins announced that their veteran goalie had been sold to Detroit. Brimsek would henceforth start in the Boston goal. Neither Thompson, his teammates, nor most of the Bruin fans could believe the news. After all, Tiny had won the Vezina Trophy four times and was still considered one of the finest goalies around even after playing ten years in the NHL.

"The team took it pretty badly," Schmidt noted. "Dit Clapper was Tiny's roommate, and he was ready to quit. We just couldn't understand Mr. Ross replacing a sure thing with a rookie."

Nothing about Brimsek altered the prevailing opinion that he would be a flop. One critic immediately denounced his potential on the grounds of his Slavic background. "Slavs," the man said, "don't have the temperament to be goalies."

Those who remembered him in Providence recalled that he had a habit of not really appearing to be "in" the game when the action got liveliest. Others decided that an American kid just couldn't make it in the Canadian-laden NHL.

Brimsek did nothing to enhance his image. He had an idiosyncrasy of wearing a pair of old red hockey pants instead of the then traditional gold, brown, and white Bruins outfit, and his footwork was less than sparkling. But his glove hand was amazingly fast and his confidence enormous.

"He's as quick as a cat," said Rangers manager Lester Patrick, who would be among the last to laud a rival Bruin. "Trying to get him to make the first move is like pushing over Washington Monument."

The doubts about Brimsek's potential were eliminated within his first dozen games. In a stretch of three weeks he scored six shutouts in seven games, was immediately dubbed "Mister Zero," and went on to win both the Calder Trophy as rookie of the year and the Vezina Trophy as top goalie.

Brimsek permanently secured the affection of Bruins fans after his first two shutouts. When Boston faced Montreal in the next game at the Garden, the kid goalie appeared destined for still another superb goalless game, as the second period ticked to a close. But the visitors organized a two-on-one rush late in the period. Herb Cain, who was later to star for the Boston club, broke free and beat Brimsek from directly in front of the net.

Once the home fans had digested the momentary tragedy, they suddenly broke into an unremitting chorus of applause for "Mister Zero," whose record had reached 231 minutes and 54 seconds of shutout goaltending. There was no question that Ross had dealt with efficacy when he sent Thompson to the Red Wings.

Boston finished first with a 36—10—2 record, 16 points ahead of New York and 27 points ahead of third-place Toronto. However, the Bruins' quest for the Stanley Cup would not be simple. Their first-round opponents were the Rangers with whom they had been quarreling all season. Ross, for one, had been ridiculing the "streamline" clever passing patterns of the light-horse New Yorkers. Rangers manager Patrick pointed an accusing finger at the Boston sextet, using a theme that would be heard many times in the future. He charged the Bruins with excessive roughhouse play.

The best-of-seven series opened at Madison Square Garden on March 21 and after the normal three periods, the teams had battled to a 1—1 tie. Now the teams pushed into the perilous waters of sudden-death overtime, and again there was no score. A second sudden death also produced no goals, the players bone weary from skating.

By now the Rangers' strategy had become apparent to Ross. The home club was determined to stifle Cowley's scoring chances with some blanket checking while keeping a watchful eye on Conacher as well. New York's hope was to force the Bruin attackers into an errant pass, snare the puck, and capitalize.

A few seconds before the third overtime, Ross summoned Cowley to his side. "We've got to fool them," he told his superb center. "They're watching Conacher so carefully it would be better to feed Hill."

There is no record of Cowley's response, but the chances are he was stunned. "Feed Hill?" This seemed a joke. Compared with Conacher, Mel Hill was a feeble shooter who had managed only ten goals over the entire season. Surely, Ross couldn't be serious. But the manager was never more concerned about a play in his life. By the time the teams took the ice Cowley realized Hill was going to get that puck if Ross had anything to say about it.

It took nearly an entire overtime period before Cowley could convert Ross' advice into action. Late in the third sudden death the Bruin center crossed into Ranger territory and lured Murray Patrick toward him. Patrick was a big, hulking skater, and the long game had slowed him down considerably. He didn't quite get to Cowley in time and the Bruin eluded him, skated into the corner and made a perfect pass to Hill who was camped in front of goalie Dave Kerr. Hill swung and Kerr missed and at 1:10 A.M. the Bruins had won the game.

The teams took a train to Boston for the second game, and after three periods of battling were tied again; this time at 2—2. The New Yorkers failed to entrap Cowley as successfully as they had in the previous game. Shortly after the eight-minute mark he charged the Ranger defense and dropped the puck behind him to Mel Hill, who scored with a forty-foot shot at 8:24 of the first overtime.

The next game was also played in Boston, and for the only time in the series, the Bruins clearly demonstrated their superiority, coasting to a 4—1 win. Now the Bostons boasted a three-game lead and confidently returned to New York for what they anticipated would be the *coup de grâce* in the first round.

Much to the Bruins' chagrin, the Rangers were unwilling to accept the obituary notices. They traded check for check and blow for blow with the Bruins and soon discovered what other teams have learned about Boston teams over the years—they don't relish retaliation in kind. When Murray Patrick disposed of Shore in a free-for-all, Brimsek completely blew his cool and rushed at the Ranger, his stick poised for a lethal blow. Dit Clapper, the big Bruins captain, intercepted the warlike Brimsek before he could swing his club. With a tremendous display of hockey guts, the Rangers came back and won the game, 2—1, forcing a fifth game, this time back in Boston.

"Boston fans showered the Rangers with firecrackers, eggs, oranges, and tin cans," reported magazine writer Lee Greene. The garbage assault bothered the visitors but didn't interfere with their play. They held Boston to a 1—1 tie for three periods and won the game late in the first sudden death on a goal by Clint Smith.

When Boston lost the sixth game, 3—1, in New York, impartial witnesses thought that the vaunted Bruins had "choked," had wilted under the mounting Ranger pressure. The verdict was supplied in the deciding game on April 2 at Boston Garden. Each team scored a goal in the second period and then played scoreless hockey until the buzzer sounded the end of regulation time.

One, then two thoroughly exhausting and traumatic sudden death periods came and went with no score. The third overtime had nearly reached the eight-minute mark when Old Man Shore captured the puck and moved it ahead to Conacher. The Bruin's shot was hard, but goalie Bert Gardiner, who earlier in the series had replaced Kerr, nabbed it in the webbing of his glove. He flipped the puck into the corner of the rink, expecting one of his defensemen to retrieve it. Somehow, Cowley got there first and continued behind the cage. The Ranger goalie thought he would retain the puck, but Cowley unexpectedly tapped it out to Mel Hill, standing in familiar territory in front of the Ranger net. Gardiner moved to stop him, but too late; the puck was in. The Bruins had won the series, four games to three, and thereafter number eighteen on the Bruins was known as "Sudden Death" Hill throughout the NHL.

The final round with Toronto was a vacation for the Bruins compared with the Ranger series. They eliminated the Maple Leafs in five games to win the Stanley Cup. Considering his age, Shore had had a laudable season. He scored 4 goals, 14 assists for 18 points during the regular season and picked up 4 assists in the playoffs. There was no reason to assume he wouldn't be wearing the Bruins uniform again. But with Shore you never could tell.

Ross, on the other hand, was never one to permit sentimentality to stand in the way of a good deal. He realized that Shore had only a couple of years left, and despite what Eddie had done for the Boston franchise, Ross was prepared to trade him to any high bidder. The New York Americans indicated they would make a handsome offer, and Ross seemed interested when they suggested a $25,000 tab.

While Ross was mulling this over, Shore was doing some business of his own and finally announced he had purchased the Springfield Indians of the International-American League for $42,000. Shore was fascinated by the prospect of running his own club and made no bones about the fact that he was moving his family to Springfield.

Ross was livid when he learned of Shore's purchase. He attempted to humiliate his star before local newsmen with the plaintive but hollow question, "Where do the Bruins come in?"

The answer was second fiddle from now on. Ross and Shore finally agreed that Eddie would play with the Bruins after December 15, 1939, in case of emergency, but he would continue playing for and managing the Springfield sextet also. Ross tried to circumvent the deal by wooing Shore to the Bruins lineup before December 15 on the grounds that the club was already confronted with an "emergency."

Eddie played in three games and scored his final goal as a Bruin on December 5, 1939. By the time the December 15 deadline arrived Shore was fed up with Ross and his chicanery. He revealed that he would no longer play for Boston because the club wouldn't permit him to fulfill his playing obligations in Springfield. Ross wasn't about to quit. It took the stubborn Scot a month to realize he no longer could dominate the man who had made hockey in Boston. At last, on January 15, 1940, Ross called a press conference and made the following announcement:

"Shore has a heavy investment with his Springfield club and we want to give him a hand."

Within two weeks of this altruistic declaration, Ross had traded Shore to the New York Americans for Eddie Wiseman and cash, thus ending the Shore era in Boston.

4. The War Years and After

Boston's total conquest of the NHL was no accident. The Bruins proved they could win big—even without the immortal Shore. They finished first again in the 1939–40 season and did it with a remarkable mortgage on the scoring championship. Schmidt finished first with 52 points while linemates Bauer and Dumart were tied for second with 43 points apiece. And right behind *them* was Boston's Bill Cowley with 40 points.

It was quite an armada but it wasn't without a flaw. The Bruins were supreme, to be sure, but they were being threatened by a constantly-improving Rangers team that finished in second place, a mere three points behind Boston. Even more significant, the Rangers lost one less game during the regular schedule than the Bruins.

Once again the Northeast rivals collided in the first round of the Stanley Cup playoffs—in that season the first- and second-place teams met in the opening round—and once again the Bruins were favorites. But this time, Davie Kerr outgoaled Frankie Brimsek, and the Rangers rebounded from a 2—1 game deficit to win the best-of-seven series in six games.

Ross had no reason to panic. New York had the young, talented players with which to depose Boston as the reigning monarch, but meanwhile, the Bruins would enjoy one more season in the sun. They won the pennant in 1940–41 with substantially the same team as they had the previous season. This time, however, Cowley won the scoring championship, finishing 18 points ahead of his nearest rival, Bryan Hextall of New York.

The Rangers of 1941–42 are regarded by impartial critics as the equal of Boston's greatest teams. Paced by the Hextall-Lynn Patrick-Phil Watson line and with young Jim Henry in the nets, the Blueshirts finished first, three points

in front of Toronto and four ahead of the Bruins. Somehow,
Boston's attack fizzled; Roy Conacher, highest scorer on the
team, was buried in thirteenth place in the standings. But the
defense, fortified by Brimsek, remained solid, and "Mister
Zero" won the Vezina Trophy for the second, and last, time
in his career.

With Shore gone, the spirit of the Bruins changed somewhat to less than vicious. Some players on the team would
actually admit privately that they didn't relish a fight, and
at least once a Bruin—Bill "Flash" Hollett—was genuinely
upset when he knocked an opponent's tooth out of his
mouth.

There wasn't much laughter, however, in the NHL after
the 1942 playoffs. The Bruins eliminated Chicago in a best-
of-five first-round series in three straight, but were ousted
in a best-of-three second-round test by Detroit, 6—4 and
3—1. Toronto eventually defeated the Red Wings for the
Stanley Cup, completing the last peacetime season for the
NHL. World War II had by now engulfed the United States,
not to mention every nation in the British Commonwealth.
The U.S. Fleet had been destroyed at Pearl Harbor and the
British had lost Singapore and Malaya. The Allies were
falling back on all fronts and troops were needed badly.

By the autumn of 1942 only the Rangers had contributed
more (nineteen) players to the Canadian and American
armed forces than the Bruins, of whom sixteen enlisted. Jim
Hendy's *Official Hockey Guide* listed the enlisted Boston
players as follows: Bobby Bauer, Woody Dumart, Alf Kun-
kel, Milt Schmidt, Eddie Wiseman, and Roy Conacher, in
the Royal Canadian Air Force, and Cliff Thompson, Gordon
Bruce, Jack McGill, J.L. Wade, Lloyd Gronsdal, Dick
Rondeau, Jack Riley, Clare Martin, Des Smith, and Frank
Mario, in the Army.

The Kraut Line had enlisted as a unit amid suitable publicity, and Brimsek was soon to join the U.S. Coast Guard.
For a time he was stationed at the Curtis Bay, Maryland,
Coast Guard Station where many other crack American
hockey players had enlisted. They soon organized a team,
affectionately known as the Cutters, or "Hooligan's Navy,"
and played two full seasons in the Eastern Hockey League.

With the Krauts gone, the Bruins finished second in
1942–43, defeated the Canadiens in the opening playoff
round, but were eliminated by Detroit in four straight games

for the Stanley Cup. That was the beginning of the end for the Bruins. Now that Brimsek was gone, the defense crumbled like a fragile wall in an earthquake. As for Ross, his magic disappeared with the first puff of smoke over Pearl Harbor and the Bruins remained a lackluster club until after World War II.

5. The Bruins' Gambling "Scandal" and Another Black Eye

Art Ross's desperate attempts at rejuvenating the Bruins to their prewar eminence continued to founder as the 1947–48 season neared its conclusion. Bobby Bauer's retirement decimated the Kraut Line once and for all and the youngsters, though promising, hardly matched the quality of those Ross had promoted in the late thirties.

Even worse, most of his deals did nothing to help the team, especially the acquisition of Billy Taylor from Detroit for Bep Guidolin. Most disappointing of all was Taylor's playing. By late January, the Bruins management was so unhappy with Taylor that they sent him home for a week, "to see," as president Adams put it, "if he could pull himself together."

It was no secret that the Bruins were anxious to trade Taylor. "I do know," said Adams, "that he will have a very tough time getting back to the form he is capable of while with Boston. The tragic thing is that he is a much better player than he has ever shown here."

Rangers manager Frank Boucher entered negotiations for Taylor on the assumption that the blond center's only problems were insufficient conditioning and general bad luck on the ice. He was not aware that Taylor might have other difficulties. The Rangers thus traded Grant Warwick to the Bruins for Taylor and an unnamed player.

"I know Billy is a good hockey player," said Boucher, "and I'm gambling that I can get the best out of him."

Boucher had unconsciously used a word—gambling— that would be heard over and over again in hockey circles.

The first scent of trouble emanated from Detroit, where the Detroit *Times* ballooned a story about two Bruins players having spoken with a Detroit gambler named James Tamer. The Boston skaters remained anonymous, and the story was at first pooh-poohed as an outrageous rumor.

Meanwhile, the Billy Taylor mystery deepened. Despite his apparent pleasure at becoming a Ranger, Taylor didn't look well. His blood pressure was down and he was given iron injections as soon as he arrived in New York, but that was the least of his worries. His name was being linked with the gambling controversy that had begun to catch fire around the league. On March 4, 1948, Walter Winchell wrote in his syndicated column:

"The two players whose names are expected to blaze in the hockey mess are Taylor of the New York Rangers and Gallinger of the Boston Bruins."

While Winchell's item flashed across the United States and Canada, NHL President Clarence Campbell conferred with Kim Sigler, governor of Michigan.

"By tomorrow," a Canadian hockey writer predicted, "the two players will be identified officially for the public and their sentences will be announced."

On March 9, the mystery was solved. The New York *Sun* ran an eight-column front page banner headline: "RANGER PLAYER EXPELLED—DON GALLINGER OF THE BOSTON BRUINS SUSPENDED FOR LINKS TO GAMBLERS." The following wire-service story accompanied the news:

Clarence S. Campbell, president of the National Hockey League, today expelled Billy Taylor, New York Ranger player, and suspended Don Gallinger of the Boston Bruins on charges of being associated with gamblers. Campbell reported the punitive action to Michigan's Governor Kim Sigler.

Campbell had returned to Michigan to announce his decision because Detroit police on Sigler's instructions last week had given the league president information pointing to a link between gamblers and professional hockey players. The hockey league president expelled Taylor for conduct "prejudicial to and against the welfare of hockey."

He charged that he had sufficient evidence to show that Taylor had "knowingly associated with and communicated with James Tamer, a criminal and known gambler." Taylor, Campbell reported in a formal statement to Sigler, "was interested with Tamer in a wager on the outcome of a National Hockey League championship game played in Chicago on February 18 between the Boston Bruins and the Chicago Black Hawks. Taylor's interest in this wager was that he authorized Tamer to place for him a bet of $500 on the Chicago Black Hawks." Boston, however, won the game in question by a 4 to 2 score.

In his investigation, Campbell made trips to Chicago, Boston, and New York. He also visited the southern Michigan prison where he talked with Tamer, a convicted bank robber who was returned to the institution two weeks ago as a parole violator. Campbell said he was suspending Gallinger indefinitely pending further investigation of his associations with Tamer. The hockey president said his investigation has "established to my complete satisfaction that no other player in the National Hockey League was involved in any gambling."

Campbell said league by-laws permitted the president "on such information and reports as he may deem sufficient" or on any act or conduct of an official or player who has been "dishonest, prejudicial to or against the welfare of the game or the league" to hand out fines or suspensions.

"A player has violated the rules of hockey by betting or being interested in any pool or wager whether or not he has any connection with the game involved," Campbell said.

"The investigation in the case of Gallinger," Campbell said, "will be vigorously pressed," but added he could not estimate how long it would require. Campbell said, "The National Hockey League will not tolerate gambling on hockey games by any of its personnel nor will it tolerate their knowingly associating with gamblers or other undesirable characters."

"There has not," Campbell's statement said, "been any charge of fixing or attempting to fix a hockey game, although that expression has been erroneously employed several times in recent publicity and the evidence completely negates that suggestion."

Campbell said that no special arrangements would be made to permit the Bruins and Rangers to replace the two suspended players. He said that the clubs, however, could sign new amateurs or call up players who are on loan. Campbell said in his formal statement that "the law enforcement authorities of the State of Michigan have been very cooperative in supplying valuable evidence upon which this investigation has been largely based." He asked Sigler for continued assistance from the State in the investigation of Gallinger's case.

Campbell added that he had discussed the charges with Taylor personally but that Taylor would not admit the bet although he admitted having telephone talks with Tamer. In Boston, Weston Adams, president of the Bruins, said he would withhold comment until officially notified by Campbell of Galliger's suspension.

Although leaks of a scandal had been seeping through the NHL's wall of silence for days before Campbell's formal announcement, the news of the Taylor-Gallinger affair stunned the league to the core. Hockey had always prided itself on being more scandal-free than its competitive major sports and this mess besmirched the game as it hadn't been in decades. The fact that no charge was made of "fixing" or attempting to "fix," as Campbell emphatically noted, hardly diminished the enthusiasm of headline writers across the continent.

Reaction to the Campbell proclamation covered the emotional spectrum. Outrage was mixed with skepticism and even some optimism about hockey's future. Tommy Munns, sports editor of the Toronto *Globe and Mail,* lauded Campbell for his investigation.

"More worthy of public confidence than ever is hockey in general and the National League in particular," commented Munns. "The vigorous handling of the involved Taylor-Gallinger-Tamer case by NHL President Clarence Campbell proved that gambling influences touched only the fringe of hockey and had no entrée to the game itself."

Although Gallinger remained suspended, the Bruins recovered from the furor and finished in third place, ahead of the Rangers. They were to meet the Maple Leafs in the playoffs, but Campbell refused to lift the ban on Gallinger. The high-scoring forward was officially expelled from the NHL for life the following September.

Boston entered the Stanley Cup semifinals against Toronto in a distinctly different position than when the clubs met in the late thirties. This time the Maple Leafs had a team that could have passed for the greatest of all time—no team ever had better center-ice strength than with Max Bentley, Syl Apps, and Ted Kennedy—whereas the Bruins were carrying a group of average players led by Milt Schmidt, who was nursing a bad knee.

The Leafs were surprised by Boston's enthusiasm for the puck in the opening game and couldn't wrap up the contest until Nick Metz scored the winning goal after seventeen minutes and two seconds of sudden-death overtime. The final score was 5—4.

Kennedy scored four goals in the second game as the Leafs came away with a 5—3 win. The first two games were unusually mild for Toronto-Boston contests, but the clearly superior Leafs did not have to resort to violence to top the Bruins.

On March 30, 1948, the teams skated out on Boston Garden ice for what was to be another black night in Bruins history. It didn't quite equal the Shore-Bailey incident for shock value, nor did it have the ethical implications of the Taylor-Gallinger scandal, but it revealed an idiosyncratic ugliness of a portion of the Boston crowd which has lasted to this day.

The game itself was nothing extraordinary. Toronto routed Boston 5—1 and dominated the Bruins in every category of play, including one memorable fight between Harry Watson of the Leafs and Murray Henderson of the home club. Husky and fast, Watson had originally come to Toronto in a deal the Leafs had made with Detroit for Billy Taylor. Calm by nature, Watson was antagonized by Henderson after a less flamboyant fight had broken out between Bill Ezinicki of the visitors and Grant Warwick of the Bruins.

"The usually quiet-mannered Toronto left-winger went berserk as he shed his gloves and peppered the Boston defenseman with a series of hard, short jabs to the face," wrote Jim Vipond. "Watson landed at least eight blows, and Henderson was forced to retire to the Boston dressing room with a broken nose."

When the final buzzer sounded, someone cracked: "The stops in the third period were Broda, six; Brimsek, nine; and Henderson, fifteen!"

The Maple Leafs mistakenly assumed that the battle had

ended when the green lights flashed at each end of the rink
and referee George Gravel had blown his final whistle, but
they should have known better. After all, they *were* in Boston, weren't they? And Boston fans had been harassing them
throughout the game. "Early in the game," said Vipond,
"Referee Gravel asked the police to remove the offending
spectators but was frustrated by a Bruins official. The Boston
representative dashed to the side of the rink and refused to
let the police interfere."

As the Toronto players attempted to make their way to
the dressing room several fans jumped coach Hap Day. Defenseman Wally Stanowski, who was one of the last to
leave, immediately rushed to the aid of his coach and fought
off several of the fans. Defenseman Garth Boesch and
center Ted Kennedy, who had walked farther along to the
dressing room, rushed back to assist Stanowski and Day.
At that point a fan ran up behind Boesch and felled the
mustachioed defenseman with a sneak punch. Dazed, the
Leaf player had to be taken back to the hotel and put to bed.

"The fight just had to happen," Day explained in the
Toronto dressing room later. "Two fans sitting behind us
kept swearing at the players, using filthy language. Perhaps I was foolish, but by the time the third period began
I could stand it no longer and started talking back to them.

"Then they concentrated on me and kept shouting,
'You're yellow, Day,' and challenging me to a fight. One
fan threatened to hit me, and I told him I'd be waiting at
the end of the game. I turned around as soon as the game
ended, and the two of us tangled. Unfortunately for Wally,
he had been beside me on the bench all evening and was the
only player to hear the challenge."

More serious damage might have been inflicted by the
Boston spectators were it not for the courageous interference
of George Hayes, a huge NHL linesman who waded into the
throng and held off the fans, enabling Day and his players
to escape to the dressing room. Help was also provided by
Bill Smith, a Boston suburbanite, who had been a member
of Conn Smythe's 30th Battery in World War II. Smith, at-
tending the game as Smythe's guest, hurried down from his
seat to assist Day.

As the Leafs finally made their way out of the Arena a
Boston policeman approached Day and offered to escort him

to a cab. "You're a little late," Day snapped. "You weren't around when we needed you. I think I can make out all right by myself now."

The ugly scene was reported on the front pages of the Boston papers. "BETTER POLICE PROTECTION NEEDED FOR THE MAPLE LEAFS," was the headline in the *Traveler*. Sports writer Art Siegel labeled the fans "mugs permitted to get away with muckerism. . . . These were fans with money enough to have the high-priced promenade seats, but lacked any of the refinements that should go with the quality of their tickets. They wouldn't dare tackle a player man to man, but they can gang-fight any individual. And the Garden police let them get away with it."

The *Herald's* headline was even more emphatic. "THUGS ATTACK TORONTO STARS," it asserted on the front page. "Most unsporting demonstration ever witnessed in Boston's hockey history . . . ," commented Henry McKenna.

One out-of-town reporter observed that police would readily eject a troublesome patron from a restaurant, a theater or, for that matter, even a race track.

"But," wrote Jim Coleman, "if your wife has been beating you and you wish to give vent to your inner bitterness, it is necessary only to attend a hockey game at Boston Garden, lean across the rail, and take a slug at the first player who gets in a tangle along the boards."

As Coleman noted, and others have since, the Boston "massacre" reflected adversely on the Bruin hockey club and gave professional hockey a black eye.

"Our original thesis," Coleman pointed out, "is that the NHL is still a bush-league outfit. Did the NHL do anything to enforce George Gravel's order that the Bostonian goon should be ejected from the Garden after grabbing Barilko? The NHL didn't do a single thing! The NHL permitted an individual club owner to flout its rule that the home team must provide adequate police protection." Coleman continued, "It's time that the money-happy team proprietors within the NHL realized that no individual owner can be bigger than the league."

Just about the only morsel of humor to be scraped up that black night was a remark made by some baritone in the Garden balcony after Bruins defenseman Pat Egan fell, permitting Nick Metz to score the Leafs' fifth goal. "Egan, ya bum," the fan shouted, "try the backstroke!"

The Bruins appeared penitent and, at least for one night, determined to behave themselves when they skated against the Leafs in the fourth game of the series on April 1. Only two penalties were called against the home team, who outscored the Leafs, 3—2, and stayed alive in the semifinal.

The teams returned to the more orderly confines of Maple Leaf Gardens for the fifth game, and the Bruins managed to hang on to a 2—2 tie until the early minutes of the third period. Then Toronto's Kid Line, consisting of Ted Kennedy, Howie Meeker, and Vic Lynn, carried into the Boston zone. Meeker sent a pass to Kennedy, who was standing in front of goalie Brimsek. The Leaf center took two swipes at the puck and finally lifted it into the cage at 5:52. Toronto won the game, 3—2, and the series, 4—1.

The series was succinctly summed up in a ditty penned by Jim Coleman the day after Boston was eliminated from the Cup competition:

> "Among America's more picturesque ruins,
> Are the shattered remains of the Boston Bruins!"

Many serious hockey fans in Boston were hoping that the outburst of hostility that pockmarked the 1948 Stanley Cup matches would have a cathartic effect on both the Bruins and their fans. Surprisingly the hockey team responded positively during the 1948–49 season, but later events proved that the hard-core rowdy element among the fans was beyond redemption.

The Bruins finished in second place in 1948–49, a point ahead of Montreal and nine points behind Detroit. Their youth movement reaped rewards as graduates of the Boston Olympics, Hershey Bears, and assorted other farm teams led the club in scoring. Paul Ronty, an Olympics graduate, was high scorer for the Bruins, and tied for fifth place in the league, with twenty goals and twenty-nine assists in sixty games, the most a team played in those days.

It was, however, the Bruins misfortune to run up against fourth-place Toronto in the opening round. Although the Maple Leafs had lost their superb captain Syl Apps and their veteran penalty killer Nick Metz through retirement, the Leafs nonetheless retained the nucleus of their Stanley

Cup champion teams of the previous two seasons. They proved that despite the standings, they were a better team than Boston and won the series in five games.

It is always a mistake to expect logic in hockey, often the most illogical of games, and so it was with the Bruins in April, 1949. The team that needed so badly to lose its dead-wood players instead lost its coach. On April 1, almost as if it were an April Fool's gag, Dit Clapper got to his feet at the team's end-of-season dinner and announced he was through as bench general of the club.

Walter Brown, president of Boston Garden, said Clapper's decision "hit me like a wet towel."

Bruins fans were soon to be hit by another wet towel when the club announced that Mister Zero, Frankie Brim-sek, had been dealt to the Chicago Black Hawks. His replacement would be a young collegian named Jack Geli-neau. It was an interesting attempt at rejuvenating the franchise, but it failed because of the spreading inferiority of the Bruins roster. The era of mediocrity had arrived with the departure of Brimsek and the continued reliance on aging players. Soon Boston fans, among the most loyal—if not stable—in the league, became disenchanted. When that happened, attendance at the Garden descended to alarming depths.

6. The Fickle Fifties

George "Buck" Boucher replaced Dit Clapper as coach of the Bruins, and Art Ross moved into the background while the younger Weston Adams became more involved with the club. Otherwise nothing much was new in Boston during the 1949–50 season, except that attendance was declining rapidly.

The most exciting aspect of the campaign developed in February, 1950, when the Maple Leafs invaded Boston, but the fury did not take place on the ice nor was it generated by a Toronto player. Managing director Conn Smythe called a press conference in his Copley Plaza Hotel suite on February 6 and categorically chided the Bruins management. The turnout of Boston writers was embarrassingly large in relation to the coverage usually afforded Adams, and one Bruins writer was moved to comment, "My gosh, look at the mob. Adams can't get more than two of the boys together at the same time these days." It didn't take long for Adams to retaliate. He popped off at Toronto writers for what he considered scathing, untrue remarks.

The Bruins president seemed baffled by Smythe's chronic criticism of his handling of the team. "I don't know why I'm always on the opposite side of the fence from Conn," Adams said, "but it's always been that way since I've been in the league. . . . Every hockey club in the United States, major, minor, amateur, is off in attendance this year. So it isn't only us. We think games bunched too closely together are too expensive for the average fan and television is murdering everything."

When Smythe arrived home in Toronto that night, he studied Adams' peroration and remarked, "That's a good thesis for a Harvard graduate."

On March 27 the Bruins, who had, by now, missed a play-off berth, made an announcement that challenged their reputation as much as any move they executed during the post-war years. They fired Boucher and then stated that the coach would have been dismissed *whether he had taken the team to the playoffs or not.*

"You only had a one-year contract," Ross told him. "We had made commitments last year for next winter. You were just a fill-in."

Boucher, a popular fifty-two-year-old ex-Ottawa star, was appalled by the treatment he received from Ross. Normally a relaxed, laconic type, the dismissed coach exploded in rare anger. "It was the dirtiest deal I ever had in my thirty-five years in hockey. . . . I had hoped I might get another chance. I thought I had done a good job and warranted another chance."

The dismissed coach's excellent reputation throughout the league seemed to reinforce the truth of his statements and the Bruin major-domos felt obliged to contradict Boucher. On April 3, the Boston club called a press conference and piously revealed, "We haven't lied to you people in twenty-six years."

Ross, sounding very much like a super-altruist, spun a tale of philanthropy, telling newsmen how he had offered to arrange another coaching job for Boucher, how Buck had been a "close friend of mine," and how he saved Boucher's job earlier in the season by not firing him.

Further dialogue was irrelevant. Boucher was gone, and the Bruins had to find a new coach and some players. Their first move was to purchase defenseman Steve Kraftcheck and Ed Reigle from Cleveland of the American League. Their second move was to hail their earlier decision to trade Brimsek and use Gelineau. The twenty-five-year-old Gelineau, who jumped from intercollegiate hockey to the Bruins, won the Calder Trophy as rookie of the year.

Meanwhile, the New York news wires were sending out a story that at first had no particular pertinence for the Bruins; Lynn Patrick had resigned as coach of the New York Rangers. Later this fact became significant for the Bruins, even up to the present.

Patrick's resignation was startling in view of the circumstances surrounding Boucher's departure from Boston. The Rangers coach had had an eminently successful year, leading the fourth-place Rangers all the way to the seventh game of the Stanley Cup finals against Detroit and losing then only in double overtime. Patrick said he was leaving New York because it was no place to raise children and he would like to get into the managing end of hockey. He planned to join his father, Lester, in the operation of the Victoria, British Columbia, Cougars.

Naive observers accepted Patrick's departure from the NHL with regrets. He *had* done so much for the Rangers; he was a Ranger through and through, having played for no other NHL team. And he was such a promising young coach. The skeptics, however, recalled that there was an opening on the Bruins' bench.

On July 1, 1950, the Bruins announced that Patrick would succeed Boucher as Boston coach, adding that Lynn was also being groomed for future managerial duties.

Patrick's debut was less than auspicious. After seven games in the 1950–51 season the Bruins were 0—4—3 and drawing sparse crowds to Boston Garden. Gelineau was playing well enough in goal, but the forwards were virtually impotent.

"We've got two players on the whole club who have scored a point in five games," said Patrick. "Sixteen of them without anything. They just can't seem to put the puck in the net."

Early in November the Bruins acquired forwards Bill Ezinicki and Vic Lynn from Toronto for Fern Flaman, Phil Maloney, and Ken Smith, as well as the rights to a junior player, Leo Boivin. In a deal with New York, Boston gave up forwards Zellio Toppazzini and Ed Harrison for Dunc Fisher.

By far the outstanding name in the collection was Ezinicki, the famed "Wild Bill," who reigned as king of the bodycheckers, one of the most feared musclemen in the league. Ezzy had lost a lot of the vigor that had characterized his play in Toronto, but he did have some sock left in his body and soon the Bruins climbed out of the cellar to make a serious bid for a playoff berth.

By mid-January, 1951, once again the Bruins looked like a respectable hockey club. And thanks to Ezinicki, they were hitting people; then one night in Detroit, Ezinicki hit Ted Lindsay, and an ignominious chapter was added to the Bruins history.

Lindsay and Ezinicki had been warring as far back as their junior hockey days in the OHA League. The Detroit left wing was a far more skilled scorer than the Bruin right wing, but Lindsay had long ago earned notoriety as a man with liberal policies about the use of his hockey stick. No angel himself, Ezinicki was renowned for his thudding, but mostly clean, bodychecks.

In the third period of the Red Wing-Bruins game at Detroit's Olympia Stadium on January 25, Ezinicki and Lindsay collided seconds after an offside whistle had blown. "He was shoving me around," Lindsay related, "and I shoved him around."

At this point in the story a split develops over who hit whom with his stick first. Detroiters contend Ezinicki was the instigator; other viewers say it was Lindsay.

"After a couple of clouts with their sticks," wrote Lewis H. Walter in the Detroit *Times,* "both threw down their weapons and their gloves and started to slug. Lindsay quickly reached across with his left hand and took hold of Ezzy's jersey. Then Lindsay poured a volly of rights to Ezzy's face and finally dropped him to the ice."

Linesmen Bill Knott and Harold "Mush" March eventually pulled them apart but Ezinicki, never afraid of Lindsay, waded in again, clouting at Lindsay. "If I let him hit me once," Lindsay said in the dressing room after the brawl was over, "he'd have thought he could hit me again later."

Ezinicki, who rarely lost a battle in his NHL career, was severely hampered by linesman Knott, who appeared to have him manacled, whereas Lindsay was released by March—a vital factor in the eventual outcome. At one point in the fracas Ezinicki, in his attempt to get back at Lindsay, dragged Knott along the ice. With the linesman draped around him, the Bruin was a sitting duck for the unencumbered Detroiter.

Whether it was the clouts landed with his stick or those with his fists, Lindsay clearly routed the Bruin. The Detroit ace dropped Ezinicki three different times, and the last time the Boston forward went down unconscious. He lay prone on the ice for two or three minutes and was still groggy when he reached the dressing room.

"Why did they keep me away?" Ezinicki asked ten minutes later in his daze. "I was all right."

Although the brawl lasted less than four minutes it has been regarded as one of the most violent in hockey history partly because of the reputation of the warriors, partly because of its one-sided nature, and, lastly, because of the damage inflicted by Lindsay. Ezinicki suffered a broken nose and cuts in three other places that required nineteen stitches to close. Lindsay took five stitches on the forehead and the knuckles on his right, punching hand were badly bruised.

The two most heavily penalized forwards in the league received the most severe penalty in the rule book for their gruesome fight—a match penalty for "deliberately injuring an opponent." The penalty is rarely called and, according to Detroit writer Paul Chandler, had never been called before the 1950–51 season.

Referee George Gravel explained that he had invoked the maximum penalty because of the stick-slashing, not the punching. "They were trying to do something really dangerous with those sticks," Gravel said. "The fight later was a plain hockey fight."

Shocked by the punishment, loss of blood, and pain of having nineteen stitches embroidered in his head, Ezinicki said he "didn't want to talk about it," when questioned in the Boston dressing room. Lindsay dressed and went to the first-aid room where Ezinicki was receiving his stitches.

"Are you all right?" the Red Wing asked.

"I'm all right," Ezinicki shot back.

At that point Lindsay walked out.

Ezinicki's worst cut was a long one down the forehead, received when the sticks were swinging. He had four stitches inside his mouth and four more on the side of his head, apparently from the bump on the ice.

The disgraceful aspect of the fight from the Boston standpoint was *not* that Ezinicki lost the battle but rather that his Bruin teammates watched the blood bath only a few feet away from the combatants. Milt Schmidt, Bill Quackenbush, and other Bruins looked on, as if wearing blinders, while their teammate was drawn and quartered. Critical observers took due note of what appeared to be the Bruins' tacit approval of the destruction of Ezinicki.

"The Wings blame the Bruins," wrote reporter Walter, "because they did not come to the aid of Ezinicki when he was beaten to the ice by Lindsay."

Only Art Ross among the Bruins personnel came to

Ezinicki's aid. "I've seen courageous guys in this game," said Ross, for a change not exaggerating to make a point, "but this Ezinicki beats them all."

By midseason there was no question that Patrick had come up with a winning combination, but that by no means assured the Bostonians popularity. Attendance was still down at Boston Garden, and Smythe continued to carp at the Bruins management. "They have 2,500,000 people in the area," he said during a February invasion, "and they can't get 14,000 out to a game."

Poor attendance notwithstanding, the Bruins beat out the Rangers for fourth place in the last days of the season and went up against Toronto in the first round of the playoffs. It took the Leafs six games to end Boston's misery; one game, a 1—1 tie, was called because of a Sunday curfew in Toronto.

The Bruins were unhappy with Gelineau's goaltending in the playoff and replaced him during the off-season with veteran Jim Henry, who previously had played for New York and Chicago. They also obtained tough defenseman Gus Kyle from New York and Adam Brown from Chicago. For spirit, the Bruins promoted dynamic young George "Red" Sullivan from their Hershey farm team. On the whole the club was a potpourri of youngsters and veterans, led by the excellent and spirited captain Schmidt, who somehow got carried away when he studied the 1951–52 roster.

"I predict," said Schmidt, "that with the promising kids here and on the farm, the Bruins are only a year or two away from being one of the really great hockey clubs of all time."

The "really great hockey club" never won a Stanley Cup nor finished first in the decade following Schmidt's prediction; they usually gained a playoff berth simply because of the greater ineptitude of the floundering Rangers and Black Hawks.

Early in December, 1951, only 4,888 fans attended a 1—1 tie with the Rangers at Boston Garden. It was the lowest crowd to attend a Bruins game since December 11, 1934. This was even more disappointing because the Bruins were tied for third place; they were a contending team.

It had become apparent to serious hockey students that the affliction which had affected the Bruins franchise could soon infect other teams and the health of the NHL in general.

"The very existence of the National Hockey League may be at stake," wrote Leonard Cohen in the New York *Post,* "as a result of the situation now confronting the owners of the Boston Bruins. Their fans are up in arms and the league must recognize that the first U.S. city in the NHL is now the worst stop on the circuit."

Smythe, moved by the Bruins' plight, traded ace forward Fleming Mackell to the Bruins for minor-league defenseman Jim Morrison. The obviously one-sided deal was made to strengthen the faltering Bruins and, as Smythe pointed out, to rectify the earlier deal when Ezinicki and Lynn went to Boston for Flaman, Smith, and Maloney.

A few days later the Bruins continued their shake-up, demoting Adam Brown, Lorne Ferguson, and Pentti Lund to Hershey in return for rookies Real Chevrefils and Leo Labine.

The Bruin management's contention that television was hurting the gate was underlined by NHL President Campbell. Appearing at a Lions Club dinner in Kingston, Ontario, Campbell asserted, "Television is the most terrible menace ever to come to the entertainment world."

On March 18 the Bruins produced their *coup* of the year —a "Schmidt-Dumart Night." By honoring the two venerable forwards the Bruins also persuaded the third member of the Kraut Line, Bobby Bauer, to emerge from retirement for one night and rejoin his old pals.

It was an interesting plan and not merely from the promotional viewpoint. Boston was still fighting for a playoff berth, and there was no indication whether chubby Bobby, who had been retired for five years, could keep pace with his better-conditioned linemates.

Financially, the idea was a gem from every angle. More than 12,000 fans filled the Garden for its second largest gate of the season, and in pre-game ceremonies Schmidt and Dumart received cash and gifts totaling close to $20,000. Bauer wasn't forgotten either. The fans gave him a portable radio, and his wife a clock. Hockey writer Tom Fitzgerald presented him with a silver pitcher on behalf of the sportscasters and sports writers.

With the ceremonies over, the Krauts then got down to

the business of winning a hockey game against the Black Hawks. Schmidt assisted on Kryzanowski's goal in the first period and scored in the second, assisted by none other than Bauer and Dumart. The score, at 12:58 of the period, was Schmidt's 200th career goal. As the happy Bruins pounded their captain on the back, Bauer dashed to the net, fetched the puck, and presented it to Schmidt as a souvenir.

The NHL pace was too much for Bauer. He'd take a half turn with his mates and then hop over the boards to be replaced by Kryzanowski. But while he was on the ice the Line betrayed flashes of its former excellence. In the third period Schmidt catapulted Bauer into the clear with a perfect pass to the right wing. Bauer cut in on goalie Harry Lumley, lured him away from the crease, and slid the puck into the far side of the net.

"The crowd," according to a United Press dispatch, "roared even louder than it did when Schmidt scored."

Boston won the game, 4—0, clinching a playoff berth, and Bauer went back into retirement.

For a few precious days in April it appeared that the Bruins would actually get past the semifinal playoffs for a change and make a serious challenge for the Stanley Cup. They had a 3—2 lead against the Montreal Canadiens and required only one more win—the sixth game was in Boston —to clinch the first round. They then proceeded to pull off a classic fold-up that some less discreet viewers have described as a "choke."

The Bruins nursed a 2—0 lead early in the second period. Ed Mazur broke the shutout for the Canadiens at 4:53 of the middle period, but Boston guarded their lead into the third period and past the ten-minute mark. Less than nine minutes separated the Bruins from a ticket to the final round. Suddenly Schmidt lost the puck, which was captured by Maurice Richard. The Rocket broke fast down the center and shot a thirty-foot drive past goalie Henry, sending the game into sudden-death overtime. Neither team scored in the first sudden death, but Doug Harvey led a Montreal rush early in the second extra period and shot another thirty-footer that bounced off Henry's pads. The puck fell six feet to the left of the Bruin goalie. Before Henry could reach it rookie Paul Masnick shot it into the cage.

The loss had an obliquely positive effect for the Bruins by sending them into a seventh game. During that game occurred one of the most spectacular goals ever scored in hockey; unfortunately for Boston, the goal was made by Richard.

The teams were tied, 1—1, from the 12:25 mark of the first period, through a scoreless second period, and past the sixteen-minute point of the third period. Sudden death appeared imminent, and there were faint suggestions that the Canadiens might, this time, be the team to fold. That suggestion was rooted in the fact that early in the second period Richard was crashed to the ice by a violent check thrown by Leo Labine. Richard lay unconscious on the ice for a full minute before he arose and skated, dazed, to the repair room. It was believed that the tip of Labine's stick opened the Rocket's eye as he hit the ice.

"I didn't remember anything after I got hit," the Rocket said hours after the game. "My legs felt fine, but my head—ow! They told me it was Labine. I don't know. I didn't even know the score when I went back to the bench."

Montreal coach Dick Irvin refused to send Richard back on the ice when he returned to the bench late in the game. "He didn't know what was going on," said Irvin.

Later it was revealed that Richard was in a partial coma before returning to the game, as Montreal *Star* writer Baz O'Meara put it, "his head fuzzed up from pain, his eyesight impaired, with dull noises ringing in his ears."

Irvin finally sent him back to the battle after the fifteen-minute mark. "He was trying to reclaim his lost senses," wrote O'Meara, "when Dumart came charging down to lose the puck in the Canadiens' zone. Bouchard grabbed the puck, sent a long pass to the Rocket near the blue line. He made a swing and Dumart, trying to bat it down, lost it.

"Richard was around him in a flash, reeled to center, then headed for the right. He was making his plays by instinct. He jabbed the puck ahead of him while Bruin defenseman Bill Quackenbush wheeled to meet the challenge. The Rocket was by him, finally got a good purchase as he swung to the right, apparently too deep for a shot, but he did a deft cut, let fly a low scorcher into a short opening and Henry, confused by his fast foray, fanned on that one."

According to veteran Forum spectators Richard was then given the loudest, most prolonged roar of his career. He staggered off the ice, slumped into his seat on the bench, and, while the crowd cheered teammate Elmer Lach, fainted —without anyone in the stands knowing it.

Billy Reay scored a final goal for the Canadiens in the last minute, bouncing the puck off Schmidt's stick after goalie Henry had been removed for an extra forward, but the man who torpedoed the Bruins was Richard. When he returned to the Montreal dressing room after the game, the Rocket broke down and cried.

"Nobody could figure out whether it was an emotional release or just the pain," said Eddie MacCabe of the Montreal *Star*. "The emotional angle was favored, though."

Bruins goalie Jim Henry himself was dazed by the defeat, coupled with injuries he suffered during the series. "One minute I was facing the Rocket," Henry explained of the winning goal, "waiting for the shot, the next he had whizzed by, and the puck was in the net."

Still the Bruin stalwart, Schmidt's commendable effort in defeat was also acknowledged. "He's surely one of the greatest," lauded MacCabe. "The guy has a heart as big as a pail."

Schmidt and Dumart were back in the Bruin lineup for the 1952–53 season, and this time they helped the club to an astonishing playoff victory after finishing in third place. Actually the Bruins and fourth-place Black Hawks had the same point total (69), but Boston was awarded third on the basis of having scored one more victory over the regular season.

On paper, this seemed unfortunate, because it meant that the Bruins would meet first-place Detroit in the opening playoff round, and it was widely proclaimed that the Red Wings boasted the strongest team ever to skate in the NHL. Gordie Howe was the runaway winner of the scoring championship; Terry Sawchuk won the Vezina Trophy with a remarkably low 1.90 goals against average; and the Wings attacked with three awesome scoring lines, supported by a hard, well-coordinated defense led by Red Kelly, Marcel Pronovost, and Bob Goldham.

By contrast, the Bruins' leading scorer, Fleming Mackell, finished in tenth place, fifty-one points behind Howe, and the Boston skaters, generally, were regarded as an attractive but hardly threatening team.

"Nobody, but nobody," said Boston *Record-American*

writer D. Leo Monahan, "figured to knock off Detroit that year."

The Bruin high command went into a top-level conference on the eve of the series' first game and mapped out strategy. "We can't expect to match Detroit offensively," said Patrick, "so I'm going to put a checking line on the Howe-Lindsay line. I've already told Schmidt, Dumart, and Joe Klukay that they've got the job. I don't care if they score a single goal, but I want them to shadow that line. If Lindsay goes out for a cup of coffee, I want somebody right out there with him."

On the drawing board, Patrick had worked out the best of all possible Bruin blueprints. Now all he had to do was put it in practice. The first game was played on March 24, 1953, at Detroit's Olympia Stadium. Suffice to say that the Red Wings were the victors, 7—0!

Patrick didn't lose his poise, which unquestionably was the most important factor in the Bruins' eventual success. "I've got to give this plan one more try," he insisted as the Boston wolves howled for his skin in the distance. "One game isn't enough time to put in a new system. We'll do it again and hope for the best."

Few but the most optimistic Boston rooters actually expected to see the Bruins come away from Detroit with anything more than their physiques in reasonable shape. The third and fourth games were to be played in Boston Garden, and it's doubtful that even Patrick, in his wildest moments of fantasy, could have anticipated what happened.

In the second game, on March 26, the Bruins thoroughly outskated and outshot the Red Wings. The Sanford-Mackell-Peirson line began clicking, and Detroit's Production Line was thoroughly nullified by Schmidt, Dumart, and Klukay. Boston won the game, 5—3.

If any one game could be credited with starting the hockey revival in Boston it was the third contest, on March 29, at the Garden. The teams were tied, 1—1, after three periods. When the sudden-death overtime began they warily pawed at each other, accenting defense. Boston was using two rookie defensemen, Bob Armstrong and Warren Godfrey, but they played flawlessly as the period passed the halfway point. If the Bruins were to win, though, they had to beat Sawchuk, and the word was he could be beaten most easily by a high shot.

In the twelfth minute of overtime, winger Jack McIntyre went into orbit for the Bruins. He hurled over the Detroit blue line and flicked his wrists. The puck took off like a jet leaving the runway and eluded the transfixed Sawchuk at 12:29. The goal sent the Bruins fans into wild transports of joy. As for McIntyre, he momentarily lost his memory.

Reporters circled him in the Bruins dressing room, pecking away with questions about his momentous goal. Suddenly, he called for time out and informed the press that they had better spell his name correctly.

"It's MacIntyre," he insisted. "Capital M, small a, small c; not McIntyre like you've been writing."

The Bruins overwhelmed Detroit, 6—2, on Gordie Howe's birthday, March 31, and did nothing to make him feel very happy about it; Dumart was shadowing Howe with unaccustomed efficiency. On April 2, the Wings broke free once more, with a 6—4 victory at home, but the Bruins earned their way into the finals, by beating Detroit, 4—2, at Boston Garden on April 5.

This time facing the Canadiens was not as threatening as it had been in previous years. Montreal was experimenting with a new goaltender in Jacques Plante, and it had taken them seven games to eliminate Chicago in their semifinal round. But Boston's momentum was soon halted when goalie Jim Henry pulled up lame early in the second game and was replaced by minor-leaguer Gordon "Red" Henry.

The teams split the first two games at the Forum; Montreal won the opener, 4—2, and lost the second, 4—1. Then Rocket Richard and his bombardiers exploited Red Henry's weaknesses, and the Bruins were dispatched in three straight games— 3—0, 7—3, and 1—0. The final game was settled with a goal by Elmer Lach at 1:22 of the first overtime, with Rocket Richard supplying the key pass on the winning goal.

McIntyre's heroics enabled him to remain in Boston for only a short time. He was soon dealt to Chicago as the Bruins continued to shake up their roster. The Black Hawks released Cal Gardner to Boston, and in time, he would play a significant role as the Bruins mucked their way through the 1953-54 season into fourth place.

For a time it appeared they weren't going to get that far. The Rangers had reunited Max and Doug Bentley, the onetime stars of the Black Hawks, and were getting exceptionally good goaltending from Johnny Bower. Boston and New York were neck-and-neck going into the homestretch run for fourth place, when Lynn Patrick used an unusual turn of insight against the Rangers.

Remembering that Max Bentley was a sensitive hypochondriac, Patrick advised Cal Gardner, who played opposite the Ranger center, to get a verbal barrage going against Bentley.

When the clubs met late in the season, Gardner remarked about Max's health. "You know something, Max," Gardner said for openers, "you're not looking well at all." Then, he began haranguing the already-worried Ranger about everything from imaginary illnesses to migraine headaches. Bentley lost his effectiveness, and the Bruins beat out the Rangers by six points.

There being no hypochondriacs on the Montreal team, the Bruins dropped four straight to the Canadiens in the playoff semifinal, and the season abruptly ended in Boston.

The 1954–55 campaign was not one Boston can be terribly proud of. More than ever, their ability to gain a playoff berth was more a tribute to the ineptitude of fifth-place New York and last-place Chicago. The Bruins' highest scorer was the tempestuous Leo Labine who was mired in sixteenth place, thirty-three points behind the leader, Boom-Boom Geoffrion of Montreal. Patrick's insistence that he wouldn't trade Labine for Jean Beliveau, the Canadiens' ace, impressed nobody, with the possible exception of Labine.

The most arresting event that took place in Boston Garden that season occurred in mid-March, 1955, during a game between the Bruins and Canadiens. In the third period, Rocket Richard was cut on the head after a collision with Boston defenseman Hal Laycoe, who opened up an eight-stitch wound in Richard's scalp that suddenly poured blood. Inflamed because he thought the Bruin would escape without a penalty, Richard charged at Laycoe as the Boston player conducted a disorderly retreat.

"The mistake we made," said Floyd Curry, the Rocket's teammate, "was failing to hold back Richard." As the Rocket broke away from peacemakers he was intercepted by Montreal linesman Cliff Thompson. Opinions differ as to Thompson's intentions as a mediator, but he appeared less than delicate in handling the Rocket, who proceeded to clout him in order to reach Laycoe. It was also unfortunate that Thompson was a home-town linesman, having played several years with the Boston Olympics and briefly with the Bruins.

More than anything, it was inefficient refereeing and improper intervention that led to Richard's explosion, but NHL President Campbell was not impressed. He suspended the Rocket, who was leading the league in scoring, for the remaining final week of the season *and* for the playoffs. Campbell's decision led to rioting on the night of March 17 at the Forum and for a mile along Ste. Catherines Street West, Montreal's main shopping area.

With Richard sidelined, the Canadiens lost first place to the Red Wings, Geoffrion beat out Richard for the scoring championship, and Detroit ultimately defeated Montreal for the Stanley Cup. Perhaps the greatest tragedy of all was that Richard, one of the most exciting players hockey has known, never won a scoring championship and missed it that year only because of an incident that should have been prevented.

Boston made a spectacular deal with the Red Wings in June, 1955, obtaining All-Star goalie Terry Sawchuk and Vic Stasiuk, Lorne Davis, and Marcel Bonin for Ed Sandford, Real Chevrefils, Norm Corcoran, Warren Godfrey, and Gilles Boisvert.

Sawchuk played brilliantly for the Bruins in the 1955–56 season, as his nine shutouts proved, but the Boston outfit was a bad team and deserved to finish fifth. A season later Sawchuk made more news for the Bruins and it was all bad. First he was sidelined with mononucleosis, and then, in mid-January, 1957, announced he was quitting hockey and suing four Boston papers for slandering him. The walkout at first seemed to be the blow that would scuttle the Bruins, but Patrick solved the problem by buying Don Simmons from the Springfield Indians. A steady, angle-playing goaltender, Simmons was an imperturbable figure who helped Boston to a third-place finish. The Bruins kept gaining momentum and eliminated the Red Wings in five games, only to be wiped out by Montreal by the same count.

Patrick's affinity for name goaltenders didn't end with Sawchuk. He obtained Harry Lumley, an ex-Red Wing, Leaf, and Black Hawk, who alternated with Simmons through 1957–58. Boston finished fourth, took the Rangers in six games, and then lost to the Canadiens, also after six, in the finals. The Bruins' energetic effort suggested that even better things were to come the following season, mostly because of the formation of "The Uke Line," composed of Bronco Horvath, Johnny Bucyk, and Vic Stasiuk.

In 1958–59, the Bruins finished second, eighteen points behind league-leading Montreal, and had the second highest-scoring team in the league with 205 goals; yet they were eliminated by fourth-place Toronto in a seven-game Stanley Cup semifinal. Thus began the worst Depression Boston hockey fans have known. Although Horvath finished second in scoring, a point behind Bobby Hull, in 1959–60, the Bruins landed in fifth. They were well on the way to their long tenancy in the NHL cellar—which started in 1960–61 and didn't end until 1964–65. Phil Watson, who had previously been fired by the Rangers, deposed Schmidt as Bruins coach in 1961–62. Watson was a bigger flop in Boston than he had been in New York, but still managed to survive through the start of the 1962–63 campaign. The Bruins actually won their opening game that year, beating Montreal at the Forum. But they then went sixteen games without a win and Watson was replaced in the game of musical coaches by Schmidt, who hardly was an improvement.

Perhaps the most surprising aspect of Boston's Depression was the Bruins' fan support. After the team finished in last place for the fourth year in a row, Bruins officials gleefully noted that attendance had actually *climbed* by 30,000 over the season before. The Bruins outdrew the Red Wings, who finished fourth and almost won the Stanley Cup, by 4,000 people. They outdrew the Boston Celtics, who were the best basketball team in the world, playing in the same arena. Finding an explanation was not easy, for these were the same fans who nearly deserted a contending team in the early fifties.

What suddenly made Boston a "wonderful hockey town"?

Peter Gzowski, the perceptive writer from Toronto, studied the Bruin scene for a few days in the 1964–65 season—at the height of the Depression—and made several cogent observations. "Boston fans seem to want to win all right," said Gzowski, "but winning just doesn't seem as important as it does in other cities—and certainly not as important as some good, rough bodychecks. . . . Win or lose, Boston fans seem to get more fun out of hockey than fans in any other city. But they like their hockey simple, and as tough as possible."

The Bruins management, perceiving this instinct for combat, early in 1963 traded high-scoring Don McKenney to the Rangers. "He just wouldn't mix it up in the corners," explained a Boston executive.

7. A Revival in Sight

The deportation of McKenney was most significant to the contemporary Bruins, because it signaled the prenatal stage of the new Gashouse Era. True, the Bruins' Depression Years were in full flower and would last through 1967, but the revival of the Bruins as a truculent, Shore-like team was slowly taking place.

Belligerent Ted Green, drafted by Boston from Montreal in June, 1960, was the new Shore as far as out-and-out conflict was concerned.

"The heroes in Boston," Gzowski analyzed in February, 1965, "tend more frequently to be defensemen like Green, a twenty-four-year-old in the Shore tradition who has had the distinction of leading the Bruins in penalties each of the three full seasons he's played with them."

But the Bruins' singular characteristic in the mid-sixties, as they tried to dig their way to daylight, was an affinity for losing. Some hockey men believe this trait, inherited by Green, Westfall, Bucyk, and Ed Johnston, all of whom played during Boston's Depression hockey years, contaminated them in big games during the 1967–68 and 1968–69 playoff seasons.

"When the big money comes out," said Gzowski, "they go down. In the poolroom they scratch on the black ball. In the hockey rink two of their players bump into each other on the power play; one gets a groin injury and an opponent gets a breakaway."

This analysis is especially pertinent in the light of what happened to the Bruins in the last two months of the 1968–69 season, when injuries decimated their lineup and cost them first place; in the playoffs Montreal got the "breaks" to defeat them in the East Division final.

The difference between today's Gashouse team and Boston's Depression skaters is, among other things, stardom.

Nearly everybody knows Bobby Orr, Phil Esposito, and Ted Green today but it wasn't that way a few years ago. In those dismal days coach Schmidt got more requests for autographs than did any of his players.

It is possible that in the mid-sixties the Bruins fans by some hockey instinct realized that the renaissance soon would take place. Or perhaps they were merely counting on the Law of Averages. Whatever it was, evidence cropped up early in 1965 that a new day was about to dawn.

The incident happened during a Sunday game with the Montreal Canadiens who, as was their custom in those days, were leading the league. But the Bruins, even in their worst days, found the home fans a tonic, and on this night, they encouraged Green and Westfall and Bucyk to an almost superhuman effort in the first period. Yet they emerged after the first twenty minutes with nothing better than a tie.

The Bruins sustained the momentum through the early minutes of the second period and then, like a toy auto whose battery has run down, they just seemed to roll to a halt. The Canadiens swarmed over the defenses, penetrated goalie Ed Johnston's net, and once more the Bruins were losers.

However, late in the third period somebody in the upper balcony kindled a spark in what had been the broken Bruins' spirit. And, before the final buzzer sounded 13,000 Boston hockey fans had swung into a resounding chorus of the anthem of another revolutionary movement, "We Shall Overcome."

The rehabilitation didn't happen overnight, mostly because Bobby Orr, Derek Sanderson, and several other youngsters were still finishing their apprenticeship in the junior leagues. It also didn't help that in 1965 the Bruin management hired sixty-year-old Hap Emms to manage the club, thereby mistakenly shunting Schmidt to the background. Under Emms' leadership the Bruins remained last and were discontented as well as inept. Emms finally was eased out in 1967.

By this time Patrick had moved to St. Louis, where he became manager. Schmidt? Nobody quite knew what was going to happen to Schmidt, and then the man most people regarded as the best center Boston has ever had was resurrected to his pedestal as general manager of the Bruins. In a way Schmidt was a fitting choice. Milt had savored the glory days of the late thirties and was a link with Shore and Clapper. He had suffered through the Bruins Depression and remembered the mistakes he had made as coach. He vowed it would not happen again.

His first move was to find bigger, tougher players. Then suddenly, the Bruins luck, which for years had been congenitally bad, suddenly turned positive. What amounted to a hockey miracle blessed Schmidt; he was able to trade Gilles Marotte, Pit Martin, and minor-league goalie Jack Norris to Chicago for Phil Esposito, Ken Hodge, and Fred Stanfield. In one swoop he had acquired three excellent and, most important, tough and big hockey players.

He named young, creative Harry Sinden from the Oklahoma City farm club as coach and, for a change, faced the 1967–68 season with infinite hope. Who could blame him? The farm teams in the OHA Junior A were working superbly. Oklahoma City had started developing youngsters, and acquisitions of earlier years began blossoming under Sinden. John McKenzie, whom the Bruins obtained from New York in January, 1966, became a piraña on the forward line and also managed to score goals with remarkable frequency.

Defensemen Don Awrey, Gary Doak, and Dallas Smith discovered confidence, that elusive element so important to young athletes, and they complemented the defense led by Orr and Green. Goalie Gerry Cheevers, drafted from Toronto in June, 1965, impressed Schmidt with his combative spirit and agility. One by one the pieces fell into place.

"I've been on a lot of teams," said McKenzie, "and I've never seen one with spirit like this."

Old-time Bruins such as Bucyk, Westfall, and Green marveled at the reformation under the Schmidt-Sinden regime. "I guess we can stop walking down the alleys and dark streets," said an enthusiastic Westfall.

At first Sinden appeared to be the Charlie McCarthy to Schmidt's Edgar Bergen. But after his rookie season Sinden's own definitive personality took hold, and he began obtaining results. Most of all, Sinden translated Schmidt's hard-hockey policy into reality. "They have changed from a small, meek team that often appeared to be merely going through the motions," wrote Pete Axthelm in *Sports Illustrated*, "into a brawling, powerful unit good enough to lead the league."

They didn't lead the league in points, but they did in

boisterousness. They were afraid of nobody and were down-right nasty to some clubs. The Rangers were a particular target for abuse, partly because of the smallness of the New York team and partly because of grudges a couple of Bruins nurtured against Rangers players. Once, in a game at Boston, Green knocked Larry Jeffrey of the Rangers unconscious and stood over his foe unchallenged by any New Yorker. Another time Derek Sanderson, then a Bruins rookie, had a fist fight with Orland Kurtenbach of the Rangers, often regarded as the best boxer in hockey, and held Kurtenbach to a draw. It proved, at least, that Sanderson wasn't afraid of *anybody*.

Ruffians seemed to emerge spontaneously in Bruins uniforms previously filled by more placid types. The unity of big men apparently brought strength and hostility. A prime example of the transformation was defenseman Don Awrey. Prior to being teamed with Ted Green, Awrey was a mediocre defenseman not especially known for his belligerence. By 1967–68 he had rapidly earned a reputation as a brawler, although some opponents suggested he wouldn't be so energetic if Green wasn't at his side on the ice.

"I always had been what you might call a borderline player," said Awrey. "Never got to play as a regular when I came up in this league. I guess I got to thinking maybe I wasn't aggressive enough. Nobody really advised me . . . although I did talk things over with Teddy Green. I'll tell you something: Just knowing I have him to back me up helps a lot. . . . All I can tell you is that things have changed on this club. In years past if somebody got into a scrap, one or two might join in. Now, on this club, anybody's fight is everybody's fight. That's the way it is."

Wherever the Bruins skated, but especially at home, a rumble was almost certain to develop. In 1967 they assaulted the Canadiens during Montreal's first two trips to Boston, inspiring demands from Montreal coach Toe Blake and general manager Sam Pollock for an investigation to determine, as Toronto *Daily Star* sports editor Milt Dunnell put it, "what kind of ugly pills the Bruins were eating."

When Toronto's general manager-coach Punch Imlach was asked to explain Boston's climb to respectable regions of the NHL, he wasted no time responding, "because they kick the daylights out of you."

Boston *Globe* writer Chris Lydon detected a cult of toughness on the team after visiting a practice. He recalled seeing Green and Gary Doak waiting near the sideboards for their turn to shoot. "Green backs Doak up against the glass barrier," reported Lydon, "and begins crashing his stick down on the top edge of the glass, inches from Doak's head. 'Let's see how close I can come to your head without you flinchin', eh Doakie?' "

Gerald Eskenazi of the *New York Times* expressed an interesting opinion as the Bruins influence made itself felt around the NHL. "They seem to be getting paranoid," said Eskenazi. "They think they're always going to be hit by somebody; so they hit first."

The new Bruins psyche had a positive effect on gate receipts in out-of-town rinks, as well as on national publications. People stopped laughing at the Bruins. Opponents viewed them with a mixture of wariness and alarm. They were, in more ways than one, a smash hit.

The Bruins were concerned about winning a high playoff position and managed to land in third place, their highest finish in nine years. They then were routed by the Canadiens in four consecutive playoff games.

"We were congratulating ourselves for finishing third," said Orr, "and before we knew it we were on our way home." Coach Sinden realized more work was needed to mold a genuine challenger for first place and the Stanley Cup.

The 1968–69 Bruins differed only slightly from the previous year's edition, like a late-model car altered only by a few pieces of chrome, some added horsepower, and bigger bumper guards. However, the changes were enough to make Boston a better team than New York and, at times, a better team than the World Champion Canadiens. Hard as it may be to believe, the 1968–69 Bruins appeared to be a more belligerent outfit than ever before, as eleven other teams were ready to testify.

8. Birth of a Dynasty

By the fall of 1968 word had filtered up and down the hockey grapevine that it was unhealthy to tangle with the Bruins. They had more big, antagonistic men than any other team in the league and they appeared to have no working knowledge of the Marquis of Queensbury rules, nor did they care.

Their basic application of hockey strategy was something like the invasion of Normandy in 1944. First they'd bomb the enemy defenses with heavyweights like Green, Awrey, and Orr; add tough middleweights like Sanderson, Hodge, and McKenzie; then allow all hands to move in and score. That the formula worked is attested to by the record-breaking scoring year enjoyed by Esposito, Hodge, and Orr, to name but a few.

Some foes weren't happy about the fact, but the Bruins undeniably intimidated a select portion of their enemy. Early in the season Mark Mulvoy of *Sports Illustrated* took note of the trend and observed, "The big, bad Bruins gave the Rangers a big, bad beating, both on the ice and on the scoreboard." On a trip west after they had pulverized the New York team, the Bruins laughed out loud among themselves about how "the Rangers didn't want any part of the puck."

Obviously, it wasn't just the Rangers. "When they drop the puck to start the game," said Bud Poile, the Philadelphia Flyers' manager, "the Bruins think it is a piece of raw meat. Do they go after it!"

Sports Illustrated observed: "The Bruins also have the league's most vociferous fans. They do not tolerate timid players. The fans particularly dislike players who wear helmets—the Bruins have none." Overlooked, however, were the two Boston goalies, Gerry Cheevers and Ed Johnston, who wore face masks. Did that make them more timid than

Montreal's Gump Worsley and Rogatien Vachon, who played without such protective gear?

The Boston players seemed to savor their Gashouse role. One of them tacked a "Peanuts" comic strip on the dressing-room bulletin board. It depicted Snoopy, the dog, holding his breath as the final bars of the National Anthem were being played. "Ten more seconds," he muttered to himself, "and I can clobber somebody." Somebody penciled in the word "Greenie." Not long afterward, another Bruin added the caption, "Snoopy could play for us." Another time forward Glen Sather of the Bruins spelled out the motto "THINK KILL" on the locker-room mirror.

While all this was going on, the team from the Hub climbed right into first place. The Esposito-Hodge-Murphy Line became the most overpowering in the league, the defense was rated by *Sports Illustrated* as the best in hockey, and the Bruins seemed hell-bent for their first championship since prewar days.

When the home stretch came into view, Peter Gzowski's interpretation of the Bruins came to mind, "They have, in fact, taken on many of the characteristics of what pool hustlers call 'losers.' Losers lose even when they win a few. They pick up some of the small change but when the big money comes out they go down."

The big money in 1968–69 was first place and the Stanley Cup. Their challengers were the Montreal Canadiens, supposedly weakened by an unknown rookie coach, injuries to starting goalies Gump Worsley and Rogatien Vachon in midseason, and the aging of their distinguished captain Jean Beliveau. There's no way, the experts insisted, that the Bruins can be caught.

Even as a first-place team the Bruins began betraying the characteristics of the losers. Esposito was suspended for two games late in February, 1969, when the Bruins could afford it least—for the foolish offense of shoving and hitting a referee. While he was sidelined the Rangers humiliated Boston, 9—0, at Madison Square Garden, to give the Bruins pause.

Injuries, which are more likely to occur on hitting teams, began crippling the Bruins. Tom Williams and Gary Doak were lost for the season. John McKenzie, Bobby Orr, Derek Sanderson, Don Awrey, Ed Johnston, one by one were sidelined for various ailments.

The Bruins farm system, which had become one of the most productive in the NHL, continued to feed reserves to the big team, and each player looked better than the last. Not surprisingly, they were tough. One of them, Jim Harrison, tangled with tough Gordie Howe, knocked the Red Wing ace's stick to the ice, and then kicked it thirty feet away from him. Schmidt remarked about the lad, "He's what you'd call a disturber."

Studying the close race, coach Sinden predicted that first place in the East Division wouldn't be decided until the final weekend of the season, when Boston and Montreal would meet in a home-and-home series opening in Montreal.

The patrons at Boston Garden could almost taste the championship. They adorned the ancient arena with banners reflecting what Toronto *Globe and Mail* columnist Dick Beddoes described as "Boston's virulent hockey psychosis."

"Play dirty and win!" proclaimed one such adornment. "Sock it to 'em, Pie!" said another in reference to "Pieface" McKenzie. "Tiny Tim doesn't like us—We hate him," announced still another.

All the banners in the world, however, couldn't stimulate the Bruins enough. They were eliminated by the Canadiens on the final Saturday night of the season and once more wound up as bridesmaids of the ice.

Conceivably, the loss of first place left Boston fans and the Bruins in an ugly mood on the eve of the first round of the playoffs. They were to meet the Toronto Maple Leafs, the fourth-place team, which had engaged the Bruins in some lively brawls only a few weeks before. In one of them Pat Quinn, a rather large but clumsy Toronto defenseman, fought with Orr and later told Toronto newsmen that Bruins ethics were far to the left of the rulebook.

Bruins fans were disturbed about the Quinn incident, especially because Orr was allegedly kicked by the Leaf defenseman. They had hoped he'd appear at the Garden once more during the season, but were disappointed when an injury sidelined Quinn for the Leafs' last regularly scheduled game in Boston.

But when the Leafs and Bruins were paired in the playoffs Quinn was back in action for the opening game and, as one might have anticipated, all hell broke loose. The major fuse was planted in the second period by Quinn and detonated by the Boston fans. For a time it appeared those in the stands would duplicate, or even exceed, their performance against Hap Day, Wally Stanowski, and Garth Boesch of the Maple Leafs more than a decade earlier.

It happened at 18:03 of the middle period, seconds after Orr had picked up speed for a rush along the right boards. "Bobby had his head down," coach Sinden admitted after the contest, "and when you have your head down you have to take your lumps."

Quinn, who had been playing defense in a very one-sided game in the Bruins' favor, detected Orr on his radar. The Leaf rookie rushed Orr from almost a right angle and deposited him on the ice with a devastating check. It remains questionable whether there was anything illegal about the check. Even subjective viewers such as Sinden allow that, at the very worst, Quinn was guilty of charging. "But," said the Bruin coach, "it wasn't a vicious check."

"Quinn hit him with his shoulder," said George Gross, assistant sports editor of the Toronto *Telegram*.

Orr fell backward on his right hip after the blow and then lay motionless on the ice, face down. Trainer Dan Canney rushed to the scene and, almost immediately, summoned Dr. Ronald Adams, the team physician. At this point referee John Ashley announced that Quinn would receive a five-minute major penalty, instead of the traditional two-minute minor, for elbowing.

"It was quite clear," Gross pointed out, "that Quinn hadn't used an elbow. At worst he should have been given a minor for charging."

In terms of its influence on the game, the penalty was totally irrelevant. Boston held a commanding 6—0 lead and was coasting to victory. Perhaps the award of a major rather than minor penalty may have suggested to the enraged crowd of 14,659 that Quinn was guilty of hyper-ruthlessness. On the other hand it's conceivable that a few bloodthirsty Boston fans merely wanted a pound of Quinn's flesh and would have started an uprising no matter what the penalty.

Seconds after the Leaf player took his seat in the penalty box some fans crowded around him. The police were conspicuous by their lack of protection for the visiting player. One fan clouted Quinn on the head with his fist while another bounced a hard object off Quinn's skull.

"Boston Garden," Gross observed, "turned into a lunatic

bin. The only thing missing was the straitjackets."

An intelligent young man, Quinn realized that his life was in grave and imminent peril, and he sought to protect himself as much as possible. The crowd wasn't satisfied and began a crescendo-like chant that reached deafening proportions. "Get Quinn! Get Quinn!! GET QUINN!!!"—who eventually was forced to seek sanctuary in the Toronto dressing room.

Orr was taken to Massachusetts General Hospital for overnight observation with a slight concussion and a slight whiplash in the neck. X-rays taken at the hospital proved negative, a factor that was unknown to the audience which remained disturbed as the third period progressed.

They wanted more Leaf scalps and got them late in the period when another brawl erupted, involving Forbes Kennedy of Toronto and several other players.

"Fans leaned over the glass to pound Kennedy," reported Red Burnett in the Toronto *Daily Star,* "while Bruins goalie Ed Johnston had him in a bear hug. . . . There were times when it appeared as if some of the kookier members of the roaring crowd would invade the ice after the Leafs."

All three Toronto papers agreed that the scene was shameful. The Boston *Globe* on April 4 not only carried a lead editorial about the fooferaw but also ran an editorial cartoon depicting Bruins and Leaf players fighting on the ice while a fan tosses beer at Quinn in the penalty box. A plainclothes investigator stands aside and remarks: "Excuse me gentlemen . . . I'm from the commission to study violence in America."

At least one Boston writer noted that the Bruins had intimidated the Leafs and there was little evidence to contradict the theory. Boston players laughed among themselves about the "timidity" of some of the visiting players. One of the stories making the rounds had it that a Bruin was mauling a Toronto forward in front of the Boston net. The Bruin expected to be counterattacked.

"Instead," the Boston player related in amazement, "the guy says to me 'what are you doing that for? I've never done anything to you.' Imagine that!"

NHL official Scotty Morrison added, "This was the dirtiest game I've seen in my four seasons as referee-in-chief and three seasons as an official. It was disgraceful."

The Bruins, a clearly superior team, defeated Toronto in

four straight games. In the East Division finals they would face the Montreal Canadiens, who had similarly swept the Rangers in four games. Although Montreal had annihilated Boston in four games during the 1968 semifinal, an air of confidence surrounded the Bruins and their followers. The *Record-American* had set the tone already with a headline: "B's WILL WIN CUP." And Bruins players were free with their predictions. Bobby Orr and others predicted four consecutive wins over Montreal.

Montreal's players and officials remained singularly quiet on the subject of the East Division finals. Some observers got the impression they were content to allow the Bruins to win the series by oratory. Then, on April 10, 1969, play began on the Forum ice.

The Bruins scored two goals and were about to win the game when John Ferguson scored at 13:28 of the third period. With less than a minute remaining, Canadiens coach Claude Ruel pulled goalie Gump Worsley and sent an extra attacker to the ice. In a matter of seconds Jean Beliveau scored the tying goal, moving the game into sudden-death overtime. Almost immediately after the face-off Orr lost the puck at his own blue line. It went to Ralph Backstrom, whose shot beat Gerry Cheevers only forty-two seconds into the period.

The second game had a feeling of *déjà vu* about it. Again Boston carried a lead down to the end of the third period, but Montreal would not be repulsed. Defenseman Serge Savard intercepted a pass from Phil Esposito, sent the puck to Ted Harris, who in turn relayed to Yvan Cournoyer. He sent it back to Savard, and Savard's shot beat Ed Johnston, who had replaced Cheevers in the Boston goal.

In overtime Green lost the puck to Backstrom, held the Montreal player, and took a two-minute penalty. Backstrom won the ensuing face-off and passed the puck back to Ferguson. Instead of shooting, Ferguson skimmed the puck to Savard. The Canadiens defenseman drove the puck at Johnston, but it caromed off Mickey Redmond's stick and past the Bruin goalie.

A team that fails to hold leads at critical moments in a game and loses successively in sudden death invites criticism and questions, which the Bruins deservedly received. Pat Curran of the Montreal *Gazette* wondered if the Bruins were "too immature under Stanley Cup pressure?"

Milt Dunnell of the Toronto *Daily Star* compared them to horses that pull up in the home stretch. "If the hockey brass ever go for fifty-minute games," wrote Dunnell, "the suspicion is that the Bruins would get tied at the forty-nine-minute mark. Then the Habs would knock them off in overtime."

When coach Sinden's skaters returned to Boston they managed to postpone their demise by defeating Montreal, 5—0 and 3—2. But the Bruins then dropped the fifth game, 4—2, at the Forum. The sixth game, played on April 24 on Bruin ice, is generally regarded as one of the finest Cup matches of all time. Sinden and some of his players had freely predicted after the opening two games that Montreal would not win again. Smaller, less belligerent Canadien skaters such as Yvan Cournoyer were being threatened by the bigger Bruins, and the inference in the Boston camp was that the Montrealers would ultimately be afraid to touch the puck.

Certainly the Bruins had their chance. Ron Murphy put them ahead at 2:29 of the first period, and Phil Esposito had glorious opportunities to add to the Boston total as the game progressed. But the Bruins still played like the "losers" Peter Gzowski observed in 1965. Whenever they appeared to have excellent chances to score they would lose the puck or shoot wide.

"Anytime the Bostons meet the Habs in the Stanley Cup shenanigans," noted Dunnell, "it's like throwing a good welterweight against the world's heavyweight champion. The welterweight may put on a rousing show, but he winds up in the resin."

Nursing their one-goal lead in the third period, the Bruins began making the loser's mistakes. Defenseman Don Awrey took a penalty at 1:05, and five seconds later Savard tied the score. The score remained 1—1 into sudden-death overtime. Boston had its chances to win the game, to be sure, but Montreal goalie Rogatien Vachon beat them to the corners whenever he had to, and the teams moved into the second extra period.

More than ten minutes had elapsed when the face-off was held deep in Boston territory. Soon the puck was behind the net. Ferguson pursued it, but a Bruin defenseman got there first. He tried to open a counterattack with a quick pass but Claude Provost of the Canadiens saw it coming as he was heading back to his zone. He trapped the puck and quickly sent it to Beliveau, who was standing in front of the net. Beliveau's shot was high to the right. "By the time I saw it," said goalie Cheevers, "it was over my shoulder."

The winning goal was scored at 11:28, leaving the crowd of 14,659 fans momentarily stunned. When they finally recovered they saluted the teams and especially the Bruins who had played well, but not well enough to win.

Manager Schmidt made it clear that nobody could tell him that the better team won the series, and there were other murmurings about the Canadiens being "lucky." But Boston columnist Tim Horgan reduced the Bruins wailing to its proper place when he denounced it as sour grapes and commended the Canadiens as the true champions.

As for the Bruins, they earned the right to proclaim, "Wait 'til next year!"

9. The Coming of the Cup

"They talk about the pressure of being
in first place. How about the pressure
of some of those losing streaks?"
—Ted Green, 1968.

Whether the Bruins, their management, fans, or writers
care to admit it or not, the Depression Years from 1959–60
through 1966–67 left an indelible scar on those who suffered through them. The compensation comes in many
ways, some acceptable and some less so. So there is reason
for the behavior of the *nouveau riche*.

Goalie Ed Johnston, defenseman Ted Green, utility man
Ed Westfall, and left wing John Bucyk endured the slings
and arrows of Boston's worst hockey misfortune and apparently emerged all the better for it. But they haven't forgotten what it was like.

"There was a time when you got used to losing," Green
related to Kevin Walsh of the Boston *Globe* at Christmas-
time, 1968. "Those were bad times. We went a couple of
years when we only won fourteen or fifteen games the entire
year. . . . One year we went something like twenty-two in a
row, and we were threatening the league record of twenty-
five winless games in a row. That was pressure."

After years of fumbling through a labyrinth of dead ends
the Bruins management realized that its hope for the future,
if there was to be one, rested in self-help. President Weston
Adams diligently supervised the reorganization of the
Bruins farm system with a clear target in mind.

"All any NHL club needs is two big men," Adams declared. "Give us two players like Bobby Hull and Stan
Mikita of Chicago and the two teams will reverse their position in the standings. Good teams come from good
material."

The evidence is irrefutable that the Adams plan succeeded. Aided by Lynn Patrick and Milt Schmidt, he
planted the seeds in such remote places as Estevan, Saskatchewan; Niagara Falls, Ontario; and Flin Flon, Manitoba. A few years were required before the first harvest, but

in time the crop included Bobby Orr, Derek Sanderson, Gilles Marotte, and Bernie Parent.

Help was required from other sources, and Schmidt provided it. He outfoxed Chicago's Tommy Ivan with the best deal in the Bruins' history when he obtained Phil Esposito, Ken Hodge, and Fred Stanfield in May, 1967.

"This is a team that will learn how to win," Esposito promised when he arrived at training camp in London, Ontario in September, 1967. "This first year, we'll make the playoffs for sure. Next year we'll be second or third. The third year [1969–70] we'll win the whole thing. Stanley Cup and all!"

In some ways Esposito has been extraordinarily clairvoyant. Boston did win a playoff berth—its first in nine years—in 1968. The Bruins were second in 1969, and many were willing to wager that they would win the whole thing in 1970. But that appears to some observers as a narrow approach. More expansive types believe the Bruins dynasty is capable of lasting through 1980.

A new crop began blossoming in 1969, and in some areas it appeared to be as bountiful as the one that produced Orr, Marotte, and Sanderson. Youngsters like Garnet Bailey, Don Marcotte, Tom Webster, Bill Lesuk, and Jim Harrison waited impatiently on the farm teams for the call to the NHL. Those who were summoned fit into the boisterous Bruins mold like perfectly meshed gears.

On January 11, 1969, one of the gears slipped when Sanderson was deactivated by a hip injury. But Schmidt summoned twenty-one-year-old Harrison to the Bruins from the minors, and it was difficult to tell that Sanderson was missing at all. Boston won the game, 6—3, and Harrison won the raves.

"The pattern of Boston mastery was established early in the game by Harrison," said Pat Curran of the Montreal *Gazette*. "The big kid with the long sideburns didn't pick his spots while throwing checks at Ted Harris, John Ferguson, Henri Richard, and others. And despite four penalties, the rookie led the Bruins in outmuscling the Canadiens. Whenever a brash rookie hits all comers and gets away with it there has to be a major reason in hockey. Either the kid has the promise of a bright new star or the opposition has taken him and the game for granted."

Harrison, like Bailey, Marcotte, and Webster, had the

beautiful promise of young talent; the Bruins so oozed with prodigies that the brass began worrying about them long before 1968–69 had ended. "The line [1969] draft," said Schmidt, "may be the most important for us. We figure to lose at least three players." Boston lost only Grant Erickson and Glen Sather in the 1969 draft.

The Bruins were able to protect fourteen players as well as two goalies. Because of the intricacies of NHL by-laws they didn't have to protect Webster, Smith, Harrison, and Orr because they were classified as "first year pros." Those who were covered had been carefully analyzed to fit into the new Bruins style. "Harrison," said Schmidt, "is my kind of player. He checks like a major leaguer."

Webster was another who exemplified the Bruins qualities, before a CBS network television audience in February, 1969. A big right wing, Webster had been elevated from the Oklahoma City farm team in the Central League. During a game against the Black Hawks at Chicago Stadium, Webster thrust his stick in the face of Chicago's Dennis Hull. The injured Black Hawk responded in a manner that commands respect among Bruins. He took a two-handed cut at Webster, like a baseball player aiming for the fences, and hit the young Bruin a grand slam in the stomach, inflicting severe abdominal bruises on him and sidelining him for several games. What mattered was that the Bruins had unearthed another volcanic type to fit the mold.

Before the June, 1969, draft the brass traded Eddie Shack to the Los Angeles Kings for a future draft choice, once again appearing to obtain something for nothing. Shack's penchant for penalties had far outstripped his usefulness as a hitter. Like Marotte, Pit Martin, and Jack Norris, Shack was expendable. The Bruins also unloaded Tom Williams, who had missed most of the 1968–69 season, and defenseman Barry Gibbs to Minnesota's North Stars for more future draft choices. By now rival managers were muttering under their breath that it would be wise for the league to "break up the Bruins."

Weston Adams retired as Bruins president at the conclusion of the 1968–69 season and was succeeded by his son, Weston W. Adams, Jr., underlining the philosophy that the Bruins will always remain in the Adams family. Perhaps it would have been more dramatic had the father handed the reins to his son at the conclusion of a Stanley

Cup victory, but nobody in Boston was about to criticize the brilliant comeback achieved by Weston, Sr.

"No man—Bobby Orr included—is as responsible for the Bruins' rise to the top as is Adams," wrote Tim Horgan in the *Herald-Traveler*. "Deposed in 1951 after serving as president since 1936, Westy swallowed his pride, packed his grip, and in 1961 volunteered to tour the farm system and try to find out why it had produced not one varsity player since Don McKenney came up in 1954. . . . If the Bruins finally have become a good team, it's because he furnished the material."

Weston, Jr. thus inherited a powerful club that was growing even stronger, motivated by the lure of two elusive goals —first place in the East Division and the Stanley Cup. Some critics believed that Boston entered the 1969–70 campaign with more young talent than any of its rivals, the Montreal Canadiens included.

"The present may belong to the Canadiens," wrote Boston *Globe* reporter Tom Fitzgerald in April, 1969. "The future definitely belongs to the Bruins."

The point was almost but not quite unassailable. The Canadiens fortress was built around aging center Jean Beliveau, who seemed irreplaceable. The Bruins were fortified with the essential hockey quality known as strength down the center, and were bubbling with confidence.

"A team is lucky to have one true leader," said Sanderson. "We have six or seven."

Perhaps, but some Bruins critics contend that they have six or seven chiefs, each one trying to run the tribe his own way. The Canadiens, by contrast, work as a team, and that's why they finished first and won the Stanley Cup.

"Sometimes," said coach Harry Sinden in the middle of the 1968–69 season, "it's easier climbing to the top than it is staying there."

The challenge now for the Boston hockey team is staying there. While they're at it, the players can take pride in the fact that they have restored dignity to the team name. Perhaps the headline on Ray Fitzgerald's column in the *Globe* on December 23, 1968, put it best:

"PURGATORY OVER FOR BRUIN FANS"

PART III

The Other Aces

1. Ed Westfall, the Super-Sub

As hockey catastrophes go, the present Bruins had regarded the loss of Bobby Orr through injury as the most telling disaster that could traumatize the team. That was a reasonable estimation until the night of February 2, 1969.

Disabled with an injured knee, Orr was forced out of the Boston lineup at a time when the Bruins were gliding along on a sixteen-game unbeaten streak; more important, they were making their first serious overtures for first place in more than two decades. On February 2, the Detroit Red Wings visited Boston Garden, motivated by the lure of a playoff berth.

The visitors smelled victory at midpoint in the game. Boston was playing two men short while the Red Wings had one player in the penalty box. Detroit's power play was nullified by the Bruins defense, and the puck fell onto defenseman Don Awrey's stick. He wound up and moved the puck ahead to Vernon Edwin "Eddie" Westfall, who is both the most ubiquitous and the least-recognized Boston skater.

Awrey's pass was too slow for Westfall, so Eddie had to decelerate, and still the puck lagged behind him. There was only one thing to do—a difficult maneuver—but Westfall executed the play as if it were second nature to him. "He caught the puck with his skate," said coach Harry Sinden, "and moved it up to his stick blade, and away he went."

True, Westfall was in motion, but he was being pursued by Frank Mahovlich on the left and Gary Bergman on the right. In that situation a less composed player would have looked frantically for a teammate or rushed a pass to nowhere in particular, as long as it freed him from danger. Instead, Westfall moved closer to the net, which was guarded by goalie Roy Edwards.

"First I had to think whether Edwards would commit himself," the pipe-smoking Westfall diagnosed after the game, "then I was hoping Mahovlich wouldn't catch up. When Edwards didn't move I had to think fast. The few times previous to that when I had breakaways I didn't score because I went high."

This 6-1, 189-pound utility player has given the banal expression "utility player" great dignity. Unlike a number of his colleagues, whose cerebration is conspicuous by its nonexistence, Westfall in that split second thought out his possibilities. Knowing that high shots were foiled by Edwards and others, he felt it was time for a change.

"This time," Westfall recalled, "I decided to go low."

The shot blurred past Edwards and nestled into the left corner of the net. It gave Westfall what he described as "a great feeling," and for good reason. The goal was his fifteenth of the season in which he would finish with 18 goals, 24 assists, and 42 points, the most he's ever collected since he became a Bruin in 1962–63. More than that, the goal represented something more than a personal record. It told the world that the utility player in his way is as relevant to the team's success as are the players with fat five- and six-figure contracts.

"The Bruins discovered," wrote John Ahern in the Boston *Globe,* "if they hadn't already realized it, that they have another super player and without him that wonderful win streak would not have reached No. 17."

The "discovery" of Westfall was not made by a single hockey expert; rather it seemed to be a happening involving many individuals, including coach and teammates.

"It wasn't only that goal," said Sinden. "He does everything and this time he was playing every position except goal. I look around on the ice and I see a lot of our guys playing well. . . . Then I look again and Westfall would be doing it all. It was a tremendous job.

"But I want to ask a question and I'll bet there's no one in hockey who can give me the answer. I just want to know when he played a poor game. If he ever did it had to be before he was in organized hockey."

Sinden's memory is limited by his relatively short tenure as NHL coach. Westfall *has* played a poor game, in fact, many poor games; but that was long ago when many of the Bruins played abysmally as if by reflex as soon as they put on the colors of the Boston club.

He became a Bruin during the 1961–62 season when Phil

Watson was the Boston coach and last place was the team's regular stopping-off place. He became a Bruin because he wanted to make it just a little bit more than the next fellow. He made a point of finding ice to practice on during the summer of 1961 so that when he arrived at training camp in Niagara Falls, Ontario, he was a step quicker than his rivals. It was that step that Bruins brass found so appealing.

"Eddie was skating in midseason form when the rest of the squad took the ice for the first time," said Lynn Patrick, then manager of the Bruins. "He caught Watson's eye and from that time on he took a regular turn."

Not having been a member of that team, Sinden, of course, couldn't recount the numerous *faux pas* that Westfall had committed in those fumbling years. But Bruins publicist Herb Ralby remembered them, and as he once noted in a magazine article, "his inexperience stood out like a beacon light."

Westfall's mistakes multiplied until the Boston management found the goals-against figure too high for the club to tolerate. He was shipped to Kingston of the now-defunct Eastern Pro League for the 1962–63 season—or at least for the start of that campaign. The demotion didn't wear well with the pleasant-smiling young man.

"At first," he revealed, "I didn't think I needed to be sent down. But it turned out the other way. I not only learned all over again how to play defense, but I regained my confidence. I found I could experiment a lot. I found out what I could do best and what I was weakest at."

It was no coincidence that the man who infused Westfall with a surplus of hockey knowledge was Kingston's coach, Harry Sinden. When Kingston's right wing was injured, Sinden tried Westfall at the forward position and discovered that his adaptability quotient was high.

"If I hadn't been sent to Kingston," Westfall admitted, "and hadn't had the chance to play, I never would have been aware of certain aspects of passing the puck up from the defense to the forward. I had never given it much thought before then. But when I had trouble digging the passes out of my skates instead of getting them right on my stick, I decided in the future to put my passes right on the forward's stick."

Westfall actually became a utility player in junior hockey, playing both forward and defense for the Niagara Falls

Flyers of the Ontario Junior A League. He usually played more than half a game for coach Hap Emms and often would be required to spend up to fifty minutes on the ice.

"As a result," said Westfall, "I never really learned to bodycheck properly until I came up with the Bruins. Leo Boivin taught me how to hipcheck when Leo was with the Bruins."

An awkward skater, whose strides reminded one of a sailor walking the deck during a hurricane, Westfall required one final demotion to the minors in 1963–64 before he acquired the poise to remain in the NHL. Even when he returned, life was not without its small tortures. There were nights when he wished there was a tunnel running straight from the dressing room to his home. Yet he nurtured the hope during those depressing seasons that some day the Bruins would see the light.

"I never wanted to be traded," he insisted. "I thought about it and then I'd think of the years ahead. I knew things couldn't stay bad forever. It had to get better and if the organization had faith in me, I felt I had to have faith in it. It certainly has paid off. Now I feel like a prosperous businessman. My life is good."

The pivotal season for Westfall was 1964–65. The Bruins had a full complement of defensemen at the start of the schedule but ran into a painful series of injuries. At first coach Milt Schmidt used Westfall as a penalty killer and then as a defenseman. When the forwards began beating a trail to the hospital, Schmidt transferred Westfall to the front line.

"Say, Eddie," a railbird mentioned one day, "you're getting as much ice time as Bobby Hull and Gordie Howe."

"Listen," Westfall shot back, "I'll take all the ice time I can get!"

In time Schmidt began employing Westfall as Hull's "shadow." It was an onerous task but one that Eddie performed so well that the role became permanent. By the 1966–67 season rookie coach Sinden began experimenting with Westfall at center, his fifth position in four and a half years with the team.

"The next move," quipped Westfall, "is to get myself some goalie equipment. I've never been in the nets before but that opportunity may arise any day and I should be ready."

His unique position as swing man complicated the possibilities of a bonus for goal scoring. "My contract is a difficult one to negotiate," he revealed late in the 1968–69 season. "There is no set price on many of the things I do, as there is with goals and assists. Perhaps in fairness to myself, I should devise some method of bookkeeping on such things as how my record stacks up against that of the man playing opposite me."

Until that day comes, Westfall must remain content with compliments, rather than statistics. "He's the big spoke out there," said defenseman Ted Green, who suffered through the Bruins' years in the NHL trough. "All he does is make the big play every time we need the big play. It's great to see him scoring. But he does so many things to stop the other team from scoring you can't name them if you spend all night trying."

Students of the new Bruins of the seventies contend that Westfall's most memorable game was the fourth match between the Canadiens and the Bruins in the 1969 East Division final. The teams were locked in a 0—0 tie early in the game when Garnet Bailey was penalized for interference. Sinden, who describes Westfall as "one of the league's best penalty killers," sent his man out to stall the Montrealers.

"We were back in our end," said Westfall, reconstructing the play, "when Dallas Smith set me up with a good pass."

Instead of wheeling back toward his own defensive zone, Westfall thought he might just fool the enemy with a surprise attack. His shot was blocked by tiny goalie Rogatien Vachon but it rebounded to the charging Westfall. "It came right back to me and I took a swipe at it with my stick."

By this time Montreal defenseman Jacques Laperriere enveloped Westfall, with his left arm over the Bruin's neck and his right around his waist. Eddie was plunging head-first toward the ice like a Kamikaze, but the damage had been done. Fully horizontal, Vachon stared longingly at the puck as it rolled into the right corner of the net.

"So long as it went in," said Westfall, "I'm satisfied. I'm not going to be fussy about how it got past him."

The Canadiens rebounded to tie the score and then Westfall went out to kill still another penalty with teammate Derek Sanderson. The 14,659 fans in the Garden had difficulty discerning which team had the penalty and which one the power play. Boston, with Westfall in command, hustled the Canadiens into the visitors' own end of the rink. The puck squirted loose behind the net. J. C. Tremblay, the Montreal defenseman, lost it to Sanderson, who sliced out in front of the net and tucked the disk behind Vachon.

Montreal doesn't die easily, and on this night they punctured the Bruins defenses in the third period as they searched for the tying goal. With less than two minutes remaining, Westfall sent Bobby Orr into the clear for what developed into the game's winning score—Montreal collected another goal before the contest was over.

What was most remarkable about Westfall's extravaganza was not so much his lucrative evening but rather the collection of headlines he gathered in the local journals. "BRUINS' WESTFALL ALWAYS A WINNER" was the banner in the *Record-American*. "WESTFALL FINALLY 'DISCOVERED' " the *Globe* disclosed.

John Ahern, who covered the game for the *Globe,* took due notice that the reporters rarely push to the far corner of the Bruin dressing room. "It has been pretty lonesome in that corner for many seasons," said Ahern, "with only an occasional scribbler stopping by to ask for a quote. On Sunday it looked like a football huddle. Silent men, bending over slightly, were taking in every word, and Eddie was talking like a quarterback."

"Sometimes," said Sinden in another part of the room, "we have to wonder why there isn't more talk about him. Probably we're to blame for it. We just expect him to do everything and he does it. What a hockey player!"

Sinden wasn't expressing a local opinion. On the other side of the ice, Montreal's coach Claude Ruel was glumly enthused about the Bruins winner. "Very good man," was the terse comment of the French-Canadian mentor. "Very good man!"

Teammate Sanderson insisted that Westfall was the unsung Bruin. "He covers up for a lot of my mistakes," said Sanderson.

The feeling about Westfall was seconded by his father Ray and his brother Howie, who happened to witness the superb performance. The other Westfalls fretted through the Depression years with Eddie, and they empathized with him as he reminisced for the newsmen.

"Only Johnny Bucyk has been here longer than I," he

said. "You can imagine what it means to us after all those awful years.

"Last year? [1968] well, I don't know about last year. We lost four straight, and for myself, I'd rather not have made the playoffs than to go out that way. You have to be able to hold your head up—it's important, you know. . . . The Canadiens know what it's like. We don't, but we will. It's something to go back home and to know—and have everybody else know—that you're the best. Yes, sir, that's something."

He looks more like a Madison Avenue executive than a battle-hardened hockey player. He wears impeccably tailored suits and often puffs a Sherlock Holmes-style pipe. He's not the type given to braggadocio, but he made an understandable slip during the Stanley Cup finals in 1969. Westfall could almost taste the champagne after Boston had tied the series, 2—2, and returned to the Forum for the fifth game.

"I don't know why we shouldn't be confident going back to Montreal," he asserted. "I think you would have to say we are getting stronger in the series while they appear to be falling back. The good thing is looking back. We were two down then and we could have fallen apart. We knew we had to fight back and we knew there was only one way to play a team like that. We had to play sixty minutes of good, strong, offensive hockey and we did. It gives us momentum and it has to tell them something. We know we can win in Montreal and there's no way they're going to beat us here."

Westfall may not have realized at the time that teammate Sanderson was injured on the second Bruin scoring play. He would miss the fifth game of the series at Montreal, creating a need for additional center-ice strength. "There's no question Westfall could do the job," said Sinden, "and do it very well, but it really messes up right wing for us."

It is history that Westfall couldn't quite compensate for the loss of Sanderson; the Bruins lost the game, and despite the guarantees of Sinden, Westfall, and others that "there's no way they're going to beat us here," the Canadiens returned to Boston and beat the Bruins for the Stanley Cup in sudden-death overtime.

When it was over Westfall walked out of Boston Garden secure in the knowledge that he is a very important Bruin.

"When they use that word 'steady,' they're leaving a great deal unsaid. There is a tendency to think of the individual things which Eddie does well without adding them all together," said coach Sinden.

"He's one of the league's best penalty killers. In an emergency we can drop him back to defense, although fortunately that has not been necessary this season. He's a remarkably good defensive forward and a two-way right winger who is contributing to the scoring of this team."

His deeds have reinforced these claims. When other, more loudly trumpeted Boston players have failed, Westfall has saved the team. As John Ahern so aptly noted on February 3, 1969, after Eddie had almost single-handedly beaten the Red Wings, "Now it is known definitely: the Bruins can play without Bobby Orr."

2. John Bucyk, the Captain

Season after miserable season during the early sixties, John Bucyk, the Bruins captain, would appear at banquets and be asked, "Listen, Johnny, if you're such a hot-shot, how come you're still with the Bruins?"

In some ways the acidic question was pertinent. Bucyk had been with the worst team in the NHL for an awfully long time, maybe too long. There were times when objective viewers wondered just who was affecting whom. But Bucyk had the best answer, and that was his scoring record.

While the Bruins floundered, the man they call "The Chief" was plodding along with the better NHL scorers, knowing that someday life would be as beautiful as it was in his youth, when he and Bronco Horvath and Vic Stasiuk marauded through the league as the "Uke Line." But that was long ago.

"I always knew the wheel had to turn some time," Bucyk remarked as the wheel *did* start moving in the Bruins' favor in 1968. "I knew we'd start winning, one of these seasons."

When the 6-foot, 207-pound left wing originally became a Bruin, via a trade with Detroit for Terry Sawchuk in July, 1957, everything was coming up roses. Boston went to the Stanley Cup finals in 1958 and finished second in 1959, while Bucyk's scoring went up and up. He was reunited with Horvath, a clever center, and Stasiuk, a bullish wing, with whom he had skated in 1954–55 at Edmonton in the Western League. Bucyk had scored thirty goals and eighty-eight points to set a rookie record in the WHL and was named rookie of the year. The reunion of the Ukes in Boston was a capital move on Lynn Patrick's part and a blessing for Bucyk.

Thanks to Horvath, Bucyk was given an identity immediately. Bronco linked Bucyk's dark complexion with that of some Indians he'd once seen and promptly knighted him

"Chief." Horvath also ladled several hundred excellent passes to Bucyk, who for the first time in his NHL life enjoyed a twenty-goal season. Horvath was repaid by Bucyk's diligent "infighting," which produced loose pucks from the sideboards where angels fear to tread.

"I always work the corners and get the puck out," Bucyk explained. "You can't score from the corners. If you pass off and the other guy scores, what's the difference? A goal is a goal."

Bucyk was so good for Horvath in the 1959–60 season that Bronco came within a couple of games of leading the league in scoring. When the shooting had finished Horvath wound up in second place, only a point behind Bobby Hull, but Bronco had played two fewer games. At this point, however, there was considerable doubt as to just how beneficial the Ukes had been to the Bruin cause. Despite Horvath's outburst, Boston dropped from second in 1957–58 to fifth in 1958–59, and the Ukes as a unit were well on their way to the scrap heap.

Chicago drafted Horvath from the Bruins in June, 1961, and Stasiuk was traded to Detroit with Leo Labine in exchange for Gary Aldcorn, Murray Oliver, and Tom McCarthy in January, 1961. Orphaned from his pals, Bucyk nevertheless responded with the same efficiency he had displayed on the Uke Line. The only problem was that his Bruin teammates were by this time exploring new depths of ineptitude.

"Bucyk," noted author Dan Proudfoot of *The Canadian Magazine*, "has been Boston's most talented individual over the past decade, even though he's never been voted a season's all-star and he's never won a league trophy."

Twice during the Depression Years, Bucyk scored twenty-seven goals, and once (1962–63) went as high as sixty-six points. Meanwhile the Bruins were scraping the bottom of the NHL. Bucyk labored through six last-place seasons in eight years and second-last the other two. When the people at banquets needled him about it, Bucyk had an answer.

"I've always considered it an honor to play in this league, that's all. I never quit even when the fans were on me. Five or six years were frustrating. But I was always proud to be in the NHL. Anybody should be proud to wear a big-league uniform. Any team's. Even then there was no shame in wearing a Bruins' sweater. Millions of kids would like to be in your position. But you're much prouder when you're in a playoff spot. Even when we were last I knew, at least, that we were last in the best."

Every so often Bucyk's name would flash over the news wires. A seasons back he surpassed Milt Schmidt's Bruin record of 575 points in 776 games. It was a very meaningful accomplishment, because Bucyk required only 673 games to do it. Not long after that he became the first Boston player to score 250 goals and one of the few to be honored with a "night" by Garden fans.

These credentials indicate that Bucyk has come a remarkably long way from his home town of Edmonton, Alberta, where he played junior hockey for the Oil Kings and skated like a retarded hippopotamus. At one point early in his career, Bucyk's skating style was so disjointed his coach, former NHL goalie Ken McAuley, ordered the left wing to figure-skating school. It was such a degrading experience that Bucyk and the Oil Kings tried to keep the episode under wraps. "We kind of kept it a secret," Bucyk later revealed to Boston writer Bob Sales. "It's not the greatest thing in the world."

The success of the pirouettes, triple axels, and figure eights is reflected in Bucyk's lyrical skating style today. His speed is enough to keep him apace with the better NHL sprinters, and his skating balance has not prevented him from becoming one of the more respected bodycheckers among forwards.

"The guy is deceptive," said veteran defenseman Allan Stanley. "He's much heavier than he looks, and he hits low, with his hip. The thing you have to remember whenever he's on the ice is that you can never afford to stand admiring your passes. Not the way Bucyk hits."

The hitting has brought destruction to opponents through the years and has also dented Bucyk's armor; more than two hundred stitches have punctured his anatomy. His most debilitating injury, however, was a slipped disk in his back. When he arrived at training camp for the 1967–68 season Bucyk had driven 3,000 miles from Edmonton to London, Ontario. The strain so disrupted his back muscles doctors ordered him to avoid skating for a week and then prescribed a heavy back brace that girdled his injury. He is known as a chronic worrier, and there was a time when his teammates regarded his professed ill health as a good omen. Bucyk usually played best when he was complaining about his condition.

His phlegmatic exterior—he's often related how nervous he is before a game—has often led Bruin fans to believe that Bucyk doesn't care whether his team wins or loses and doesn't try hard enough. It is a mistaken impression that viewers have had of other big players whose loping style is deceiving.

"Besides," Bucyk has replied in a legitimate self-defense, "how many players are fired up all the time? Hull isn't. Frank Mahovlich isn't."

Criticism of Bucyk's style has not been limited to the fans. Management removed him from the captaincy after the 1966–67 season and named three alternate captains— Bucyk, Ted Green, and Phil Esposito. The front office countered that they were doing Bucyk a favor by "lessening the burden" but the fact is that losing a "C" on a man's NHL jersey is like being told you're not good enough to run the ship anymore.

The barbs continued into the 1967–68 season, even when the Bruins began challenging for first place. Coach Sinden described his play as "terrible" after the halfway point in the campaign. "No hockey player has ever baffled me the way Bucyk does," Sinden was quoted in *The Canadian*. "A guy with his talent languishing. Hell, if he doesn't pick up, we won't make the playoffs. He's the key."

Bucyk had scored 18 goals in the first twenty-three games and then only 3 more in his next twenty-three. He collected 9 more in the remaining twenty-six games for a personal high of 30 goals, 39 assists, and 69 points, and a personal low of 8 penalty minutes.

While Esposito and Orr were capturing the ink in the heralded climb to second place in 1968–69, Bucyk was unobtrusively going about getting the job done. Despite threats of a back operation he showed up at camp and skated in Uke Line form.

"From what I've seen," enthused Sinden, "he couldn't be playing any better. He's skating hard, he's checking, he's digging the puck out of the corners. He's doing everything a coach could ask of a man and sometimes a lot more."

Explaining the Bucyk phenomena is confusing to some and simple to others. "Nothing ever changes with him," a teammate revealed. "He's always been a streak player."

Bucyk finished the 1968–69 season with 24 goals, 42 assists, and 66 points, a tie with his 1962–63 mark and the second highest in his career. He was, as they say, a brick, coming up with key goals when needed most. Typical was his effort one night during that season when the rest of the Bruins were taking it easy against the Los Angeles Kings. Bucyk scored twice, including the insurance goal, in a 6—4 win over the visitors.

"The way things had been going," commented Tom Fitzgerald in the *Globe,* "the 13,615 onlookers derived much relief from the Chief's contribution."

The Chief didn't diminish his effort against Toronto in the East Division Stanley Cup semifinal round, moving with rabbitlike alacrity.

"Much has been made of the contributions of goalkeeper Gerry Cheevers, center Phil Esposito, winger Ken Hodge, defenseman Bobby Orr, and a clutch of others," wrote Leo Monahan, "but Bucyk and Ron Murphy have played roles as large as anybody's."

Sinden added: "Another area where Bucyk has been doing a great job for us but hasn't been given much credit is on the power play."

One would think that with everyone waxing lyrical about him, Bucyk would rest assured that his job is secure in Boston; but he knows better. For too many years to suit any professional athlete, Bucyk had been disturbed by persistent word that he was being traded here and there, but mostly to Toronto. If his apparent lethargy had any roots it was in these trade rumors.

"It can't help but shake you up," he once admitted after a spate of Bucyk-to-Toronto reports had circulated around the NHL. "Read something like that, and then go out and play in a couple of hours' time, and you find yourself asking what's the use of trying."

For Bucyk to have survived more than a decade in the Bruins uniform and maintained his composure is a feat in itself, which has not been overlooked by careful students of the game. "It's been a rough decade," said Dan Proudfoot, "let it be said, roughly equal to the meanest endurance test ever devised by man."

Maybe it has been a trying period in a man's life, even though he's only playing a game and getting paid for it. But

Bucyk knows it has had its rewards, and for him, none better than the night of December 8, 1967, when he raced down the ice a few feet behind teammate John McKenzie. When they moved to within forty feet of Ranger goalie Ed Giacomin, McKenzie lifted his stick and allowed the puck to fall behind him.

Bucyk leaped at the puck and moved it to the backhand side of his stick. Giacomin sprawled to block the cage but Bucyk hurled the rubber from the thick, heel portion of his blade into the net and then crashed into the end boards. The goal, his second of the game, ensured the Bruins a 3—1 victory and brought thunderous applause from the upper sections of old Boston Garden. Fans realized that the goal gave Bucyk a lifetime NHL point total of 576, beating Schmidt's old mark by one point.

The arena thumped with sound like a mammoth rock 'n roll concert. "Chief, Chief, Chief," the people screamed and chanted as if they were proclaiming an ancient tribal rite. "Chief, Chief, Chief!" It continued for several minutes, and it made all the years of pain disappear.

"First you think you're dreaming," Bucyk said when it was over. "Then it hits you: they're cheering for *you*. It hits hard—but it's wonderful!"

3. Derek Sanderson, the Dead-End Kid

"LES CANADIENS FRANÇAIS ONT DES VISAGES
QUI NE ME REVIENNENT PAS." *

—Derek Sanderson

The message was carried across the top of a story in the French-Canadian weekly, *Sport Illustre*. Just to be sure everyone understood how the brash Bruins center supposedly felt the editors of the Montreal publication splashed a photo of mod Derek on the front page. There the headline was more blunt: "JE DETESTE LES CANADIENS FRANÇAIS."—Derek Sanderson.

There is no substantive evidence why "Turk" Sanderson should hold the Canadiens in contempt beyond their annoying habit of depositing the Bruins out of the Stanley Cup playoffs. More than likely the French-speaking author, François Dowd, was merely capitalizing on the Sanderson personality, which certainly is the most fascinating of the Bruins, even including Bobby Orr, Ted Green, and Phil Esposito.

In a world of squares and self-censored individuals, where hockey players are expected to be seen and heard as little as possible, Sanderson has sprouted into a hippie-oriented, loquacious chap who wears big flowery ties and will deliver a peroration at the drop of a puck. He is also a clever center of the tough, little Stan Mikita type who may well overshadow his teammate Esposito and blossom into the best pivot in the NHL.

Only those whose attentions are riveted on the past will fail to acknowledge Sanderson's potential. They will point out that he was a hostile skater more concerned with mayhem than mature playmaking and, in that, they are right. But Sanderson broke out of his angry cocoon late in the 1968–69 season and by playoff time was the best all-around forward the Bruins had; and that includes the highly praised but somewhat overrated Esposito.

* The French-Canadians have faces which I don't like.

Sanderson has more to say than the entire Bruins team put together—and he says it. More often than not, his dialogue rambles. One afternoon, late in February, 1969, he delivered a typical monologue on several dozen well-chosen subjects. It went something like this:

"When this team is right—everybody healthy—it can't be beaten. . . . Last year I predicted we'd mop up the Canadiens in the playoffs, and it happened the other way around. This year [1969] I'll say this: if we get by the first round, we'll go all the way. . . . People—no matter what type of work they do for a living—can't get 'up' for their jobs every day. It's impossible, no matter how hard they try. It's the same with us. . . . There's nobody on this team who's afraid of anyone. A lot of the people in this league—including some of the really good ones—have a tendency not to want to pay the price. When the going gets tough, they don't. They see a game get a little rough and say to themselves, 'Oh, oh. Forget this one. We'll get two points next game.' It's not a question of courage, really, just a tendency to look for the easier way. That doesn't happen on this club, believe me. None of our guys are afraid of anyone."

Sanderson's penchant for pronouncements, combined with his boutique wardrobe, have given him the aura of a Joe Namath. Teammates call him "Little Joe" and have threatened to paint his brown skate boots white so he can further emulate the Jets' quarterback. He is the chief protagonist in the Bruins drama, as the perceptive ones have discovered.

"Sanderson," observed Gary Ronberg of *Sports Illustrated,* "is the classic poor boy who makes it and buys the big Cadillac, pals with the swingers, and hits the spots. His sideburns are down to here and his bell bottoms out to there. He goes through money the way Sherman explored Georgia. He has a $350-a-month apartment on Beacon Hill, with a white rug on the floor like you-know-who."

It surprised no one in Boston sporting circles that Sanderson gravitated toward Ken Harrelson, and vice versa, when "The Hawk" played for the Red Sox. "The Hawk and the Seagull," needled Esposito when Harrelson was traded to Cleveland in April, 1969. "He's the hawk and you're the scavenger."

Sanderson was not exactly pleased about the trade and talked about boycotting Fenway Park. "Those guys [the Bruins] are telling me I should get myself traded to the Cleveland Barons," said Sanderson. "But, listen, the Hawk is my pal. With this kid, whatever he does is right. He's a personality, right? He's not some hunk of merchandise to be traded around. I don't blame him for what he's doing [Harrelson's brief holdout]—I guess I'd do the same thing if I were in his place."

Such candid impudence is fortified by the knowledge that the Bruins would hardly consider trading Sanderson unless they could obtain a superstar or something close to a million dollars in return. Boston's hockey brass watched Derek develop in the junior Ontario leagues with as much uneasiness as they watched Bobby Orr. They worried about Orr injuring himself, but they fretted about Sanderson injuring others.

In the 1965 Memorial Cup finals for Canada's junior championship, Sanderson, who was playing for Niagara Falls, knocked out Bob Falkenburg, an Edmonton defenseman. There were two arresting aspects of the incident. To begin with, Sanderson stood just under six feet and weighed less than 170 pounds, while Falkenburg was a six-footer, weighing about 190 pounds. And to conclude, Sanderson rendered his foe *hors de combat* with a single punch.

Sanderson didn't escape from the series unscathed. After the game six Edmonton rooters descended on the Niagara Falls belligerent, drove him into a dressing room, and proceeded to give him the most one-sided beating of his young life.

The incident in no way deterred Sanderson from future uprisings. Late in December, 1966, he played on a junior All-Star team against the Czechoslovak National squad, which was touring Canada on a good-will mission. Sanderson did the cause of international amity absolutely no good by drawing four penalties, including a major for spearing Jiri Holik of the visiting team.

"Holik spit in my face three times," Sanderson explained in defense. "I shoved him, but I didn't spear him."

Derek must have been doing something wrong during his junior days to inspire the wrath directed at him. Once when he played in Hamilton, a fan hurled a container of hot coffee in his face. And when he skated along the side-boards in Kitchener one evening a spectator leaned over and punched him in the mouth.

"What would you do if this happened to you?" Sanderson wondered. "You'd retaliate, the same as I did."

His disputatious personality never curbed his ability in juniors, but Sanderson experienced some self-doubt when he arrived at the Bruins training camp in September, 1967. A few of his new teammates sensed they had a winner among them and also perceived their rookie was worried.

"One night," Sanderson fondly recalled. "Esposito, Green, and Shack took me out for a talk to convince me I could make the team. They said 'don't lose that cockiness. Just keep your cool.' "

On the whole, Sanderson obeyed his mentors and completed his freshman year with superior grades. He was voted the Calder Memorial Trophy as rookie of the year, scored 24 goals and 25 assists for 49 points in seventy-one games and fought enough to collect 98 minutes in penalties.

"I guess," he said, "I was tough because I had to prove myself. I hope I've proved something. I like those goals better than the penalties, even though a lot of people won't believe me."

Needless to say, most observers doubted that Sanderson would play closer to the rulebook. His 130 minutes in penalties for the 1968–69 season were hardly consonant with pacifism, nor were a few of his thrusts into enemy territory.

Sanderson achieved the height of irreverence during the third game of the East Division semifinal round for the Stanley Cup in April, 1969. The Bruins were playing Toronto at Maple Leaf Gardens and appeared certain winners of the series. The Maple Leaf goaltender that night was John Bower, the oldest player in the league and a man whose age at the time was variously estimated as somewhere between forty-five and fifty. Bower, because of his friendliness and general durability, was a much revered hockey player and certainly not one to incur an opponent's anger, no matter how volatile the player.

But that night, Sanderson astonished the onlookers with what many regarded as a contemptible attack, "carelessly skating through the goal crease," as Dick Beddoes wrote in the *Globe and Mail,* "and bowling Bower over."

Sanderson escaped from the scene of the crime before any of the Toronto enforcers could get a piece of his abundant scalp, but the Leafs couldn't be faulted for trying. Bruins coach Harry Sinden detected a potential assault on his man and, just as Pat Quinn of the Leafs invited Derek to battle, instantly ordered him off the ice.

"I get myself under control when a lot of guys got a lot of bread on the line," said Sanderson. "Hell, Harry made me look bad when he took me off. Quinn wasn't worth retaliating with. Not when it's close, anyhow."

Observers have marveled at Sanderson's desire to play when his metabolism indicates he should be in the hospital. The Bruins recall the home-and-home double-header with Montreal in December, 1968, when the teams played a 0—0 tie at the Forum and returned to Boston for the Sunday night return match at the Garden. Sanderson was enjoying life immensely until after he ate some tuna fish after arriving from Montreal. In a few hours his innards were being tortured with food poisoning.

"I've never been so sick in my life," said Derek.

He phoned his coach at noon on Sunday and detailed his problem. Sinden knew he had to find another center. "I wasn't counting on him being in uniform," Sinden remembered.

At precisely 7:35 P.M., as the teams lined up for the National Anthem, there was Sanderson on the ice and itching to give the Canadiens a hard time. "I hadn't eaten since yesterday," Derek reported later. "But I knew we only had three centermen. I wasn't going to come, but I slept from four to six, and then I decided to try the warm-up. The doctor gave me a couple of pills which settled my stomach some, so I gave it a try. It was a big game and I hated the thought of missing it."

His performance, if not overwhelming, was certainly memorable. Montreal amassed a three-goal lead while Sanderson's stomach rumbled as he watched from the bench. "We gotta break the shutout," he said to teammate Green.

"I think," Green replied, "it's time to get to work."

By the end of the second period Montreal was nursing a 4—3 lead. Exactly one second after the opening face-off in the third period Glen Sather leaped out of the penalty box in pursuit of the puck. Sather's shot was stopped by goalie

Tony Esposito, but Sanderson arrived on the scene and batted the rebound over the goaltender's shoulder to tie the game. The crowd of 14,653 cheered so fervently Sanderson would have been forgiven if he thought for the moment he was Bobby Orr.

"When you hear that," he said, "you don't feel like coming off. You don't feel tired. You're too happy to be tired."

At 9:51 of the final period Sanderson scored again, a goal that turned out to be the game-winner and a goal that firmly established him as a vital Bruin. It was an opinion that grew as the season progressed toward playoff time, finally crystallizing into print once the Montreal-Boston series began. On the eve of the opening game the Toronto *Daily Star* carried a headline: "HABS FEAR SANDERSON MORE THAN ESPO."

Red Burnett, the *Star's* veteran hockey analyst, explained that the figures—Esposito finished the season with 126 points while Sanderson had 48—were somewhat deceptive. "It is even more strange," Burnett noted, "when you figure Sanderson didn't get a point in the two league games he played at the Forum. It could be, though, that the Canadiens have heard how Sanderson took the Maple Leafs apart in Toronto."

Montreal defeated the Bruins in the first two games at the Forum, winning both contests in sudden-death overtime. The second defeat appeared to put Sanderson into a temporary state of shock.

"He skated off the ice looking like a kid who had been hit by lightning," wrote John Ahern in the Boston *Globe*. "He stared straight ahead, transfixed. He sat on the bench in the locker room, still staring and saying not a word. It was more of the same on the plane home and even at the airport, where a surprisingly large crowd welcomed the team. There wasn't even a hint of animation."

A day later Sanderson was returning to normal. When he talked to his friend Ahern, he freely predicted that Boston would win the series. He sprinkled his monologue with that assertive "right," convincing the newsman he had fully recovered.

"This was the sign," wrote Ahern. " 'Turk,' when he's hitting on all cylinders, uses the word 'right' ten times in one sentence."

The Bruins routed Montreal 5—0 in the third game, but

Sanderson's masterpiece was the fourth match, played at the Garden. Dispatched to the ice in the opening minute of the game as a penalty killer, Turk immediately set up the first Bruins goal. A few minutes later Sanderson was in the penalty box for elbowing when the Canadiens tied the score. After he returned to the ice John McKenzie of Boston was whistled off for two minutes, and once again Sanderson did his thing.

"Besides shooting a pretty good stick," commented *Sports Illustrated*, "Sanderson is a tremendous forechecker and a brilliant penalty killer."

Midway through the 1968–69 season Derek had developed a theory about the Canadiens—"if you play the man, they won't get started"—which he put into practice while killing the McKenzie penalty. The puck had skimmed behind the Montreal net and seemed to be closest to Canadiens' defenseman J. C. Tremblay. But Sanderson was swooping down on him like a dive bomber, and the normally-poised Montrealer appeared to rush past the puck. Sanderson easily pushed his stick blade against the rubber and then moved directly out in front of the net, which was guarded by Rogatien Vachon. As the goaltender attempted to push the puck away with his oversized stick, Sanderson looped the disk around the goalie's leather pads and into the net.

This extraordinary example of perseverance and grim determination was embellished by the follow-up play. As Sanderson swung his stick toward the goal, sending the puck into the cage, Montreal's John Ferguson lumbered from behind, crashing Sanderson amidships. The blow sent the Bruins center falling to the ice in obvious pain, a toppling rather like what Boston deals out to opponents who dare park in the vicinity of the goal crease. Most of the viewers expected Sanderson to regain his feet and return to the game. Derek did finish out the first period, but when the second began he was absent, temporarily if not severely damaged.

"It was Ferguson, all right," he said after the Bruins had won the game, 3—2. "He got me good with his knee. It was intentional. There couldn't be any doubt. I saw the replay on television. Just as I was putting in my goal, he came running at me and up went the knee. Got me right in the thigh. Hell of a charley horse."

The damage was severe enough to force Sanderson out of the critical fifth game. "Because of Sanderson's importance," wrote Jim Proudfoot in the Toronto *Daily Star*, "you must wonder whether the Bruins can succeed without him."

A few hours later Boston had lost the contest, 4—2, to the Canadiens, and the Bruin hierarchy wondered just how Sanderson could be rehabilitated in time for what might be the final game of the series at Boston Garden.

The medical report indicated that Sanderson would be too crippled to play for about a week. It wasn't merely a charley horse in the left thigh. Muscles and ligaments had been damaged badly, and this news cast a pall over the Bruins camp prior to the sixth game on April 23. But if Sanderson was ever going to lace on a pair of skates it would be on this night.

"Nothing short of amputation will keep him off the ice tonight," predicted John Ahern, and Derek confirmed the evaluation.

The ailing center explained, "There's no tomorrow if tonight's bad, so the kid's got to be in there, right? We can win this one and go back to Montreal even again, right! And we can win up there. No question about it. So I might take a shot and see how it works out. The kid has to be out there playing hockey and look like a hockey player. Just putting the suit on doesn't make you one. Or me either."

The Turk returned and played as far as his guts would carry him, which was pretty far. He fought with Henri Richard early in the game and pecked away at goalie Vachon as the teams battled through a 1—1 deadlock in the third period. Late in the third period he nearly shot the puck past the Montreal goalie when teammate Westfall crashed into Vachon. When Terry Harper of the Canadiens was sent off for tripping at 13:42 of the third period, coach Sinden inserted Derek on left wing with Phil Esposito and John McKenzie; but the line couldn't muster a shot on goal. As the game ticked on into a first and then a second sudden-death overtime, Sanderson's pain-killing medication wore off, and his effectiveness was curtailed. At 11:28 of the second overtime Jean Beliveau, the Canadiens' captain, ended the Turk's discomfort by shooting the puck past Bruins goalie Gerry Cheevers.

Montreal had again won the Stanley Cup, but Sanderson just wouldn't believe it. Long after his teammates had departed he sat on a bench trying to fathom the events of the previous two weeks.

"How do you explain it?" he wondered. "They don't have the team, the defense, the talent, or the guts. But they get the goals."

It was a gratuitous remark, but one that was echoed by others connected with the Bruins—men who are considerably older and should know better than Sanderson. "In his bitterness," commented Gary Ronberg, "Sanderson was being decidedly unfair to the Canadiens."

If he was unfair, he certainly didn't appear concerned; but then, that's Derek Sanderson. He is his own man and he proves it by wearing the longest sideburns, by picking on bigger men than himself, and by being as different as possible.

One night he told Toronto writer Dick Beddoes that sometime he just might skate out on the ice wearing a pair of *white* skates! And he just might be the target of every tough square in the NHL.

"What's it matter how long your sideburns are, if you can produce," he reasoned. When it was suggested that white skate boots would be like a red cape in front of the opposition bulls, he dismissed the thought with a few phrases of unassailable logic.

"Maybe that'll make me more of a target than I am. But they've got to come through my stick to get me, right? And they can bleed l;ke me, right?"

And Derek Sanderson is the most colorful young man in the NHL, right?

RIGHT!

4. Phil Esposito, the Artful Dodger

Of all the big, "bad" Bruins, the least likely member of the cast is sloe-eyed center Phil Esposito, who is big but not bad at all. The six-foot-one, 195-pound Italian-Canadian is truly an anachronism on the Bruins because, as the Toronto *Daily Star* once noted, he "hits the puck and not the players." Physically he appears incapable of dashing around a hockey rink because of his terrible foot problems. And at least one of his teammates has questioned whether he has the frame to be the NHL's leading scorer.

"Look at that body," goalie Gerry Cheevers kidded one evening late in the 1968–69 season. "Can you imagine that body scoring more than 100 points?"

Well, that body scored 126 points by March 31, 1969 on 49 goals and 77 assists. That body had put together a collection of records that may never ever be broken. These include:

Most assists one season, including playoffs—77.

Most points one season—126.

Most goals one season by a center—49.

Most assists one season by a center—77.

Most points one season by a center—126.

Most points one line, one season (with Ron Murphy and Ken Hodge)—263.

Esposito became a Bruin prior to the 1967–68 season, when Chicago manager Tommy Ivan became disenchanted with Esposito the person as well as Esposito the player. The Black Hawks boss added Ken Hodge and Fred Stanfield to the package and received defenseman Gilles Marotte, goalie Jack Norris, and center Pit Martin.

At first Esposito was dismayed at the prospect of becoming Bobby Hull's opponent when he had been enjoying himself as center for "The Golden Jet."

"In Chicago," he revealed, "they called me a garbage collector. They said I picked up Bobby's garbage for points."

But hockey purists realized that Esposito was a creative center who had developed many interesting plays for Hull.

"We knew at Chicago that Espo was a good player," said Hodge, "but I never expected him to play this well. They gave him an added responsibility here—they gave him an A (for alternate captain). . . . Phil has a lot of hidden talent, you know. Don't forget, Bobby scored 100 goals in two seasons with Espo as his center."

Esposito scored 35 goals and a league-leading 49 assists for 84 points in 1967–68, his first season as a Bruin. He placed second in scoring behind Stan Mikita, making it seem that the Black Hawk management had been rather poorly advised to trade him.

"It may have been the worst trade in the history of the sport," said Jim Proudfoot of the Toronto *Daily Star*. Events of 1968–69 subsequently underlined Proudfoot's point.

It wasn't only his scoring that sparked the Bruins to second place; he bubbled with a *joie de vivre* that sometimes arose in quips and other times in pure practical jokery, such as hiding the luggage of general manager Milt Schmidt in a hotel lobby. In Chicago they might have denounced such tomfoolery, but the Bruins endorsed it with a laugh.

"We need his loosey-goosey style around the dressing room," said coach Harry Sinden.

On the ice Boston Garden patrons reacted to Esposito's scoring with awesome turbulence. During the weekend of March 1, 1969, he scored his record ninety-eighth point against the Rangers on a Saturday night, and the next evening against Pittsburgh he became the first player to score 100 points in a season.

The Sunday event was singularly significant because not only were some two hundred hats tossed on the ice, but down from the far regions of the balcony fluttered a woman's pink brassiere. No other Bruin—or NHL player, for that matter—can claim to have been so honored. Esposito also collected plenty of bonus money for winning the Art Ross Trophy as leading scorer and for being named to the First All-Star Team for 1968–69.

"I feel like Midas, you know?" he said at the conclusion

of his biggest season. "The fact the club was offensive-minded helped. I mean, if we're stressing defense I'm not going to get half the shots."

Esposito helped galvanize the Bruins from last place in 1966–67 when he was with Chicago, to third in 1967–68, and second in 1968–69. Meanwhile, the Black Hawks described a downward spiral that landed them last in the East Division in 1968–69. Also, Esposito's inflationary scoring apparently cultivated dissension among the Black Hawks, who resented his being traded in the first place.

"All that trade did," said one Chicago player, "was take money out of *all* our pockets."

Even though Bobby Hull continued to flourish, personally, he wasn't bashful about admitting he missed his old pal, Esposito.

"He was my right arm," Hull declared. And then, just in case a listener didn't get the message, he reiterated a few decibels higher, *"MY RIGHT ARM!"*

Esposito has been equally lavish in his praise of Hull. "I give the guy all the credit in the world," he said. "Not just because I played with him but for another thing. In practices Billy Reay made me and Kenny Hodge skate with Hull. I mean we'd do circuits of the rink following him. You skate fifteen times around a rink with Hull setting your pace and you're skating!"

When it became apparent in 1968–69 that Esposito would outscore his former teammate, Mikita, a story broke in Los Angeles insinuating that Esposito wanted to beat Mikita because he too is a center. The story infuriated Esposito, who claimed he said no such thing; he did admit, however, to Paul Rimstead of *The Canadian Magazine* that he enjoys talking.

"I like to think I'm honest," Esposito asserted. "I say what I think. Maybe I talk too much."

One time most Esposito-watchers admit he talked too much was the night of February 8, 1969 during a game with Philadelphia at Boston Garden. About five minutes had elapsed in the third period when Esposito and visiting defenseman Larry Hale were penalized for slashing; they continued their argument en route to the penalty box. As referee Bob Sloan moved in to announce the penalties to the timekeeper, Esposito shouted at the official, who then added a ten-minute misconduct penalty to Esposito's infraction.

According to a report delivered by NHL President Clarence Campbell, these events followed:

"When Esposito heard the referee report the misconduct penalty, he charged at the official, giving him two good shoves with his gloved hands. The official immediately signaled that Esposito was out of the game and turned to get away from him. Esposito managed to brush aside the linesmen, followed the official for a couple of strides, and then delivered a solid left-hand punch which landed on Sloan's shoulder."

Bruins players and the linemen, Bob Frampton and Ed Butler, then hauled Esposito away from Sloan before any further blows could be struck. The Bruins center was dismissed from the game and fined a total of $75—the automatic $25 and $50 assessments that accompany a misconduct and game misconduct penalties.

Although the incident occurred on February 8, Esposito was permitted to play for the Bruins until February 14, when Campbell conducted a hearing in his Montreal office and announced his decision to suspend the player for two games. Esposito was thus able to play in all Bruins games until February 19, when Boston visited Pittsburgh, and again on Sunday, February 23, when the Bruins played at New York. Opponents, especially the Montreal Canadiens, were critical of Campbell's delay and the fact that he permitted Esposito to continue playing before issuing his suspension. Others contend that the sentence was extraordinarily light, compared to previous penalties Campbell had issued against players who struck officials. In March, 1955, the league president had suspended Maurice "Rocket" Richard of Montreal for the final week of the season and the *entire* playoffs after Richard struck a linesman in Boston.

Speaking in his own defense, Esposito claimed he had sworn not at referee Sloan but rather at defenseman Hale, but Campbell apparently was unimpressed. "Regardless of whether Esposito was swearing at the referee or someone else," said Campbell, "there is no possible excuse for his subsequent conduct in assaulting the official by charging toward him and delivering two crisp shoves and then following these up by a valid punch."

Esposito returned to the Bruins lineup somewhat more penitent but no less a scoring threat. His accurate shooting helped demoralize the Toronto Maple Leafs in the opening round of the East Division Stanley Cup series and nearly—but not quite—dissuaded critics that Esposito was just an average player in Stanley Cup matches; that rap had been affixed to him when he was with Chicago and was held scoreless in six games in the 1967 playoffs.

"Esposito has destroyed the myth that he's not there in the clutch," commented Trent Frayne on the front page of the April 5, 1969 edition of the Toronto *Daily Star*. "In fact, he has found virtual anonymity in the truculence of the series so far by scoring a record-tying 4 goals and 2 assists in the first game, and adding a goal and two assists in the second."

But handling the disintegrating Maple Leafs was one thing and scoring against the World Champion Montreal Canadiens was another. Montreal coach Claude Ruel assigned his diligent veteran center Ralph Backstrom to shadow Esposito in the first two games at the Forum. The Bruins ace was completely neutralized; Backstrom managed to score the winning goal in the first game and was the architect of the winner in the second. The whispering about Esposito's ineffectiveness in clutch games was heard once again.

When the teams returned to Boston for the third game of the series Bruins coach Harry Sinden was able to have last call on placing men on the ice for every shift; consequently, he was able to get Esposito away from Backstrom. Boston routed Montreal, 5—0, on April 17 with Esposito scoring twice and assisting on the remaining three scores. But the lanky center refused to concede that the escape from Backstrom accounted for his new success.

"I had my chances in Montreal," he declared, "but I just wasn't getting it. But I knew it would come sooner or later."

Esposito failed to score in the fifth game and was shut out in the sixth and final game. Even more disastrous, he was on the ice when Jean Beliveau scored the Cup-winning goal for Montreal. Also arresting was an unobtrusive item buried near the bottom of Toronto *Star* sports editor Milt Dunnell's column that "Canadiens scored fifteen goals in their playoff victory over Boston and Esposito was on the ice for eight."

The combination of his subdued scoring against Montreal and his defensive work provoked questions about Esposito's value. Ben Olan, the respected columnist of *Pro Sports*

Weekly, raised the point—"Esposito A Choker?"

"The sad part," wrote Olan, "is that some will be thinking, 'Did Phil Esposito choke in the playoffs?' . . . I remember they said it, too, years ago about baseball sluggers Johnny Mize and Ted Williams. Then Mize was traded by the New York Giants to the Yankees and helped the Yanks win five consecutive pennants and World Series, and Williams busted up an All-Star Game with a ninth-inning homer and slammed two more homers in another All-Star Game. . . . Esposito will come through, too, with clutch goals when the Bruins win the Stanley Cup, maybe next year [1970] or the year after."

Esposito explained how he was constantly foiled by Montreal's agile goalie Rogatien Vachon in the fifth and sixth games. "I don't want to downgrade Vachon," said Esposito. "He was great. But half the time I was just standing there in front of him. All I had to do was shoot. So what did I do? Fire wide or straight into his pads, that's what. I wish I knew what was wrong.

"It happened again in the sixth game. I could have had at least two goals and I missed them. That makes it a million for me in the last two games. I had the chances and couldn't do it. All I know is that if I had to play the series against the Canadiens over again, I wouldn't do it differently. You think it's easy? The puck is on the ice and a few guys are going for it. Do you think anybody has time to make up his mind where he's gonna shoot it? Get it away as fast as you can, that's all that counts. In the overtime in Boston, Vachon makes a great stop. If I score, I'm a hero. The goalie makes a great stop, so I'm a bum. What does everyone want from me?"

Obviously, more than the Art Ross Trophy, the First All-Star nomination, and a handful of records. Possibly they want the unattainable.

5. Gerry Cheevers and Ed Johnston, the Goalies

During the early sixties a story made the rounds that two Bruins goalies, walking along a street in downtown Boston, came upon a fire-alarm box at the intersection. A red globe crowned the fire box and, on this day, a blaze was reported in the immediate vicinity of the players. As the goaltending pair approached the street corner the red light atop the fire box began flashing, signaling the alarm.

One goalie grabbed the other about the shoulder blades and began frenetically shaking him, sobbing, "Goal! Goal! Goal! Get me outa here!"

Apocryphal it may be, but the episode illustrates the valid point that goaltending for the Bruins in the Depression years from 1959 through 1967 was not conducive to sound mental health. And conversely, the quality of Bruin netminding during most of those years was what Jim Hernon, an excellent amateur hockey player, described as "minus the radical fifty—or about as worthwhile as a complete foul ball."

Early in the 1962–63 season *Sports Illustrated* wrote, "The only team in the NHL that has lacked a distinguished goalie over the past decade has been Boston."

Some of the Bruins netminders were plain awful. Others were average, and still others alternated between bad, average, and funny. It was difficult and yet imperative for a Bruins goaltender to retain his sense of humor in those days. One who did was Bobby Perreault.

"All you have to do to play goal," Perreault once explained, "is be fast and close your eyes." After he defeated Montreal, 5—0, Perreault reported, "I have my eyes shut all the time."

Once Perreault was strolling around Cadillac Square in Detroit, when he noticed a policeman's horse—minus policeman. So, the goalie did what came naturally; he mounted the horse and cantered around the square until the enraged cop whistled him down.

After a week in which the Bruins won one game, lost one, and tied two, Perreault withdrew a long stogy from his breast pocket and announced to his teammates, "If we make the playoffs, I smoke cigars all summer."

It was a seventy-game schedule in 1962–63 and Perreault managed to play through twenty-two games, thereby ending his major league career. The roly-poly French-Canadian was replaced by Ed Johnston, a husky Montreal-born youngster who had previously belonged to the goalie-rich Montreal Canadiens. Johnston stepped between the goal pipes at the start of the third period on November 14, 1962 and again on December 15. He played a total of forty-nine games and finished the season with a poorer goals-against record than his humorous predecessor. However, for reasons known only to management, Perreault was dismissed to the minors and Johnston was given the Bruins goaltending job; a dubious triumph.

With exclusive rights to the Bruins nets in the 1963–64 season, Johnston gave up 211 goals for a 3.01 average. Boston won only eighteen games that year and finished dead last. It was difficult to determine just how good—or bad—Johnston's goaltending was because Boston's defense seemed to be competing with its offense for some sort of ineptitude award. He did manage six shutouts and was sturdy enough to play all seventy games, but the feeling persisted that he would be, at best, an adequate goalie; and that was that.

The following year the Bruins alternated Johnston with Jack Norris, a relative unknown who was useful only in that he provided a comparison with Johnston. If Johnston was inept with a 3.47 goals against average, Norris was worse at 3.70, and the Bruins again finished in sixth place. But the new order was coming, and in 1965–66 there was evidence that Boston's goaltending deficiencies would soon be remedied, even though they still had Johnston, whose record was getting worse rather than better.

The source of hope was Bernard Parent, another Montrealer, who had an admirable record as a junior goaltender in Niagara Falls. For a while it appeared that Parent might be more than an average player, but a couple of severe beatings altered his reputation. He finished his rookie season with a 3.69 average to Johnston's 3.72 and a reputation as a potential star.

That same season the Bruins drafted Gerald Michael Cheevers, a witty young man who had bounced around the minors, from the Toronto Maple Leafs. Cheevers had played two games for Toronto in 1961–62 and showed no evidence of being anyone's salvation, let alone the Bruins.

"Toronto had Johnny Bower," said Cheevers, "who was playing very well for them and then in 1964, they picked up Terry Sawchuk in the draft. I knew there was no way I was going to win a job from a pair of greats like that. Actually, when they drafted Sawchuk, they dropped my name from the protected list. But nobody claimed me. The next year they left me unprotected again, and Boston grabbed me for the $30,000 draft price. I was glad of it."

A knee injury was, perhaps, the best accident that befell Cheevers and the Bruins in his rookie season with Boston. The Bruins demoted him to Oklahoma City where he met coach Harry Sinden. The young mentor was sensitive to the new goaltender's problems and helped put him back in the groove.

"He was a bit down on himself for not having stuck with the Bruins," Sinden recalled. "But I figured we could straighten him out at Oklahoma, and we did. The team seemed to rally in front of him, and we went on to win our first championship that year."

Sinden was promoted to the Bruins the following year but he didn't forget Cheevers. In November, 1966, Johnston suffered an eye injury. Normally the substitute goaltender, Parent, would replace the starter, but Sinden wasn't following the book. He elevated Cheevers from Oklahoma City and immediately started him in the Bruins goal. He tied New York, 3—3; shut out Toronto, 4—0; and beat Montreal, 2—1, in his first three games. He was returned to Oklahoma City in January, 1967, finished the season there and won the Harry Holmes Memorial Trophy as the Central League's outstanding goaltender.

During the summer of 1967 the Bruins were compelled to make a serious decision about which goaltenders they would protect in the draft. It wasn't a simple matter because they owned Johnston, Cheevers, and Parent—as well as the very promising young Doug Favell. Only two could be retained. Parent appeared to be the first choice, followed by

Cheevers, Johnston, and Favell, but Schmidt and Sinden protected Johnston and Cheevers and lost the other pair to the Philadelphia Flyers.

"That put pressure on Eddie Johnston and myself," said Cheevers, "but as far as I was concerned, I was anxious to prove that I belonged in this league as a matter of general principle, anyway."

Superficially at least, it appeared that Cheevers had not only won himself an NHL job but managed to bump Johnston in the process. The kid played forty-four games while the veteran played twenty. Cheever's average was 2.83 and the veteran's record was 2.87, but management's feeling about the pair was tacitly expressed during the playoffs with Montreal. Sinden stubbornly stuck with Cheevers as the Canadiens won four straight games. It was a bit of strategy that invited—and received—criticism.

"I probably cost our team one game in that series," Cheevers told Montreal author Gil Smith. "But we lost two of those games by the margin of a single goal, and a break or two might've made the difference."

Management was not persuaded that it had committed an error by not using Johnston in at least one game, claiming that many of the Bruins had never played in playoff competition before. They came right back with Cheevers and Johnston in 1968–69. In many ways the pair had come along neatly, if not splendidly, as a goaltending tandem. Both were good gag men and, like Bobby Perreault, enjoyed exploring the lighter side of life.

One afternoon Cheevers was sitting at a restaurant table with teammates Dallas Smith, Phil Esposito, and Ed Johnston when a middle-aged man approached the Bruins and nudged Cheevers on the shoulder.

"You're Phil Esposito, aren't you?" the man mistakenly asked Cheevers.

"Yes, Phil Esposito," the goalie replied without a smile.

"Well," the man continued proudly, "I want to congratulate you. Keep up the good work."

Cheevers nodded agreement as the man turned away. Esposito then turned to the goalie and added, "Way to go, Phil. Keep it up."

Cheevers nodded again, "I certainly will."

Johnston was laughing along with Cheevers until the night of October 31, 1968. Sinden had advised the man they call "Eddie J." that he would be starting that night in Detroit's Olympia Stadium. Johnston was handling some routine warm-up shots when he was suddenly struck down by a flying puck that came from the corner. He was hit on the side of his head above the left ear and was carried to the dressing room.

At first Johnston's injury seemed to be a routine pre-game accident that would soon heal. He was dispatched to Detroit's Osteopathic Hospital, where doctors kept him under observation for four days. When he was released, ostensibly recovered, he took an early evening flight back to Boston.

"They got me on the plane," said Johnston, "but anything I know about arriving home is what I've learned from Ted Green and Sammy Videtta, who met me at Logan Airport."

Johnston didn't remember being ill on the flight, but all indications were that he was terribly ill. When Green greeted him at the airport he was appalled at Johnston's appearance.

"Teddy has told me," Johnston added, "that I looked so bad there was only one thing to do."

Green rushed the goaltender to Massachusetts General Hospital, where doctors pondered whether or not to perform an operation to relieve a blood clot. They eventually rejected the idea but kept Johnston in the hospital until December of that year.

Time proved a great healer for Johnston, and by January 4, 1969, he told Sinden he was ready to play. He held the Minnesota North Stars to a pair of goals in a 2—2 tie at Bloomington, Minn., and found his old groove with a two-goal tie with Detroit at Olympia on January 23.

Meanwhile Cheevers was playing like an All-Star and acting like a comedian. He collected three shutouts—he hadn't achieved one in his previous NHL work—and was invited to play in the All-Star Game. The solemn occasion didn't curb Cheevers' wit. While sitting next to Montreal's terribly serious captain Jean Beliveau, Cheevers offhandedly asked whether any other teams were playing that night, knowing full well that *nobody* plays on All-Star Game night except the All-Stars. Beliveau began explaining that he didn't imagine there were any other matches, then realized that Cheevers had just given him a rather large verbal needle.

The Bruins are constantly amused by Cheevers' antics. One afternoon the goalie walked into the dressing room and, when nobody was looking, contrived a sign reading

"SECOND STAR." He then affixed it to defenseman Gary Doak's locker, knowing, as the other Bruins did, that Doak had only played a couple of minutes in the previous night's game.

A horse fancier, Cheevers has mentioned that one of his ambitions is to write a fictionalized account of horse racing. "I'd never be able to do it on my own," he told Gil Smith, "but my wife is a college graduate with a degree in literature. That helps."

Another of his ambitions is to goal the Bruins to first place and the Stanley Cup. He had opportunities to do that in March and April, 1969 and failed both times. The Bruins played the Canadiens in a home-and-home series on March 29 and 30; if they could win both games they would clinch first place. Instead, they lost the key game, on March 29 at the Forum, 5—3, and the goaltending was less than exceptional.

Cheevers rebounded to play superbly against Toronto in the East Division's Stanley Cup semifinal round. Boston defeated the Maple Leafs, 10—0 and 7—0, in the first two games. Cheevers' two consecutive shutouts were the first since Glenn Hall accomplished the feat in April, 1961, against Montreal.

As expected, Toronto was wiped out in four games. Now Cheevers was to get the test of his life, and for a time, it appeared he would, as they say in Montreal, "gagne ses epaulettes." With Cheevers in goal for the opening game of the East Division final at the Forum, the Bruins held a 2—0 lead until John Ferguson broke the shutout at 13:28 of the third period.

"From the press box," noted Red Burnett of the Toronto *Daily Star*, "it looked as if Cheevers had moved late with his left hand."

Boston tenaciously held its one-goal lead until the final minute of the period, when Jean Beliveau snatched the puck from Phil Esposito and passed it back to Jacques Laperriere at the left point. Laperriere moved the puck in to Serge Savard, whose shot was blocked by Cheevers. The Bruin goalie then stopped Beliveau's rebound thrust, but the Montreal center captured the puck again and this time lifted it over Cheevers to tie the score with only fifty-six seconds remaining.

Cheevers was screened by teammate Bobby Orr when

Ralph Backstrom beat him with a shot after only forty-two seconds of sudden-death overtime. To what extent Cheevers was culpable in the defeat that should have been a victory, according to many neutral observers, is debatable. Many experts contend that the truly great goaltender makes the big saves, no matter what; this time, Cheevers didn't.

In any event, coach Sinden departed from his 1968 policy and benched Cheevers in the second game, replacing him with Johnston, who was working his very first playoff game. Once again, the Bruins held a one-goal lead until the final minutes of the third period. But Ted Harris recovered the puck for Montreal, passed ahead to Yvan Cournoyer who, in turn, relayed to Serge Savard in front of the Boston net. The shot went into the left corner of the goal, past a diving Orr and past Johnston's right leg. Then once again, Montreal won the game in overtime when Mickey Redmond deflected Savard's shot past Johnston.

It was unanimously agreed that Johnston played capably for the Bruins and had little opportunity to block Redmond's difficult deflection. "Eddie was super," commended Sinden. "He played so well that he never deserved to be a loser."

His compliments suggested that Sinden would start Johnston again when the teams returned to Boston for the third game of the series on April 17, but Cheevers was the goaltender that game and stopped the Canadiens, 5—0. Veteran Boston writers called it one of the best games he's ever played, if not the best. Tom Fitzgerald of the *Globe* called it "sensational" and left it at that.

Cheevers was less complimentary to himself. When a reporter mentioned he was using an unusual goalkeeper's stick, he looked up and replied, "Who said I was a goalkeeper?"

Cheevers showed what kind of goalkeeper he was a few days later as the Bruins defeated Montreal, 3—2, to tie the series. His staying power wasn't enough, though, on April 22, when the clubs returned to the Forum. The Canadiens, after taking a 3—0 lead on two long shots by defensemen and a weird ricochet off Orr, went on to win, 4—2. The star of the game was Cheevers' opposite, Rogatien Vachon, who stopped 24 shots in the second period alone and 40 in the entire game.

Sinden decided to stick with Cheevers for the sixth game,

this time at Boston Garden. The goalie justified the decision —at least up to a point early in the third period, when Boston led, 1—0. Savard then shot a forty-footer that struck the ice and fooled Cheevers. The game was tied and moved into sudden-death overtime. For the second consecutive night Vachon out-goaled Cheevers with one spectacular save after another, especially in the overtime. Finally, in the second sudden death the puck came to Jean Beliveau at the rim of the face-off circle.

"As soon as the puck hit Beliveau's stick," Cheevers related, "it was gone. By the time I got organized the puck was going over my shoulder and into the net."

A second after Beliveau's stick swiped up in the air in the victory salute Cheevers dropped his head and then slammed his stick against the sideboards. Johnston sat on the bench with his grief-stricken teammates.

Several minutes later in the morgue that was the Bruins' dressing room, the goaltending pair slowly unstrapped their fat leather pads. Cheevers patiently tried to reconstruct the play for persistent reporters. Then he walked out into the corridor where the players' wives stood, softly sobbing.

It was a stunning defeat for young Cheevers, but youth is still with him. "For him and all the other young Bruins," commented a Toronto writer, "there are plenty of next years remaining."

6. Ted Green, the Policeman

On a brisk winter night in Manhattan early in January, 1969, a taxicab stopped on the corner of West 33rd Street near Eighth Avenue, not far from the players' exit from Madison Square Garden. A soft drizzle began to increase in its intensity, driving most of the people for cover. At that moment three members of the Boston Bruins trotted to the waiting cab, slammed the door, and waited for the auto to make its way through the Manhattan traffic morass. But the light was red, and the cab waited.

Without warning a pack of young boys descended on the taxi and began pounding fists and palms against the left rear window. They accompanied the frenzy with the chant, "Get Green! Get Green! Get Green!"

At first, Bruins defenseman Ted Green laughed contemptuously at them. He feigned opening the door, and almost as one, the tribe turned and ran. Then, as the cab began accelerating, they counterattacked and pounded the rear of the cab as it sped north along Eighth Avenue.

The fans' burst of hostility was harmless in its immaturity, but profound in its symbolism. Of all the big Gashouse Bruins, none has generated so much raw dislike among New York hockey fans over the years as Edward "Ted" Green. Some observers who have talked with Green contend that the feeling is mutual. What seems most unusual is that the hostility has lasted so long. The taxicab incident could just as well have occurred three years earlier or even more.

In December, 1966, Bob Waters, writing in *Sport Magazine,* asserted that Green had two health problems. One was his injured right knee. "The other problem," wrote Waters, "is keeping New York Ranger fans from sending him to Bellevue for treatment of a severe headache caused by a bashed-in skull."

Whether or not the anti-Green sentiment is limited to New York, the roots of this particular rivalry make for intriguing analysis.

The first hint of trouble erupted in the 1961–62 season, Green's rookie year and a season in which Andy Bathgate of the Rangers was the leading scorer and one of the classiest performers in the NHL. On one or two occasions Bathgate mentioned to reporters that he took a dim view of Green's deportment; when the Ranger's remarks got into print Green did some dim-viewing of his own.

Although he was most renowned for his stick-handling and shooting, Bathgate was also a skilled boxer, a fact that never eluded Green. From time to time the two would collide, but one evening Green made the mistake of running at Larry Cahan, Bathgate's teammate and a man of enormous strength. A good-natured sort with the temperament of a reluctant dragon, Cahan had not intended to fight Green, but he was goaded into combat. He then proceeded to render the Bruin horizontal in a matter of seconds and could easily have sunk Green's head through the ice and into the 50th Street subway station below—but Cahan was far too genteel for such behavior.

The event could well have been a great embarrassment for Green. Here he was upended by Cahan in front of 13,000 New York fans. The photo was displayed coast to coast by the wire services and was constantly reprinted, even in a two-page spread in a national magazine over a story about Green. Not long after that Green, persistent chap that he was, tried Cahan again and wound up in virtually the same position. Perhaps the worst move the Rangers ever made in the sixties was the demotion of Cahan to the minors in 1963–64. With Big Larry gone, the New York sextet had nobody who could cope with Green, and soon the Rangers paid the price for their transgression.

Green mauled the New York players virtually single-handedly and practically without retaliation, until Green knowingly or otherwise goaded the New Yorkers into counter-attack by felling a harmless little center named Phil Goyette.

The event, which blew up into a *cause célèbre*, took place at Madison Square Garden on December 26, 1965. Goyette was advancing the puck near center ice when Green turned to attack him.

"Green saw Goyette's blur peripherally," described Bob Waters in *Sport Magazine,* "and whirled quickly to meet it. He thrust his stick blade instinctively and it sank into Goyette's abdomen. The 15,925 fans screamed in unison. Goyette sagged to the ice, clutching his middle. Green skated casually, trying to appear uninterested."

It seemed absurd for Green to assault Goyette, a player who rarely received more than three penalties a season and was not likely to disturb Green other than by wearing an enemy uniform. But there was the little Ranger being carried off the ice, and there was Green sitting in the penalty box with a five-minute major for "deliberate attempt to injure." It was inevitable that the fans would bellow. "Get Green!"

The best the Rangers could do on the ice was attempt a few charges and high sticks, which Green seemed to dismiss as so many dust particles. But once off the ice, the Rangers and their management unloaded a barrage of verbs, adjectives, nouns, and pronouns to describe the Bruin as a not very lovely fellow.

Rangers president Bill Jennings was livid as he stormed around the press room. He described Green as an "animal" and suggested that a bounty be placed on his head, inferring that the Ranger who "got" Green would win a handsome bonus. For a time there were rumblings in Boston that Green, in turn, would sue the Rangers president, who was a member of the NHL Board of Governors. In this case, discretion proved to be the better part of Green's valor.

Although Green never sued Jennings, he gave the impression of being sincerely wounded by the accusations emanating from New York. As the bashing defenseman told it, he was being grossly misunderstood. Hockey writer Bob Zak questioned him about it, and Green gave a vivid description of the events that led up to Goyette's downfall.

"May I say that this was my first spearing penalty in seven years of pro hockey," Green told Zak. "I went into the corner for the puck. I got control of it, but then two guys were on me—one in front of me and one behind. I was fighting for control of the puck with both of them when the stick of the guy behind me just missed my ear. So, I turned to bodycheck him first and in turning, my stick accidentally caught him. I didn't know it was Goyette. Now that I know it was him, I'm very sorry that it was."

"Badman" hockey reputations don't grow up overnight, nor are they inspired by single incidents. Green was notorious as a hard-nosed player before he struck Goyette. The difference was that now he was being labeled, and he didn't like it. Prior to a game in Detroit, a paper heralded Green's arrival with a headline, "The Animal's Coming." Green was dismayed by the insinuation, but if it hurt him personally it also helped him on the ice. With each new season opponents became more and more wary of the five-foot-ten, 200-pound defenseman.

"If Frank Mahovlich, who comes down the left, has to get by Ted, he'll think a little bit about coming in on him," said Tom Johnson, the Bruins' assistant general manager. "So what happens? Mahovlich will shoot from farther away."

This action-reaction process did not escape Green's attention, and he appreciated its value, as evidenced by statements reported by Chris Lydon in the Boston *Globe*. "I get a lot of advantages because of the way I play," Green told Lydon. "It's not because I'm tough, which I really don't think I am. But I play an aggressive game." At this point Lydon editorialized, "Aggressive is the hockey word for savage."

Green went on, "Take yourself. If you were playing hockey against me and you knew you weren't going to get hit, you'd free-wheel, fancy-dan, and deke all over the place. But if you knew I was out there waiting for the right opportunity to crank you, you'd be worried about getting hit, right? Lots of times, because of the reputation I've picked up in the past, I can go into the corner after the puck and come right out with it without ever getting bodychecked at all—lots of times. Maybe a guy figures if he hits me I'm going to turn around and rap him with the stick. I probably won't, but . . . he doesn't know that."

During his early boisterous years Green betrayed a few moves that hinted he could be more than just a hatchet man, if he put his mind to it. Mostly though, he was crude, given to errant passing in his own end of the rink and to being easily duped by the more cerebral members of the opposition. Except for one season—1966–67, when he played only forty-seven games—his penalty minutes were always over the 100 mark.

Anything was apt to happen with the "old" Green.

Former Bruins goalie Bob Perreault told about the time Green belted him with a hockey stick—accidentally, of course—and nearly knocked him unconscious.

"Greenie swing at Eddie Shack," said Perreault, "two hands!—missed and hit me. I thought I had a broken jaw." The Bruins called for a ten-minute time out. Perreault's jaw wasn't broken but he had cut his tongue.

By 1968–69 Green had experienced a reformation of sorts. His penalty minutes dropped from 133 the previous season to 99, and he went around telling people that this was not the Green of bygone days. One of these people he told was Alan Grayson, sports writer for the *Christian Science Monitor*.

"I used to play a lot of aggressive hockey because the fans seemed to like it, and the Bruins weren't going anywhere," said Green. "But people don't realize that when you're throwing bodychecks all the time and getting into scraps, it saps quite a lot of your energy. Then last season [1967–68] it seemed as if we'd have a real good chance to win the league and take the Stanley Cup. So I decided I wasn't going to help the team if I was in the penalty box half the time. I used to take runs at players. I'm still ready if the right opportunity arises, but I'm not looking for it the way I used to. Some of the fans may have preferred the way I played before, but it's a lot more important to get first place and to win the Stanley Cup than to set some stupid record for getting penalties. Besides, I'm enjoying making passes, lugging the puck, and manning the point on the power play. I find it easier to play the game the way I'm doing, and I'm going to last a lot longer."

While it is true that Green has improved defensively and that the Bruins have a superb defense, the record indicates that neither Green nor the defense is close to the best in the league, as some have claimed. The Boston club's goals-against record was among the worst in the East Division during the 1968–69 season, and Green was indirectly responsible for the winning goal scored by the Canadiens in the second game of the 1969 East Division finals.

The Bruins defenseman lost the puck to Ralph Backstrom, then fouled the Montreal center and was sent off with a two-minute penalty. While Green was sitting in the penalty box Montreal won the game. Green was also on the ice in the sixth and final game when Jean Beliveau beat goalie Gerry Cheevers in the second sudden-death period.

Such performances have not diminished Green's value in the eyes of his employers. The Bruins management realizes that Green, in his turbulent way, is as important to the team as Bobby Orr, and maybe even more important now that he has learned to control his temper.

Whether because of internal or external forces, Green's change to the more positive brand of hockey coincided with the arrival of Bobby Orr as a Bruins star. Once the Golden Boy defenseman arrived in Boston the balance of headline power shifted from Green to Orr. Added to that was the fact that Orr immediately received a fabulous salary, whereas Green had had to stumble along unnoticed with losing Bruins teams.

Green has played for five last-place Bruins teams and one fifth-place club, so it's not surprising that he once doubted he'd make an All-Star Team. "I can skate damned near as fast backward as I can forward," he said to Bob Waters during the 1966–67 season. "I skate well enough to be on any forward line in this league. They use me to kill penalties, don't they? But what kind of recognition do I get?"

Late in the 1968–69 season he told Alan Grayson he doubted he'd ever make a First or Second All-Star Team. "Too many people still think of me as a clobberer," he said.

Perhaps they do, and perhaps Ted Green is all the better for it. But when all the ballots were in at the conclusion of the 1968–69 campaign, Ted Green was one of the two defensemen on the Second NHL All-Star Team.

As Stan Mikita has for so long had to play Number Two to Bobby Hull in Chicago, so Green has been the Avis to Bobby Orr's Hertz. When Green made it to the Second All-Stars, Orr was on the first team.

"Green has been playing well all along," said coach Harry Sinden, "but you just don't notice it as much with Orr out there."

It is an onerous situation for such a proud warrior, but as Green insightfully remarked after the New York fans had stormed his taxicab, "You must be able to adapt to all situations."

He has proven he does it very well.

During the long drive from Toronto to Parry Sound in September, 1968, Bobby Orr went to great lengths to explain that reporters should keep an eye on Dallas Smith during the 1968–69 season. "He's a helluva good young defenseman," said Orr. "It's a shame he doesn't get more attention."

Smith, unobtrusive like the "other half" of the Bruins, is one of the many unsung heroes of the squad. When Orr conducts a solo rush, captivating an audience, Smith quietly drops back to the Bruins blue line, ready to single-handedly protect the defense. And skating next to the headline-grabbing Ted Green is fast-developing Don Awrey.

While Phil Esposito was breaking scoring records in 1969, his sidekick, Ken Hodge, was doing plenty of heavy work along the boards.

"Let's face it," said Esposito, "if Kenny wasn't having the season he had, where would I be?"

Fans didn't take much notice in February, 1969, when John McKenzie was sidelined with an injury, but his teammates realized they were missing a good man.

"He ignites the rest of us," said Derek Sanderson. "John works so hard he makes you feel guilty."

The success of the Bruins is the sum of its parts, and the parts that include the Bucyks, Westfalls, McKenzies, Hodges, Smiths, and Awreys have been as important as the Espositos, Greens, and Orrs.